# DYNASTY High

A guide to TV's "Dynasty"
and "Dynasty II: The Colbys"

Book 1 in the BRBTV fact book series

Billie Rae Bates

BOOKSURGE
PUBLISHING
North Charleston, S.C.

Copyright © 2004 by Billie Rae Bates
All rights reserved.

ISBN: 1-59457-713-7
First print edition, July 2004 (first electronic edition: October 2003)
Second print edition, October 2006

This compilation is evolved from the popular **BRBTV** website "Dynasty High," created by Billie Rae Bates. Part of the World Wide Web since 1998, **BRBTV** is an outgrowth of a love for, and many years of research into, several classic television shows of the late '70s and early '80s. The information contained here is compiled and / or written by Billie Rae Bates and the complete volume is copyrighted as such.

No part of this work may be reproduced or transmitted in any form or by any means, electronic or mechanical, including photocopying, recording or by any information storage or retrieval system without written permission from the author, except for inclusion of brief quotations in a review.

This work has not been approved, licensed or sponsored by any entity involved in creating or producing the "Dynasty" or "The Colbys" TV series.

"Dynasty" is a registered trademark of the Oil Company, composed of Aaron Spelling Productions Inc., E. Duke Vincent Productions and Douglas Cramer Productions Inc. of California, along with Esther Shapiro and Richard Shapiro of California. All rights reserved.

TV Guide is a registered trademark of TV Guide Magazine Group. US Magazine is a registered trademark of US.

**BRBTV** makes no claims, expressed or otherwise, on the trademark properties of "Dynasty" or "The Colbys" or any other registered trademarks listed in this book.

Most photography by Billie Rae Bates, with various exceptions: Back-cover photo of the author by K.Ross Newland; photo of Peter Mark Richman courtesy of Peter Mark Richman; photo of Diahann Carroll from 1955 in the public domain; photo of a young Rock Hudson licensed through CreativeCommons.org; photo of Charlton Heston at the Civil Rights March from the National Archives and Records Administration.

**Spreading peace, love and useless information about television!**

**BRBTV**

*Since 1998*

To see other books available from **BRBTV**,
check out the home page at
www.brbtv.com

To contact Billie Rae Bates, email
BillieRaeBates@yahoo.com
or check out
www.billierae.com

*Dedicated to Grace, the most "Krystle-like" of all my friends.*

# Contents

*Foreword* .................................................................... *7*
*Introduction* ............................................................... *9*

Cast ............................................................. 11
Characters ................................................. 25
Episodes — "Dynasty" ............................... 66
Episodes — "The Colbys" ........................ 134
Credits ....................................................... 150
Up for Debate .......................................... 154
Fun & Useless Information ..................... 157
Birthdays .................................................. 180
Websites ................................................... 182
Merchandise ............................................ 185
Acknowledgments ................................... 191

Dynasty High: A Guide to TV's "Dynasty" and "Dynasty II: The Colbys"

# Shoulder pads, ahoy!

OK, so ....

Can you ever talk about "Dynasty" without bringing up the shoulder pads?

Oh, Mr. Nolan Miller, what a legacy you left, tucked away back there in the beautiful '80s. Reaganomics. Excess. Capitalism. Yuppies and preppies and ... *ooooh*, those shoulder pads.

There was something so poetic about that linebacker look, wasn't there? Strong and imposing, weren't all of those Carrington gals, in those wonderfully shoulder-padded suits?

BILLIE RAE BATES

And they linger ... those bold shoulder pads, in my closet, they linger ....
*oh*, if only it weren't so! Because I'm afraid they crept into the fashions of
the '90s, and perhaps even beyond! In fact, I dare say they became a
staple of women's fashions! How could it be????

Yet, there was something about those shoulder pads that seemed to give
dear Krystle and cunning Alexis a powerful boost. Those shoulder pads
signified females capturing a man's world, and so much of "Dynasty" was
about that, wasn't it? Because while you had Blake and Jeff and Adam
and Dex and whoever wheeling and dealing, you really had so much of
the *female* perspective, too.

From a chick exec of the new millennium, *hurrah for the female
perspective!*

Because (with our apologies to all you men out there – you know we'll
always love you!), it was those young female viewers of the '80s,
watching Alexis and Krystle and Sable and Monica and Sammy Jo prancing
around in their shoulder-padded duds (with a little mink thrown in), who
have become the power chicks of today.

So you boys better look out .... *Meow!!* .....

BRB

*October
2003*

# Introduction

"Dallas" was a hit. There was no denying it.

It was 1980, and the TV-viewing world had already ridden the wave of obsession with "Who Shot J.R." and other Ewing trials and tribulations. The climate was ripe for another juicy primetime soap to pop onto the airwaves.

The writing and producing team of Richard and Esther Shapiro had collaborated on TV work such as NBC's late-1960s "Tarzan," 1977's "Minstrel Man" and the same year's "Intimate Strangers," a drama about family relations that ironically starred Larry Hagman. But now they were turning their attention to a new project, one that perhaps the Shapiros weren't anticipating would explode quite the way it did.

"The title was originally 'Oil,'" Esther Shapiro explained on the CBS special "Dynasty Reunion: Catfights & Caviar" in May 2006, "and ABC hated that title, so they came up with 'Dynasty.' The beginning of the show was really the entrance of this secretary, Krystle, into this extraordinary life, being married to a real tycoon."

"Dynasty" premiered on January 12, 1981 on ABC (with a pilot that picked up that original rejected name, "Oil") and ran until May 11, 1989. Rather than the ranches, Texas barrooms and ten-gallon hats of its CBS rival, it focused on the sleek limos, the boardrooms, the fabulous furs and finery of the Denver wealthy. To the fans who eagerly awaited each Wednesday-night installment, "Dynasty" presented a glossier land of 1980s excess, a place where corporate deals were cut over caviar, not bourbon and branch, a place where cool clothing outclassed the breakfasts on the ranch patio. It was a place we all wanted to be. In a way. A place with a different sort of "charm." Richard Shapiro explained, "Blake Carrington was, as we suggested all the characters were, on the side of the angels, and if he did some things occasionally, like kill his son's gay lover, those things happen."

"Dynasty" experienced a slow start but then rose quickly in the ratings chart. And we all know what kicked it up a notch, now don't we?

"The network really wanted a kind of a J.R. character," Esther Shapiro said of the entrance of Alexis Carrington at the end of the first season, "and we felt that this actress, whoever she was, had to be beautiful."

Beautiful, powerful, sinful, prideful, lustful ... all that and more describes this groundbreaking female character, played by Joan Collins, who gave J.R. a run for his money, so to speak, and kept the soap humming in basically fine form (oh, sure, there was a little knock in the engine here or there) all the way to the end.

"The drama," said soap authority Christopher Schemering in "The Soap Opera Encyclopedia," "lacking even the merest hint of verisimilitude, was seen as refreshingly irreverent, fun and funny – escapist entertainment shrewdly executed. Much of the suspense lay not in what would happen next but what Alexis and Krystle would *wear* next."

Through the Moldavian Massacre, through so many catfights, through divorce and marriage and birth and evil twins and UFO abduction and megawatt costars and interesting recasting and on and on, we loved the soapy escapades of the Carringtons. In the fall of 1984, for instance, before the ratings drop that accompanied the Krystle / Rita storyline, the show had 100 million regular viewers in 70 countries. From the moment Fallon bit into that sugar couple off the opulent wedding cake, to the moment Alexis and Dex went diving over that balcony, we were enthralled, pure and simple.

The story behind the scenes of "Dynasty" has already been told, in countless magazine articles, web features and books. What **BRBTV** offers you here is a fun reference guide — a place where you can look up the actor who played that obscure character in that one episode, or who's the long-lost child of whom, and other assorted little facts and such. The **BRBTV** fact book series follows a formula — cast list, character guide, episode guide, and so on, in an easy-to-page-through format that you can have at your side while you're watching the show. So step into the limo and c'mon along for the ride ... and enjoy.

## Cast

Who played whom? Here they are, all the characters you'll find on "Dynasty" and "The Colbys." This listing includes folks who only made one appearance on the show(s), to make this as complete a list as possible. You'll see a few names here of characters who came along later, in the postseries TV reunion movie, too. They're arranged alphabetically by first name. You'll note that some characters only had one name, and sometimes the same first name was given to different characters in different episodes. Name spellings are taken directly from actual on-screen credits or any printed appearances the names made within the episodes. A "**C**" denotes characters unique to "The Colbys." Enjoy!

Ace Hudson ... **Mark Thomas**
Adam Carrington ... **Gordon Thomson / Robin Sachs**
Adelle ... **Barbara Whinnery**
Adriana ... **Viveca Lindfors**
Adrienne Cassidy ... **Shanna Reed** **C**
Afferton ... **Vernon Weddle**
Aldo ... **Andrew Masset**
Alexis Colby ... **Joan Collins**
Alfred ... **Robert Balderson**
Alfred Grimes ... **R.G. Armstrong**
Alfred Sorenson ... **Bradley White**
Alice ... **Bebe Kelly**
Alice ... **Tracy Cunningham**
Allison Atkinson ... **Aubrey Starns**
Aly Samarkian ... **Jack Heller**
Amanda Carrington ... **Catherine Oxenberg / Karen Cellini**
Amos ... **Robert Davi**
Amy ... **Brynia Willis**
Andrew Laird ... **Peter Mark Richman**
Andy ... **Wade Wallace**
Angela ... **Patricia Mullins**
Angelo ... **David Lane Baker** **C**
Anna Gregory ... **Cynthia Leake**
Anna Rostov ... **Anna Levine** **C**
April ... **Natalia Nogulich**
Archbishop of Moldavia ... **John Van Dreelen**
Arlon Marshall ... **Michael Brandon**

Arnie ... **Rocky Giordani**
Arthur Cates ... **Peter White**
Arthur Whitcomb ... **Sandy McPeak**
Audrey Fredericks ... **Doris Singleton**
Avril Dawson ... **James Karen**
Baker ... **Peter Crook**
Barbara ... **Peggy Walton Walker**
Barbara Davis ... **Barbara Davis**
Barbie ... **Jennifer Wallace**
Bart Fallmont ... **Kevin Conroy / Cameron Watson**
Bartell ... **Joe Horvath**
Beaumont ... **Joseph Chapman**
Bedelia ... **Christina Hart**
Ben Carrington ... **Christopher Cazenove**
Ben Carson ... **Jon Sharp**
Ben Reynolds ... **Joey Aresco**
Bennett ... **Tom Ohmer**
Bessie Matthews ... **Virginia Capers**
Beth ... **Ellen Sweeney**
Bethany ... **Sandra McCabe**
Betty Ford ... **Betty Ford**
Betty Kingsley ... **Anne Haney**
Bill ... **Colby Chester**
Bill ... **Kenneth Phillips**
Bill ... **Ted Lehmann**
Bill Cochran ... **Dawson Mays / Jordan Charney**
Bill Mahoney ... **Steve Eastin C**
Bill Rockwell ... **Peter White**
Billy Dawson ... **Simon MacCorkindale**
Billy Joe (Sam) Erskine ... **John Dehner C**
Billy Waite ... **Kevin McCarthy**
Blake Carrington ... **John Forsythe**
Blanchard ... **James Hornbeck**
Bliss Colby ... **Claire Yarlett**
Bob Ashmore ... **F.J. O'Neil**
Bobby ... **Ken Martinez**
Boyd Curtis ... **Duncan Gamble**
Brad Milburn ... **Barry Cahill**
Brady Lloyd ... **Billy Dee Williams**
Brent ... **Larry Horowitz**
Bubba ... **Mickey Jones C**
Buck ... **Patrick Wright**

DYNASTY HIGH

Buck Fallmont ... **Richard Anderson**
Buck Houser ... **John Rixey Moore**
Buddy ... **James Carrington**
Burrell ... **James Parkes**
Burt McCann ... **Taylor Lacher**
Captain Chabria ... **Jay Reinhardt**
Captain Cordillo ... **Gerald Castillo**
Captain Harris ... **Taylor Lacher**
Captain Lockwood ... **James Wainwright**
Caress Morell ... **Kate O'Mara**
Carl Creighton ... **Richard Roat**
Carlos ... **Edwin Gerard  C**
Carol Marshall ... **Wendie Malick**
Cash Cassidy ... **James Houghton  C**
Cecil Colby ... **Lloyd Bochner**
Channing ... **Ferdy Mayne**
Channing Colby ... **Kim Morgan Greene  C**
Charles Dalton ... **George DiCenzo**
Charles Hampton ... **Ben Piazza**
Charles Matthews ... **Al Fann**
Charley ... **Don Maxwell**
Charlie ... **Ben Marino**
Charlie ... **Jack Axelrod**
Charlie Braddock ... **George Murdock**
Chen Ling ... **James Hong**
Cheryl ... **Cheryl Crandall**
Chester Smythe ... **Keith McConnell**
Chris Deegan ... **Grant Goodeve**
Christine ... **Dinah Anne Rogers**
Christopher ... **Tony O'Dell**
Cindy ... **M.E. Loree**
Claire Maynard ... **Joanne Linville**
Claire Prentice ... **Kimberly Beck**
Claire Tennyson ... **Stella Hall**
Clarence ... **Eddie Quinlan**
Claudia Blaisdel ... **Pamela Bellwood**
Clay Fallmont ... **Ted McGinley**
Colonel Saban ... **Aharon Ipalé**
Conrad ... **Don Torres**
Constance Colby ... **Barbara Stanwyck  C**
Cora Van Heusen ... **Carole Cook**
Count Pierre ... **France Benard**

BILLIE RAE BATES  13

Cray Boyd ... **Ed Marinaro**
Crenshaw ... **Anthony Zerbe**
Curtis ... **Read Morgan C**
Cyril ... **Nelson Welch C**
Dan ... **Chris Kriesa**
Dan Cassidy ... **John Crawford**
Dan Crane ... **Gary Wood**
Dan Franklin ... **William Traylor**
Dana Waring ... **Leann Hunley**
Daniel Reece ... **Rock Hudson**
Danny Carrington ... **Jameson Sampley / Justin Burnette**
Dave Alden ... **John McCann**
David ... **Kelly Elias**
David Prescott ... **John Considine**
David Soames ... **Bruce Gray C**
Davis ... **Tricia O'Neil**
Dean ... **Robert Parucha**
Dean Caldwell ... **Richard Hatch**
Dean Harris ... **Dennis Howard**
Debbie ... **Wendy Kilbourne**
Denise ... **Kiva Lawrence C**
Dennis Champlin ... **Jack Bannon**
Dennis Grimes ... **Jeff Kaake**
Deselles ... **James MacKrell**
Detective Coe ... **Mitchell Edmonds**
Detective Harrison ... **Bert Kramer**
Dex Dexter ... **Michael Nader**
Dina ... **Tracy Leah Ryan**
Dina Hartley ... **Natalie Core**

*"Dynasty" has been featured in many different soap-opera guides over the years, such as this 1991 one, "Soap Opera History" by Publications International.*

DYNASTY HIGH

Dirk Maurier ... **Jon Cypher**
Dobson ... **Ted Toll**
Dominique Deveraux ... **Diahann Carroll**
Dona ... **Diane Behrens C**
Doris ... **Claudia Bryar**
Doris ... **Molly Cheek**
Dorji Rinpoche ... **Ernest Harada C**
Dottie ... **Victoria Carroll**
Doug ... **Doug Simpson**
Douglas ... **James J. Levine**
Dr. Albans ... **Conrad Bachmann**
Dr. Ames ... **Lou Felder C**
Dr. Bowden ... **Ed Winter**
Dr. Braddock ... **Ed Coupee**
Dr. Chase ... **Kenneth Kimmins**
Dr. Chen ... **Clyde Kusatsu**
Dr. Davis ... **Thomas Ryan**
Dr. Eggleston ... **Robert Sampson**
Dr. Ganton ... **Milt Tarver**
Dr. Gavin ... **David White**
Dr. Hampton ... **Ben Piazza**
Dr. Hayes ... **James Greene C**
Dr. Holton ... **Barbara Tarbuck**
Dr. Jobinet ... **Tony Jay**
Dr. Jordan ... **Rick Lenz**
Dr. Louden ... **Don Dubbins**
Dr. Mansfield ... **Linda Thorson**
Dr. McNaughton ... **David Spielberg**
Dr. Morrell ... **Allyn Ann McLerie**
Dr. Robinson ... **Edward Winter**
Dr. Rossiter ... **John Findlater**
Dr. Solis ... **Bonnie Keith**
Dr. Tully ... **Toni Attell**
Dr. Walcott ... **Robert Hooks**
Dr. Waverly ... **Georganne Johnson C**
Dr. Webb ... **Michael Prince**
Dr. Westhaven ... **Michael Fairman**
Dr. Wilton ... **Chip Johnson**
Drew Mayfield ... **Basil Hoffman**
Duane ... **Steven Marachuk**
Earl ... **Curtis Credel**
Earl Cunningham ... **Christopher Cary**

Earl Thomson ... **Russell Johnson**
Ed ... **Ron Ray**
Ed Linden ... **Alex Henteloff**
Ed McFadden ... **Ivan Bonar**
Ed Queens ... **Paul Jenkins**
Eddie ... **Michael Harrington C**
Edna MacReady ... **Rachel Ward**
Edward P. Langdon ... **Robert Cornthwaite**
Edward Prusky ... **Joris Stuyck**
Elaine Carter ... **Jennifer Nairn-Smith**
Elena ... **Kerry Armstrong**
Ellen ... **Linda Phillips**
Elsworth Chisolm ... **John McLiam**
Emily ... **Dana Kimmell**
Emily Fallmont ... **Pat Crowley**
Emily Grimes ... **Marlyn Mason**
Emily Laird ... **Barbara Beckley**
Emma ... **Kathleen O'Malley**
Enid Palmer ... **Alison Evans C**
Eric ... **Frank Zagarino**
Eric Grayson ... **Lawrence Pressman**
Ernesto Pinero ... **Richard Yriguez**
Fabrice ... **Alain St. Alix C**
Fallon Carrington ... **Pamela Sue Martin / Emma Samms**
Farouk Ahmed ... **Kabir Bedi**
Father Shea ... **Pierrino Mascarino**
Ferguson ... **Lorry Goldman**
Fielding ... **Peter Browne C**
Florence ... **Mary Baldwin**
Francesca Colby ... **Katharine Ross C**
Frank ... **Ben Marino**
Frank Carter ... **Don Matheson**
Frank Dean ... **Matt Clark**
Frank Linaver ... **Angus Duncan**
Fred ... **John McCook**
Fred ... **Woody Brown**
Fred Hughes ... **John Gowans**
Fred Mason ... **Nick Angotti**
Fred McHenry ... **Michael McGuire**
Fred Merrill ... **David Ackroyd**
Frederick ... **(Joshua) Dean Stewart**
Fritz Heath ... **Kenneth Tigar**

Gail Kittredge ... **Lisa Aliff C**
Galloway ... **Charles Knapp**
Garrett Boydston ... **Ken Howard**
Gary Tilden ... **Madison Mason**
Gavin Maurier ... **Neil Dickson**
George ... **Robert Rockwell**
George Samuels ... **Ed Lottimer C**
Georgina Sinclair ... **Nana Visitor C**
Gerald ... **Alan Pass**
Gerald Ford ... **Gerald Ford**
Gerald Wilson ... **John Larch**
Gerard ... **William Beckley**
Gibson ... **Stan Sells**
Gifford ... **Rance Howard**
Gloria Wilby ... **Fran Benett**
Gordon Wales ... **James Sutorius**
Gregory Farnsworth ... **Vernon Weddle C**
Griff ... **Corey Young**
Griffin ... **Jon Cypher**
Hal Lombard ... **Bradford Dillman**
Hall ... **Frank Schuller**
Hamilton Stone ... **Christopher Neame**
Han Li Su ... **Dana Lee**
Handley ... **Colby Chester**
Hank ... **Billy Long**
Hank Lowther ... **Drew Snyder**
Hardesty ... **Cliff Murdock**
Harold Chadway ... **Alan Haufrect**
Harold Jessup ... **William Bogert C**
Harry Donalds ... **Mark Roberts**
Harry Thresher ... **Daniel Davis**
Hawkins ... **Brion James**
Heidi ... **Lou Hancock**
Helen ... **Viviane Lord**
Helen Pomeroy ... **Neva Patterson**
Helen Webster ... **Fran Ryan C**
Henderson Palmer ... **Ivan Bonar C**
Henry Kendall ... **John Randolph**
Henry Kissinger ... **Henry Kissinger**
Henry Logan ... **Steven Lambert C**
Henry MacReady ... **Mickey Cherney**
Henry Marlis ... **Robert Sampson C**

Hilda Gunnerson ... **Betty Harford**
Horatio Quinlan ... **Lloyd Haynes**
Houser ... **Frank Schuller**
Hoyt Parker ... **Michael Parks**
Huang ... **Alvin Ing**
Hutch Corrigan ... **Joseph Campanella C**
Ilene Robson ... **Concetta Tomei**
Inspector Verlakis ... **Anthony DeFonte C**
Jack Crager ... **Bert Remsen**
Jack Fowler ... **Michael Greene C**
Jack Lyons ... **Jesse D. Goins**
Jackie Deveraux ... **Troy Beyer**
Jake Dunham ... **Brian Dennehy**
James Beaumont ... **Bill Cort / Joseph Chapman**
James Rayford ... **Robert Harland**
Jane ... **Evelyn Guerrero C**
Jane Matthews ... **Marguerite Ray**
Jason Colby ... **Charlton Heston C**
Jason Dehner ... **Paul Shenar**
Jay ... **Gary Costello**
Jay Bradley ... **Clayton Landey**
Jeanette Robbins ... **Virginia Hawkins**
Jeff Colby ... **John James**
Jeffrey Ames ... **Mike Garibaldi**
Jennifer ... **Belinda Montgomery**
Jennifer ... **Greta Blackburn**
Jennifer ... **Kathryn Leigh Scott**
Jennifer ... **Merrill Leighton**
Jensen ... **Hedley Mattingly**
Jeremy Thatcher ... **Chip Lucia**
Jeremy Van Dorn ... **Jeroen Krabbe**
Jeri ... **Debra Satell**
Jerry ... **Ben Mittelman**
Jerry ... **Patrick Dollaghan**
Jesse Atkinson ... **Christopher Allport**
Jim Ellison ... **Richard Herd**
Jim Wilkerson ... **Philip English**
Jimbo ... **Dick Durock**
Jimmy Lee Parris ... **Ray Stricklyn C**
J.J. ... **John Reilly**
Joanna Sills ... **Kim Terry-Costin**
Joaquin Palmas ... **George Clifton**

Joe Westhaven ... **Michael Fairman**
Joel Abrigore ... **George Hamilton**
John Moretti ... **Vincent Baggetta C**
John Zorelli ... **Ray Abruzzo**
Jonas Edwards ... **Robert Symonds**
Jonathan Lake ... **Calvin Lockhart**
Joseph Aynders ... **Lee Bergere**
Josh Harris ... **Tom Schanley**
Jud ... **Scott Cooper**
Jud Barrows ... **Royce D. Applegate**
Judge Barham ... **Philip Abbott C**
Judge J. Therom ... **Carlos Romero**
Julia ... **Bunky Young**
Kai Liu ... **Soon-Teck Oh**
Karen Atkinson ... **Stephanie Dunnam**
Kate Torrance ... **Lurene Tuttle**
Katherine Malley ... **Bettye Ackerman**
Katie ... **Orly Kate Sitowitz C**
Keith ... **Keith Jones**
Kelly Atkinson ... **Kimberly Holman**
Kevin ... **Gerald Berns**
King Galen ... **Joel Fabiani**
Kirby Aynders ... **Kathleen Beller**
Kolya (Nikolai) Rostov ... **Adrian Paul C**
Kostas ... **Jack Bruskoff C**
Kotey ... **Garrett Davis**
Kristina Carrington ... **Jessica Player**
Krystle Carrington ... **Linda Evans**
Kyle Bert ... **Sam Chew Jr.**
La Salle ... **Alain St. Alix**
Lady Ashley Mitchell ... **Ali MacGraw**
Larry ... **Clay Winters**
Larry ... **Reid Smith**
Larry Atkins ... **Robert Burton**
Lars Nordstrom ... **John Milford**
Lauren Colby ... **Brittany Alyse Smith**
Laurie ... **Christine Kellogg**
Lawrence Baskins ... **Christopher Thomas**
L.B. Colby ... **Timothy McRutt / Ashley Mutrux / Brandon Bluhm**
Lee ... **Richard Herkert C**
Leon ... **Paul Napier**
Leslie Carrington ... **Terri Garber**

Less Osgood ... **John Carter**
Liam Farley ... **Bruce Gray**
Lillian ... **Cynthia Steele**
Lin ... **Jim Ishida**
Lin ... **Peter Kwong**
Linda ... **Ava Lazar**
Lindsay Blaisdel ... **Katy Kurtzman**
Ling ... **Jose DeVega**
Lisa ... **Connie Hill**
Liz ... **Janet Adams**
Lois Dern ... **Dawn C. Abraham**
Louise Dunham ... **Bonwitt St. Claire**
Lowell Sherman ... **Vanessa Bell C**
Lt. Calder ... **Robert Pine**
Lt. Cobb ... **Arlen Dean Snyder**
Lt. Dawes ... **Christopher Pennock**
Lt. Evans ... **Brett Hadley C**
Lt. Gilman ... **Christopher Lofton C**
Lt. Holliman ... **Ken Swofford**
Lt. Lopez ... **Fausto Bara**
Lt. Olsen ... **Barney McFadden C**
Lucas Carter ... **Kevin McCarthy C**
Lucy ... **Madlyn Rhue**
Luke Fuller ... **William Campbell**
Marcia ... **Sally Kemp**
Margaret ... **Davey Davison**
Marie ... **Marie Berry**
Marion ... **Judy Levitt**
Marion Loomis ... **Barbara Beckley**
Mark Jennings ... **Geoffrey Scott**
Martha ... **Dorothy Patterson**
Martin Gaines ... **Don Dubbins**
Martin Holland ... **Matthew Faison**
Marvin ... **Randy Hamilton**
Marvin Davis ... **Marvin Davis**
Mary Hackford ... **Harriet Medin C**
Matthew Blaisdel ... **Bo Hopkins**
Maurice Boland ... **Nicholas Pryor C**
Maxwell Allen ... **James Horan**
Maya Kumara ... **Bianca Jagger C**
Meg ... **Lora Staley**
Melanie ... **Stepfanie Kramer**

Melman ... **Milton Selzer**
Michael Culhane / Cullinan ... **Wayne Northrop**
Michael Cunningham ... **Jeff Pomerantz**
Michael Grogan ... **Sam Melville** **C**
Mike ... **Mike Norton**
Miles Colby ... **Maxwell Caulfield**
Miss Lindquist ... **Carolyne Barry**
Monica Colby ... **Tracy Scoggins**
Morgan Hess ... **Hank Brandt**
Mother Blaisdel ... **Diana Douglas**
Mrs. Charles ... **Louise Fitch**
Mrs. Davis ... **Tricia O'Neil**
Mrs. Gordon ... **Janet Brandt**
Mrs. Johnson ... **Michelle Davison**
Mrs. McAllister ... **Salome Jens** **C**
Mrs. Parker ... **Susan French** **C**
Mrs. Pomeroy ... **Neva Patterson**
Mrs. Wrigley ... **Carol Ann Henry** **C**
Nadine ... **Holly Lynn**
Nadine Craig ... **Diana Webster**
Natale ... **Eugene Peterson**
Nate Pencroft ... **Patrick Omeirs**
Neal McVane ... **Paul Burke**
Neil Kittredge ... **Philip Brown** **C**
Nick Kimball ... **Richard Lawson**
Nick Toscanni ... **James Farentino**
Nicole Simpson ... **Susan Scannell**

## Behind the scenes

"I viewed the 'Dynasty' tape but thought it was a pale imitation of 'Dallas.' ... The 'Dynasty' cast were competent but, with the exception of Pamela Sue Martin who played the feisty daughter, there wasn't much bite to the characters."
— Joan Collins, in her autobiography, "Second Act," on being approached by Aaron Spelling to play Alexis

Nikolai ... **Michael Gregory**
Nikos Livadas ... **Tito Vandis C**
Nurse Johnson ... **Jill Andre**
Officer Hansen ... **Jed Gillin**
Oscar Stone ... **John McLiam**
Owen Bancroft ... **Philip Coccioletti**
Pamela ... **Stephanie Williams**
Pat Dunne ... **Gary Wood**
Penelope Shane ... **Maggie Roswell**
Pete ... **Walt Scott**
Pete Davis ... **Nigel Bullard**
Pete Dawson ... **Percy Rodrigues**
Pete McWhorter ... **Jonathan Perpich**
Peter ... **Alexander Petale**
Peter DeVilbus ... **Helmut Berger**
Peter Duchin ... **Peter Duchin**
Peter Hackford ... **Guy Doleman C**
Peters ... **Carol Locatell**
Phil ... **Craig King**
Phil Thorpe ... **Alan Fudge**
Philip Spaulding ... **James David Hinton**
Phillip Colby ... **Michael Parks**
Phoenix Chisolm ... **Lezlie Deane**
Polly Trumble ... **Healy Cunningham C**
Prasad ... **Kavi Raz C**
Prince Michael of Moldavia ... **Michael Praed**
Ralph Dunbar ... **Brian Avery**
Ranger ... **Bill Zuckert C**
Rashid Ahmed ... **John Saxon**
Ray Boning ... **Lance LeGault**
Ray Montana ... **Harvey Jason**
R.D. Fleming ... **William H. Bassett**
Rebecca Payne ... **Lise Hilboldt**
Reverend Carlton ... **Ivan Bonar**
Richard Daniels ... **Phillip Clark**
Richard Winfield ... **Don Eitner**
Rick ... **Tony DeCarlo**
Rita Lesley ... **Linda Evans**
Robert ... **Robert L. Benwitt**
Roger Grimes ... **J. Eddie Peck**
Roger Langdon ... **David Hedison C**
Rollings ... **Liam Sullivan C**

Rosalind Bedford ... **Juliet Mills**
Rudy Richards ... **Lou Beatty Jr.**
Russ Kelton ... **Michael Goodwin**
Sable Colby ... **Stephanie Beacham**
Sacha Malenkov ... **Judson Scott C**
Salvador Ramon ... **Henry Darrow**
Sam ... **Marcus Mukai**
Sam Dexter ... **David Hedison / Ed Nelson**
Sammy Jo Reece ... **Heather Locklear**
Sarah Curtis ... **Cassie Yates**
Sarah Pat Beecham ... **Tisch Raye**
Scott Cassidy ... **Coleby Lombardo C**
Sean McAllister ... **Charles Van Eman C**
Sean Rowan ... **James Healey**
Sen. Adams ... **Arthur Adams**
Sen. Brady ... **John Terry Bell**
Sgt. Benson ... **John Howard Swain**
Sgt. Cooper ... **Jonathan Goldsmith**
Sgt. Landers ... **Michael Durrell**
Sgt. Roscoe ... **John Cedar**
Sharen ... **Arlene Banas C**
Shelley ... **Greta Blackburn**
Sister Agnes ... **Kieu Chinh**
Sister Teresa ... **Ronnie Claire Edwards**
Skip Maitland ... **Gary Hudson**
Spiros Koralis ... **Ray Wise C**
Stan McAllister ... **Joe Kapp**
Stanley ... **Arlen Dean Snyder**
Stanley Thurlowe ... **Warren Munson**
Steven Carrington ... **Al Corley / Jack Coleman**
Stevens ... **Robert Ackerman C**
Steward ... **Clayton Norcross C**
Sung ... **Cary Hiroyuki C**
Susan Farragut ... **Christina Belford**
Susan Aames ... **Marsha Clark**
Sydney Tyler ... **Preston Hanson**
Tania ... **Dawn Jeffory**
Tanner McBride ... **Kevin Bernhardt**
Taylor ... **Hari Rhodes**
Ted Dinard ... **Mark Withers**
Terry ... **Michael Meyer**
Terry Toscanni ... **Carol Bagdasarian**

Tess Harrison ... **Kiva Lawrence**
Thomas Crayford ... **Tim O'Connor**
Timothy Holmes ... **Robert Hogan C**
Tom ... **Don Reid**
Tom ... **Jerry Ayres**
Tom ... **William Tucker C**
Tom Bradfield ... **Ian Abercrombie**
Tom Carrington ... **Harry Andrews**
Tom Loomis ... **Stacy Keach Sr.**
Tony ... **Robert Wilson**
Tony Driscoll ... **Paul Keenan**
Tony Nelson ... **Frank Schuller**
Tracy Kendall ... **Deborah Adair**
Ty Meredith ... **Robert Clotworthy**
Val ... **Paul Provenza**
Vera Nesbit ... **Joy Garrett**
Verna ... **Barbara Pallenberg C**
Veronica Miller ... **Bibi Besch**
Victor Eckland ... **James Ray**
Victor Miller ... **William Prince**
Victoria Aynders ... **Patricia McPherson**
Vince Harrison ... **Mace Barrett**
Vincent ... **Tom Everett**
Virginia Metheny ... **Liza Morrow**
Vlachos ... **Zitto Kazann C**
Volkert ... **Curt Lowens**
Walt Tyson ... **George D. Wallace**
Walter Lankershim ... **Dale Robertson**
Warnick ... **Theodore Bikel**
Warren Ballard ... **Clive Revill**
Wayne Masterson ... **Gary Morris C**
Wesley Arnold ... **Christopher Coffey C**
William Handler ... **John Brandon**
William Todd ... **Michael Ensign**
Williams ... **Rodger LaRue**
Winston Towers ... **Tom Hallick**
Yuri ... **Carl Strano**
Zach Powers ... **Ricardo Montalban**

## Characters

Who was whom? Who did what to whom? Who was the child of whom, or the sister of whom? These and other tantalizing questions will be answered, if you read on. Birthdates and death dates are included, when known. These dates are in the "real time" that the shows aired (assuming, for instance, that if Fallon was mentioned as being 26 years old in an episode that aired in 1983, then the character was likely born in 1957). Spoiler warning: If you haven't seen all the episodes of both shows, these character descriptions might reveal some shockeroo plot lines!

### Adam Alexander Carrington (Michael Torrance)  *b. February or March 1957*
**Parents:** Blake & Alexis Carrington (assumed: David Torrance)
**Siblings:** Fallon Carrington, Steven Carrington, Amanda Carrington, Kristina Carrington
**Spouses:** Claudia Blaisdel, Dana Waring
**Children:** miscarried daughter, surrogate son
Smooth, dark-haired, handsome lawyer with a bit of a mean streak. Was kidnapped when he was six or seven months old, around September 29, 1957 (later stated by Alexis as "just before his first birthday") and raised in Billings, Montana, as Michael Torrance. Educated at Yale University and chaired political debates there. Jealous of Jeff Colby and tried to poison him with toxic paint fumes at Jeff's office. Raped Kirby Aynders and fell in love with her. Married Claudia Blaisdel in October 1985. Shown "evidence" that he wasn't a Carrington by Neal McVane, which was later refuted by McVane's source. Involved with Virginia Metheny after Dana Carrington left him; treated Virginia like dirt after finding out she was a former prostitute. Fed a compromising photo of Jeff Colby and Monica Colby to a tabloid in 1989. Recruited by an evil consortium to spy in his father's company in May 1988. Became engaged to Kirby in 1991.

### Adrienne Cassidy
**Spouse:** Cash Cassidy
**Child:** Scott Cassidy (adoptive)
Shrewd, sniping senator's wife who had to fight off Monica Colby's interest in her family.

### Afferton
Snooty wedding planner for Krystle Jennings and Blake Carrington in 1981.

## Aldo
Hotel bagman in Italy encountered by Alexis Carrington.

## Alexis Morell Carrington Colby Dexter Rowan
**Parent:** Steven Morell
**Sibling:** Caress Morell
**Cousins:** Sable Scott, Francesca Scott, Rosalind Bedford
**Spouses:** Blake Carrington, Cecil Colby, Dex Dexter, Sean Rowan
**Children:** Adam Carrington, Fallon Carrington, Steven Carrington, Amanda Carrington
**Grandchildren:** L.B. Colby, Danny Carrington, Lauren Colby, surrogate son of Adam Carrington

Ruthless, powerful tycoonette in smart suits and fabulous furs. Born in London and schooled in Switzerland. Met Blake Carrington when she was 17. A painter. Cheated on Blake with Roger Grimes and with Cecil Colby, even suspecting for years that Cecil fathered her daughter, Fallon Carrington. Married to Blake for nine years. Banished from Denver by Blake for her indiscretions in October 1963 or 1965 (depending on which episode you believe). Lived in Acapulco for several years. Had a one-night stand with Jason Colby in the late 1970s. Had an affair with Zach Powers aboard his yacht in Venezuela. Had an affair with King Galen of Moldavia. Returned to Denver in 1981 after a "16-year absence" to testify in the Ted Dinard murder trial. Hated Krystle Carrington and fired a shot to scare Krystle's horse, thereby causing her to fall and lose her unborn child. Called on Mark Jennings to make trouble for Krystle's marriage to Blake. Shipped Kirby Aynders off to Paris, fearing Kirby might become her daughter-in-law. Framed for Mark's murder by Neal McVane. Hid the fact that Amanda Carrington was her daughter, even from Amanda. Tracked down Ben Carrington in the Australian outback and plotted with him to steal Blake's South China Sea oil leases. Purchased and ran the Denver Mirror newspaper in her vendetta against Blake. Rescued by Sean Rowan when her car plunged into a river in 1986. Ran for governor against Blake in 1987. Often at odds with Sable Colby (their "mummys were sisters"), particularly over Dex Dexter. Told Jason Colby in 1987 that the twins were not really his children. Purchased the Fashion Fury company from Arlon Marshall in 1991.

## Alfred Grimes
**Child:** Roger Grimes
**Grandchild:** Dennis Grimes
Kidnapped L.B. Colby in 1982 for the vengeance of his son's death.

### Alfred Sorenson
Magazine reporter in Denver.

### Aly Samarkian
Casino owner in Denver.

### Amanda Bedford Carrington   b. April 1964
**Parents:** Blake & Alexis Carrington (assumed: Hugh & Rosalind Bedford)
**Siblings:** Adam Carrington, Fallon Carrington, Steven Carrington, Kristina Carrington
**Spouse:** Prince Michael of Moldavia
Spoiled princess who was Alexis Carrington's best-kept secret until the girl came to Denver at age 20 to find her mother. Married through her mother's arrangement with King Galen; this royal wedding was the "Moldavian Massacre," where several people died. Had an affair with Dex Dexter and attempted suicide after Alexis found her and Dex in bed together. Involved with Michael Culhane. Went to Europe in 1987.

### Amos
Worker on the drilling crew of Matthew Blaisdel and Walter Lankershim.

### Amy
Blond floozy that Jeff Colby slept with after Fallon Colby's alleged death in 1984.

### Andrew Laird
**Spouse:** Emily Laird
Former criminal attorney who was Blake Carrington's chief legal counsel.

### Anna Gregory
High-school friend to Dana Waring.

*Photo courtesy of PeterMark Richman.com*

### Anna Rostov
**Sibling:** Nikolai (Kolya) Rostov
Pretty blond ballerina from Russia.

### April
Prostitute picked up by Adam Carrington in 1987.

### Arlon Marshall
**Spouse:** Carol Marshall
Owner of the Fashion Fury company who employed and slept with Sammy Jo Reece.

### Arthur Cates
Longtime lawyer to Sable Colby.

### Arthur Whitcomb
Colorado entrepreneur and former colleague of Tom Carrington. Donated his timberland to the state for a wildlife preserve project that Blake Carrington spearheaded in 1987.

### Audrey Fredericks
Stylist for Fallon Colby's nursery.

### Avril Dawson
Banker whom Blake Carrington appealed to for an extension on his $100 million loan for the China Sea oil leases in 1984.

### Baker
Reporter for World Finance magazine who filled in for Gordon Wales on an assignment involving the Carringtons and Colbys.

### Barbara
Executive assistant to Blake Carrington.

### Barbara Davis
**Spouse:** Marvin Davis
Denver socialite actively involved in the Carousel Ball charity event.

### Bart Fallmont
**Parents:** Buck & Emily Fallmont
**Sibling:** Clay Fallmont
Handsome and homosexual political man who became friends with Steven Carrington after being "outed" by the tabloids. They later became involved and lived together in Washington, D.C.

### Bartell
Foreman of the oil rig that exploded with Steven Carrington on it.

## Bedelia
Trailer-trash significant other to Frank Dean.

## Ben (Benjamin) Carrington
**Parents:** Tom & Ellen Lucy Carrington
**Siblings:** Blake Carrington, Dominique Deveraux
**Spouse:** Melissa Saunders
**Child:** Leslie Carrington
Conniving man who accused his brother Blake Carrington of causing their mother's death. Cheated his father out of oil leases in a deal with Jason Colby. Was abandoned by his wife and daughter in 1972. Plotted with Alexis Colby to steal Blake's South China Sea oil leases. Blamed by his daughter Leslie Carrington for making her mother unhappy; eventually made amends with Leslie.

## Ben Carson
Oil-rig worker fired by Blake Carrington for drinking on the job.

## Ben Reynolds
Friend of Steven Carrington on an oil rig that exploded.

## Betty Kingsley
Editor at Creighton Publishing Co., which worked on Caress Morrell's tell-all book about Alexis Colby.

## Bill Cochran
Banker associate of the Colbys. Advised Blake Carrington in his gubernatorial bid in 1987-88.

## Bill Mahoney *d. February 1986*
Engineer who was the pump-man aboard the Trident, a Colby Enterprises tanker that was responsible for the San Miguel oil spill. Was in a bar fight with Miles Colby after the incident.

## Bill Rockwell
Chief of public relations for Denver Carrington until he resigned in 1983. Rewarded Tracy Kendall with her job as his assistant after she slept with him. Started his own business, then tried to woo Tracy to work for him.

## Billy Dawson
Manager at the LaMirada hotel who worked with Fallon Colby to remake it into LaMirage. Enjoys mountain-climbing.

## Billy Joe (Sam) Erskine
Sleazy lawyer to Lucas Carter.

## Billy Waite
Snakish business associate of Blake Carrington and Alexis Colby.

## Blake Carrington
**Parents:** Tom & Ellen Lucy Carrington
**Siblings:** Ben Carrington, Dominique Deveraux
**Spouses:** Alexis Morell, Krystle Jennings
**Children:** Adam Carrington, Fallon Carrington, Steven Carrington, Amanda Carrington, Kristina Carrington
**Grandchildren:** L.B. Colby, Danny Carrington, Lauren Colby, surrogate son of Adam Carrington

Wealthy, at first ruthless, then later compassionate, oil magnate. Owner of the Denver football team, the 45- or 48-room (depending on which episode you believe) Carrington mansion, the Carrington Mall in Aspen, the Carrington Plaza in Denver, a cabin on Manchester Lake, a lake itself, and other goodies. Worked as an oil-rigger by day and went to school at night to eventually found Denver Carrington. Injured in an oil-rig explosion in Denver in 1964. Lost his temper when discovering his wife Alexis Carrington with one of the Carrington staff, Roger Grimes, in 1965, and had her sign papers and leave town. Often at odds with his son Steven Carrington. Raped wife Krystle Carrington in a drunken rage. Convicted of the manslaughter of Ted Dinard and put on probation. Blinded (temporarily!) by mobsters for a botched business deal in 1982. Challenged son Steven for custody of grandson Danny Carrington. Lost his memory in a Hong Kong oil-rig explosion in 1986 and was wooed by Alexis. Ran for governor against Alexis in 1987. Questioned for the killing of Roger Grimes in 1989 and in hoarding a fortune in World War II Nazi artwork. Imprisoned in 1989 until late 1991, when he was pardoned by the governor.

## Blanchard
Reporter for the Denver Chronicle.

## Bliss Colby  *b. 1965*
**Parents:** Jason & Sable Colby
**Siblings:** Jeff Colby, Monica Colby, Miles Colby

Youngest Colby child and beautiful blonde who was involved with Sean McAllister, then Spiros Koralis and later Kolya Rostov. Nicknamed "Rabbit" by her father. Competes in surfing events.

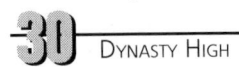

## Bob Ashmore
Business partner of Blake Carrington who offered him cash for his ELC holding in 1986.

## Brad Milburn
Sleazy associate of Blake Carrington who murdered his own wife in 1978.

## Brady Lloyd
**Spouse:** Dominique Deveraux
Charming, debonair recording executive with a way with words.

## Buck (Buckley Clayburn) Fallmont
**Parent:** Clayburn Fallmont
**Spouse:** Emily Fallmont
**Children:** Bart Fallmont, Clay Fallmont
Seasoned senator with a problem with alcohol. Hates Carringtons. Told his son Clay Fallmont, who was involved with Leslie Carrington, that Clay's real father was Ben Carrington, to drive the two lovers apart.

## Captain Lockwood
Police officer who took over the case of L.B. Colby's kidnapping.

## Caress (Cassandra) Morell
**Parent:** Steven Morell
**Sibling:** Alexis Morell
**Cousins:** Sable Scott, Francesca Scott, Rosalind Bedford
Jealous, angry woman who served five years in a prison in Caracas, Venezuela, writing an incriminating book, "Sister Dearest," about Alexis Colby. Loved Zach Powers and resented Alexis for "sailing off" with him when she was imprisoned. Put back in prison through the machinations of Ben Carrington.

## Carl Creighton
Editor / agent at Creighton Publishing Co. who handled Caress Morell's book.

## Carlos
Butler to Zach Powers.

## Carol Marshall
**Spouse:** Arlon Marshall
Long-suffering and smart wife of a fashion industry mogul. Bonded with

Alexis Colby and benefited from her expertise.

## Cash Cassidy
**Spouse:** Adrienne Cassidy
**Child:** Scott Cassidy
Senator, son of one of Jason Colby's adversaries, and former love of Monica Colby who secretly adopted the son she had by him. Reunited with her in 1986.

## Cecil Baldwin Colby  *d. November 1982*
**Parent:** Andrew Colby
**Siblings:** Constance Colby, Jason Colby, Phillip Colby
**Spouse:** Alexis Carrington
Oldest Colby son, powerful magnate of Colbyco and rival to Blake Carrington. Promised Fallon Carrington he would bail Blake out of financial trouble if she married Jeff Colby. Assumed the alias "Logan Rhinewood" to torment Blake. Formed a business deal with Alexis Carrington and had a heart attack while they were making love; married her on his deathbed.

## Channing Carter Colby
**Uncle:** Lucas Carter
**Spouse:** Miles Colby
Member of the publishing family of Carter Publications and slinky, sneaky reporter who was writing an expose about the Colbys when she fell in love with Miles Colby. Desperately afraid of becoming pregnant because of watching her own mother die after giving birth to her baby brother.

## Charles Dalton
Legal counsel and right-hand man to Daniel Reece.

## Charles Hampton
Neurologist based at the California Neurological Medical Group. Assessed Krystle Carrington's condition and the effects of her horse-riding accident.

## Charles Matthews
**Sibling:** Laura Matthews
**Niece:** Dominique Deveraux
**Spouse:** Jane Matthews
Man approached by Sgt. John Zorelli for information in the Roger Grimes murder case.

### Charlie Braddock
Kidnapper of the baby Adam Carrington in the 1950s.

### Chen Ling
Plastic surgeon who operated on Steven Carrington after the oil-rig explosion in late 1982.

### Cheryl
Assistant to Steven Carrington in 1987.

### Chris Deegan
Homosexual lawyer who was involved with Steven Carrington.

### Christine
Secretary to Blake Carrington.

### Claire Maynard
Aggressive columnist for the Denver Chronicle who met with Blake Carrington about a feature story on L.B. Colby's kidnapping in 1982.

### Claire Prentice
Therapist who cautioned Steven Carrington that little Danny Carrington was emotionally troubled in 1986.

### Claire Tennyson
Assistant to Steven Carrington.

### Claudia Mary Johnson Blaisdel Carrington Carrington   b. 1951; d. 1986
**Spouses:** Matthew Blaisdel, Steven Carrington, Adam Carrington
**Child:** Lindsay Blaisdel
Emotionally unstable woman who married Matthew Blaisdel when she was a pregnant teen in March 1966. Was discharged from a sanitarium in 1981. In love with Steven Carrington. Spied at Denver Carrington for Cecil Colby when he promised to locate her missing daughter. Shot in a struggle over a gun with Krystle Carrington. Obsessed with dead daughter Lindsay Blaisdel and hovered atop a roof with a doll in a blanket that everyone thought was the kidnapped baby L.B. Colby. Recuperated at the High Meadow Sanitarium. Slept with Jeff Colby. Married Steven Carrington in November 1983. Took over for the absent Fallon Carrington as head of LaMirage. Slept with Dean Caldwell. Involved with Adam Carrington as she was divorcing Steven, and married him in October 1985. Accidentally set fire to LaMirage and died there.

## Clay (Clayburn) Fallmont
**Parents**: Buck & Emily Fallmont
**Sibling:** Bart Fallmont
**Spouse:** Sammy Jo Reece
Handsome, athletic demolitions expert and often playboy. Hired by Dex Dexter for a pipeline project. Married Sammy Jo Reece in 1986 when she believed she was pregnant. Was involved with Leslie Carrington until suspecting they were brother and sister.

## Constance Colby Patterson  *d. January 1987*
**Parent:** Andrew Colby
**Siblings:** Jason Colby, Phillip Colby, Cecil Colby
Solid, kind matriarch of the Colby clan. Favored Jeff Colby. Involved with Hutch Corrigan. Killed in Nepal, with all suspicion focused on Hoyt Parker, alias Phillip Colby, not really dead.

## Cora Van Heusen
Brothel owner who provided information on Ben Carrington's whereabouts on the day Ellen Carrington died.

## Count Pierre
French pal of Fallon Colby and former acquaintance of Kirby Aynders.

## Cray (Creighton) Boyd
Soldier of fortune hired by Alexis Colby to recapture her fleet of oil tankers in 1989. Educated in international law at Yale and a former schoolmate of Adam Carrington. Former Green Beret.

## Crenshaw
Ben Carrington's attorney in his legal pursuit of Tom Carrington's estate in 1986.

## Dan Cassidy
Pilot / worker in Bali consulted by Blake and Alexis Carrington in their search for the missing Steven Carrington in 1982.

## Dan Franklin
**Spouse:** Marie Franklin
Employee of Tom Carrington. Helped Blake Carrington rescue an injured rigger on the day that Ellen Carrington was killed in a house fire. Testified years later for Ben Carrington's pursuit of Tom's estate.

### Dana Bethany Waring Carrington
**Spouse:** Adam Carrington
Schoolmate and former lover to Michael Torrance / Adam Carrington in Billings, Montana; had an abortion by him. Came to Denver to be near him. Unable to have children and arranged to have a surrogate child through Karen Atkinson.

### Daniel Reece   d. May 1985
**Child:** Sammy Jo Reece
Wealthy owner of Delta Rho Stables who was raised around horses. Owns newspapers. Was involved with Iris Grant Dean. Had an affection for Krystle Carrington and left his fortune to Sammy Jo Reece, with Krystle as executor, when he died in Libya.

### Danny (Steven Daniel Jr.) Carrington   b. 1982
**Grandparents:** Blake & Alexis Carrington, Daniel Reece & Iris Grant Dean
**Parents:** Steven & Sammy Jo Carrington
Sweet young boy with a love for horses.

### Dave Alden
Coach of Steven Carrington's football team in 1987.

### David
Administrative assistant at Colbyco.

### David Prescott
Executive of the architectural firm that did a renovation of the Carrington mansion in the 1960s.

### Dean Caldwell
Handsome art gallery owner in Denver who took an interest in Claudia Carrington in 1984.

### Dean Harris
Physician to Kristina Carrington.

### Dennis Grimes   b. around 1961
**Grandparent:** Alfred Grimes
**Parents:** Roger & Emily Grimes
Ex-con who came to Denver in 1989 to terrorize the Carringtons for the murder of his father and to obtain the secret Nazi art treasure. Was 4 years old when Roger Grimes was killed.

> **Behind the scenes**
>
> "Dex will leave Alexis, not the other way around. He'll see that they no longer fit."
> — Michael Nader, telling Playgirl magazine in 1985 how he thought Dex and Alexis would part ways

## Dex (Farnsworth) Dexter
**Grandparent:** Farnsworth Dexter
**Parent:** Sam Dexter
**Sibling:** Marilyn Dexter
**Spouse:** Alexis Colby

Dashing, handsome, young businessman and son of a Denver Carrington board member who took over his father's post in November 1983. A Rhodes scholar and honors graduate of the School of Mines. Former Green Beret, adventurer and sometimes foreign mission partner to Daniel Reece. Formed Lex-Dex corporation with Alexis Colby, whom he always loved. Involved with Amanda Carrington and Sable Colby behind Alexis' back. Shot in the back while trying to flee a hostage situation at the Carrington mansion in 1987. Fell over the bannister at the Carlton hotel in 1989 but survived.

## Dirk Maurier
**Nephew:** Gavin Maurier

Businessman who made $400 million in a few years through investments of junk bonds. Called a "financial genius" by World Finance magazine.

## Dominique Deveraux Lloyd (Millie Cox)
**Parents:** Tom Carrington & Laura Matthews Cox
**Siblings:** Blake Carrington, Ben Carrington
**Aunts:** Bessie Matthews, Jane Matthews
**Uncle:** Charles Matthews
**Spouse:** Brady Lloyd
**Child:** Jackie Deveraux

Beautiful, wealthy owner of Titania Records and some nightclubs whose birth name was Millie Cox and whose mother died when she was 13. Had an affair with Garrett Boydston as a young singer while performing on a ship in the Mediterranean in November 1965. Came to Denver to tell Blake Carrington she was his half-sister, the daughter of his father's black maid. Pursued in 1985 by Garrett ; eventually became engaged to him.

Hired Monica Colby to head the Los Angeles division of her company.

### Dona
Receptionist to Dr. Waverly.

### Doris
Friend to Krystle Carrington.

### Dottie
Prostitute whom Steven Carrington met at a club in late 1981.

### Douglas
Assistant to Alexis Colby at Colbyco.

### Dr. Jordan
Psychiatrist to Claudia Blaisdel.

### Dr. Mansfield
Pediatrician to Kristina Carrington.

### Dr. Waverly
Obstetrician to Fallon Colby and Channing Colby.

### Drew Mayfield
Judge in the Mark Jennings murder case in 1984.

### Earl Thomson
Defense attorney for Blake Carrington when Blake was accused of arson in the LaMirage fire in 1986.

### Ed
Barber to Blake Carrington in 1982.

### Ed Linden
Cosmetics company executive whom Sammy Jo Carrington was involved with in New York.

### Ed Queens
**Spouse:** Nell Queens
Jerky, antigay worker on the drilling crew of Matthew Blaisdel and Walter Lankershim. Framed coworker Steven Carrington for the rig breakdown.

### Elena
Duchess of Brana who was engaged to Prince Michael.

### Elsworth Chisolm   d. April 13, 1989
**Grandchild:** Phoenix Chisolm
Elderly man who once worked on the construction crew at the Carrington property in the 1960s. Answered a newspaper ad to provide information on the Roger Grimes murder. Lived in the Catalina Apartments.

### Emily Fallmont   d. December 1986
**Spouse:** Buck Fallmont
**Children:** Bart Fallmont, Clay Fallmont
Meek society woman who trained for the Olympics in equestrian events in her younger days. Had an affair with Ben Carrington. Gave Blake Carrington the evidence he needed that Ben, not Blake, was responsible for their mother's death. Hit and killed by a car after a fight with Buck Fallmont.

### Emily Grimes
**Spouse:** Roger Grimes
**Child:** Dennis Grimes
Nurse and tolerant wife of the philandering Roger Grimes. Approached by Dex Dexter and Jeff Colby in the Roger Grimes murder investigation.

### Emily Laird
**Spouse:** Andrew Laird
Attractive wife of Blake Carrington's chief attorney.

### Enid Palmer
Secretary to Jason Colby.

### Ernesto Pinero
Architect and associate of Peter DeVilbus. Worked on a building project with Fallon Colby at LaMirage.

### Ernie Braden
Lieutenant investigating the Bill Mahoney murder; arrested Miles Colby at the second wedding of Jeff and Fallon Colby.

### Everett Maurier
Attorney to Peter DeVilbus.

Dynasty High

### Fallon Carrington Colby Colby  b. 1957
**Parents:** Blake & Alexis Carrington
**Siblings:** Adam Carrington, Steven Carrington, Amanda Carrington, Kristina Carrington
**Spouses:** Jeff Colby (three times), Miles Colby
**Children:** L.B. Colby, Lauren Colby
Spoiled daddy's girl and flighty, sharp-tongued, promiscuous woman in her younger years. Killed Roger Grimes as a child after witnessing him beating her mother Alexis Carrington; repressed the memory. Graduated in 1976 from Miss Drew's School. Fell in with former summer-camp-mate Jeff Colby after her father suggested their pairing as a business deal. Established the hotel LaMirage. Temporarily paralyzed after being struck by a drunken driver. Lost her memory after she was presumed dead in a plane crash in 1984; wandered through California as "Randall Adams." Involved with Miles Colby, then raped by him out of his desperation after she regained her memory. Got into a mud fight with Sammy Jo Reece over Jeff Colby in 1988. Married and divorced Jeff a third time, then was involved with Miles again briefly.

### Farouk Ahmed
**Sibling:** Rashid Ahmed
Middle Eastern businessman who knew Nick Toscanni briefly when Nick's brother committed suicide in an Indonesian prison.

### Father Shea
Clergy associate of, and mentor to, Tanner McBride.

### Ferguson
Assistant district attorney in Denver.

### Francesca Scott Colby Hamilton Langdon
**Sibling:** Sable Scott
**Cousins:** Alexis Morell, Caress Morell
**Spouses:** Phillip Colby, Peter Hamilton, Roger Langdon
**Child:** Jeff Colby
**Grandchildren:** L.B. Colby, Lauren Colby
Compassionate woman who loved Jason Colby and was envied by her sister Sable Scott. Lived in California with her father after her parents' divorce. Wed Phillip Colby around 1957, and was only 18 when Phillip went off to the Vietnam War. Gave birth to Jeff when she was still very young, returned to her family to raise him, but then was pressured by

Cecil Colby to give up the 3-year-old Colby heir. Later married a diplomat, Peter Hamilton, and lived in London. Became widowed again and returned to California. Finally admitted to Jason that Jeff Colby was his son, not Phillip's.

### Frank Dean
**Spouse:** Iris Grant
**Child (assumed):** Sammy Jo Dean
Lower-middle-class racecar driver who shipped his daughter off to the Carrington mansion after discovering that his sister-in-law Krystle Carrington had married wealthy. Came to the Carrington mansion in 1983 after hearing about Steven Carrington's assumed death in an oil-rig explosion.

### Frank Linaver
Attorney who testified for Logan Rhinewood at the crime commission in 1982.

### Fred
Sleazy modeling contact to Sammy Jo Carrington in 1983.

### Fred Mason
Colonel and mission coordinator at Air Civil Control in Denver when the plane carrying Blake Carrington and Daniel Reece was missing in 1984.

### Fred McHenry
Police chief who helped Blake Carrington in the hostage situation with Matthew Blaisdel in 1987.

### Fred Merrill
Denver police lieutenant investigating the cabin fire that trapped Alexis Colby and Krystle Carrington in 1983.

### Fritz Heath
Colbyco controller and 20-year employee. Conspired with Sean Rowan to swindle Alexis Colby.

### Gail Kittredge
**Spouse:** Neil Kittredge
Beautiful blonde married to Monica Colby's Titania coworker and lover.

## Garrett Boydston b. 1940
**Spouse:** Jessica Boydston
**Child:** Jackie Deveraux
Levelheaded though sensitive lawyer who loved and pursued Dominique Deveraux. Had an affair with her on a ship in the Mediterranean in November 1965. Lied to her about being married, causing a rift between them. Worked for Jason Colby. Found out after many years that Jackie Deveraux was his daughter. Became engaged to Dominique.

## Gary Tilden
Former associate to Michael Culhane.

## Gavin Maurier
**Uncle:** Dirk Maurier
Wealthy, adventurous businessman who tried to woo Alexis Colby.

## George
Employee to Sable Colby at the Colby Collection.

## Georgina Sinclair
Ballerina and old friend of Kolya Rostov.

## Gerald Wilson
Attorney to Cecil Colby.

## Gerard
Butler to the Carringtons.

## Gloria Wilby
Attorney for Karen Atkinson.

## Gordon Wales
Reporter at World Finance magazine who interviewed Blake Carrington in March 1984. Hired by Alexis Colby to work at the Denver Mirror.

## Gregory Farnsworth
Handwriting expert in the case of Phillip Colby's letter concerning Jeff Colby's parentage.

## Hal Lombard
Grimy, Oklahoman business associate of Blake Carrington who came on to Krystle Carrington when staying at the mansion in 1984.

### Hall
Private investigator hired by Blake Carrington in 1986 to find the woman who was with Ben Carrington on the day their mother died.

### Hamilton Stone
Bank executive in Denver. Once was undersecretary of state. Once was an ambassador.

### Han Li Su
Chinese minister handling Blake Carrington's South China Sea oil leases.

### Hank
Ranchhand at Delta Rho.

### Harold Chadway
Physician who transplanted a new heart into Kristina Carrington in 1987.

### Harry Thresher
Man involved in a gunrunning scheme with Sean Rowan in 1988.

### Hawkins
Foreman at Lex-Dex. Fired by Dex Dexter in 1986 and started a fight with him.

### Helen
Nanny / nurse to Kristina Carrington in 1987.

### Helen Pomeroy
Court-appointed social worker in the custody suit over little Danny Carrington. Holds a bachelor's degree in sociology and a master's degree in social work.

### Henderson Palmer
Butler to the Colbys.

### Hilda Nielson Gunnerson
Longtime maid to the Carringtons who's "fed her relatives" on Carrington food, as Blake Carrington once surmised. Nanny to Kristina Carrington.

### Horatio Quinlan
Judge in the Ted Dinard murder case.

### Hutch Corrigan  *d. January 1987*
Rugged, aged cowboy and boyfriend of Constance Colby.

### Inspector Verlakis
Investigator on the scene of Nikos Livadas' murder.

### Irene
Maid to the Colbys.

### Jack Crager
Trainer of the horse Allegre, which was owned by Peter DeVilbus and Krystle Carrington.

### Jack Fowler
Man who bought Miles Colby's totaled sportscar.

### Jack Lyons
Police detective in Denver.

### Jackie Deveraux  *b. 1966*
**Grandparents:** Tom Carrington & Laura Matthews Cox
**Parents:** Garrett Boydston & Dominique Deveraux
Bright, impressionable young woman who was raised to believe her father was a racecar driver killed in a crash. Befriended by Garrett Boydston and later learned that he was her father. Injured in the LaMirage fire.

### Jake Dunham
Deputy district attorney in Denver who prosecuted the Ted Dinard murder case. Played football in college with Matthew Blaisdel.

### James Beaumont
Clothier to Krystle Carrington.

### Jane Matthews
**Spouse:** Charles Matthews
**Niece:** Dominique Deveraux
Middle-class woman who, with her husband, was questioned by Sgt. John Zorelli in the Roger Grimes murder case.

## Jason Colby
**Parent:** Andrew Colby
**Siblings:** Constance Colby, Phillip Colby, Cecil Colby
**Spouse:** Sable Scott
**Children:** Jeff Colby, Monica Colby (assumed), Miles Colby (assumed), Bliss Colby
**Grandchildren:** L.B. Colby, Lauren Colby
Commanding Colby son, strong but caring businessman and head of Colby Enterprises, which includes the subsidiaries of Colby Properties in San Francisco, Colby Industries in Houston, Colby Aerospace Labs in San Jose, Colby Timber in Eureka (where his "granddad" started the empire), Colby Petroleum and Colby Marine Transportation. Based at Colby Enterprises headquarters in Los Angeles. Personal wealth: $1.2 billion. Drinks single malt whiskey. Educated at Stanford. Fought in World War II. Loved Francesca Scott before and after he married her sister Sable Scott in 1958. Had a one-night stand with Alexis Carrington in the 1970s. Battled Zach Powers over business and over Zach's interest in Sable. Learned that Jeff Colby was his son decades after Jeff was born. Reunited with Francesca. Cut off twins Miles and Monica Colby in 1987, after Alexis told him they were not really his children.

## Jason Dehner
Psychic contacted by Blake Carrington in the disappearance of Steven Carrington, then again when Fallon Colby was assumed dead.

## Jay
Assistant to Alexis Colby at Colbyco.

## Jay Bradley
LaMirage hotel manager in 1986. Fired by Blake Carrington, then influenced by Ben Carrington to plot against Blake.

## Jeanette Robbins
Downstairs maid in the Carrington mansion, employed by the family since 1969.

## Jed Barrows
Foreman at the High Ridge chemical company in Montana. Spoke with Fallon Colby and Jeff Colby about the court case involving mercuric oxide poisoning, a case that Michael Torrance was involved in as an attorney.

## Jeffrey Broderick Colby  *b. 1957*
**Parents:** Jason Colby & Francesca Colby
**Siblings:** Monica Colby (assumed), Miles Colby (assumed), Bliss Colby
**Spouses:** Fallon Carrington (three times), Kirby Aynders, Nicole Simpson (assumed)
**Children:** L.B. Colby, Lauren Colby

Impulsive businessman who started out in media relations at Colbyco Oil. Educated at Princeton in the 1970s. Likes to drink. Became a sort of surrogate son to Blake Carrington. Often at odds with Adam Carrington, who tried to poison him with toxic paint fumes. Slept with Claudia Blaisdel. Married Kirby Aynders in March 1983. Involved with Ashley Mitchell after his "divorce" from Nicole Simpson. Fought rival Miles Colby for Fallon Colby, his one true love. Worked with Jason Colby at Colby Enterprises. Received $500 million in Colby shares from Connie Colby. Had a one-night stand with Leslie Carrington. Involved with Sammy Jo Reece in 1988. Was the subject, along with good friend Monica Colby, of a compromising photo fed to a tabloid by Adam Carrington. Wed and divorced Fallon three times.

## Jennifer
Londoner who was secretary to Cecil Colby.

## Jennifer
Assistant to Alexis Colby Rowan in 1988.

## Jensen
Owner of the jewelry store that fashioned Adam Carrington's silver baby rattle in 1957.

## Jeremy Van Dorn
Leader of a large public-relations firm, mastermind behind an international, evil conglomerate, and thorn in Alexis Colby's side in 1991.

## Jesse Atkinson
**Spouse:** Karen Atkinson
**Children:** Kelly Atkinson, Allison Atkinson

Man who was approached by Sean Rowan and convinced to reconcile with ex-wife Karen Atkinson, so that Adam and Dana Carrington would not get custody of their surrogate son.

## Jim Ellison
Powerful money broker from the East Coast.

### Jimmy Lee Paris
Psychiatrist and friend to the Colbys who treated amnesiac Fallon Colby.

### J.J.
Manager of many of Dominique Deveraux's business affairs.

### Joanna Sills
Woman whom brokered the sale of the Carlton hotel from Alexis Colby to Sable Colby. Dex Dexter turned to her when having troubles with Alexis in 1988. Romanced by Adam Carrington and joined forces with him to combat Sable.

### Joel Abrigore
Dark, conniving film director and abusive mate of Rita Lesley. Conspired with Sammy Jo Reece to kidnap Krystle Carringon, using Rita as her double. Disappeared in 1986.

### John Moretti
California assistant district attorney with a vendetta against Jason Colby who put Jeff Colby and Miles Colby on separate murder trials. Also accused Jason of beating Sable Colby, with Sable's false testimony.

### John Zorelli
Italian sergeant at the Harmon Springs Police Department who investigated the Roger Grimes murder. Raised in Philadelphia. Holds a Ph.D. in psychology. Worked at the Philadelphia Police Department and was wounded in his rookie year. Became sergeant after four years on the force. Loved Fallon Carrington.

### Jonas Edwards
Longtime physician to Kate Torrance. Came to Denver from time to time out of concern for Adam Carrington.

### Jonathan Lake
Assistant undersecretary of state. Intrigued by Dominique Deveraux. Hired by Bart Fallmont in his environmental campaign against Blake Carrington's pipeline.

### Joseph Arlington Aynders  d. October 1983
**Spouse:** Alicia Aynders
**Children:** Sean Rowan, Victoria Aynders, Kirby Aynders
Snobbish majordomo of the Carrington household and long-suffering nemesis of Alexis Carrington, who hired and taught him. Served in the military in the 52$^{nd}$ artillery in his younger years. Set fire to a cabin with Alexis and Krystle Carrington trapped inside after Alexis threatened to reveal to his daughter Kirby Aynders the "dirty" secret that her mother was in an insane asylum. Committed suicide.

### Josh Harris  d. December 1987
Football player who became involved with Sammy Jo Reece. Died of a cocaine overdose.

### Kai Liu
Asian businessman whom Alexis Colby appealed to in 1986.

### Karen Atkinson
**Spouse:** Jesse Atkinson
**Children:** Kelly Atkinson, Allison Atkinson, surrogate son
Surrogate mother to a child for Adam and Dana Carrington. Changed her mind about the baby and was awarded custody.

### Kate Torrance
**Child:** David Torrance
**Grandchild:** Michael Torrance (assumed)
Woman who raised the kidnapped baby Adam Carrington as her grandson, as Michael Torrance.

### Katherine Malley
Secretary to Cecil Colby.

### Katie
Maid in the Colby household, fired by Sable Colby, then reinstated by Connie Colby.

### King Galen
**Child:** Prince Michael
Ruler of Moldavia who cut a deal with Alexis Carrington and married off his son to her daughter, Amanda Carrington.

## Kirby Alicia Aynders Colby
**Parents:** Joseph & Alicia Aynders
**Siblings:** Sean Rowan, Victoria Aynders
**Spouse:** Jeff Colby
**Child:** miscarried daughter
Young, sometimes-naive daughter of a Carrington servant. Graduated with a humanities degree from the Sorbonne in France and came to the Carrington mansion to live in late 1982. Raped by Adam Carrington and was carrying his baby, later miscarried. Married Jeff Colby in March 1983. Convinced to move back to Paris by Alexis Colby after showing an interest in Adam. Worked as a translator overseas. Returned to Denver in 1991 to help the Carringtons recover Krystle Carrington from European captors. Became engaged to Adam.

## Kolya (Nikolai) Rostov
**Sibling:** Anna Rostov
Defecting Russian ballet dancer who was involved with Bliss Colby.

## Kotey
Minister official in Natumbe, West Africa.

## Kristina Carrington   b. December 5, 1984
(Note: Her name appears as "Kristina" on a cake in an episode, though it's often spelled "Krystina," as it was for the Eugene collector doll.)
**Parents:** Blake & Krystle Carrington
**Siblings:** Adam Carrington, Fallon Carrington, Steven Carrington, Amanda Carrington
Bright, friendly child. Received a heart transplant in 1987. Unknowingly helped Fallon Colby find the secret Nazi art treasure in 1989.

## Krystle Grant Jennings Carrington
**Sibling:** Iris Grant
**Cousin:** Virginia Metheny
**Spouses:** Mark Jennings, Blake Carrington
**Child:** Kristina Carrington
Compassionate, attractive, down-to-earth woman of humble roots in Dayton, Ohio. Raised on a farm. Came to work as a stenographer for Blake Carrington in May 1978. Involved with Carrington geologist Matthew Blaisdel before becoming engaged to Blake. Raped by Blake when he was in a drunken rage. Became a formidable opponent to Alexis Colby. Threatened numerous times by Alexis and suffered a miscarriage

> ## Behind the scenes
> "I loved the characters. I mean, I read the script, and I just thought it was a gift from God. I was so excited, because the people were so intriguing to me."
> — Linda Evans, in an appearance on CNN's "Larry King Live" in March 2004

when falling from a horse that was spooked by Alexis. Pursued by Nick Toscanni. Pursued by Daniel Reece, who once had an affair with her sister Iris Grant Dean. Pursued by Joel Abrigore and secretly replaced by lookalike Rita Lesley. Became mentally disturbed and ran away to stay with cousin Virginia Metheny in Ohio in 1987. Left the country for a specialized neurological hospital. Held captive in Europe as she slowly recovered in 1991.

### Kyle Bert
Lambda Corp. representative from Boston who came to check out LaMirage for a possible convention site in 1984, and didn't appreciate it when Claudia Carrington refused his slimy advances.

### Lady Ashley Mitchell  d. 1985
**Spouse:** Maynard Mitchell
Famous photographer who pursued Blake Carrington. Friend of Dominique Deveraux. Involved with Jeff Colby. Shot and killed at the "Moldavian Massacre."

### Larry
Oil-rigger hired by Blake Carrington in 1986.

### Lars Nordstrom
Tanker captain employed by Harry Thresher.

### Lauren Constance Colby  b. February 1987
**Grandparents:** Jason Colby & Francesca Colby, Blake & Alexis Carrington
**Parents:** Jeff & Fallon Colby
**Sibling:** L.B. Colby
Colby heiress born prematurely at Cedars-Sinai Medical Center, at 3 pounds 2 ounces. Paternity questioned before birth, until test results proved she was not Miles Colby's child.

BILLIE RAE BATES

## Lawrence Baskins
U.S. government customs agent in the situation with Kolya Rostov's quest for freedom.

## L.B. ("Little Blake") (Blake Carrington) Colby  *b. February 1982*
**Grandparents:** Jason Colby & Francesca Colby, Blake & Alexis Carrington
**Parents:** Jeff & Fallon Colby
**Sibling:** Lauren Colby
Sweet, blond, Carrington heir. Kidnapped by Alfred Grimes in 1982.

## Leslie (Saunders) Carrington
**Parents:** Ben & Melissa Carrington
Spirited, begrudging woman who, with her mother, left her father and moved to Canada in 1972. Went to engineering school. Worked for Dex Dexter. Involved with Michael Culhane. Blamed her father for her mother's unhappiness, but eventually made peace with him. Involved with Clay Fallmont before finding out he might be her brother. Had a one-night stand with Jeff Colby. Involved with Sean Rowan in the Natumbe operation.

## Lin
Butler to Alexis Colby.

## Lindsay Blaisdel  *b. 1966 or 1967; d. 1981*
**Parents:** Matthew & Claudia Blaisdel
Youth saddened by her mother's institutionalization; sent to live with her grandmother while her father was on assignment in the Middle East. Troublesome as a teenager. Died in a Jeep crash with her father in a Peruvian jungle.

## Lt. Gilman
Investigating officer when Sable Colby was accidentally shot aboard Zach Powers' yacht.

## Lt. Holliman
Denver police officer investigating Claudia Blaisdel's shooting.

## Lt. Olsen
Investigator in Bill Mahoney's death.

DYNASTY HIGH

## Lucas Carter
**Niece:** Channing Carter
Chief of the Carter publishing empire.

## Luke Fuller  d. 1985
**Parents:** Jake & Bonnie Fuller
**Spouse:** Carrie Fuller
Executive assistant to the public-relations director at Colbyco, and gay lover to Steven Carrington. Educated at Yale University. Was married for six years. Shot and killed in the "Moldavian Massacre."

## Marcia
Secretary to Blake Carrington.

## Margaret
Friend of Krystle Carrington and coworker of hers at the Carrington refinery.

## Mark (Howard) (Samuel) Jennings  d. April 1984
**Spouse:** Krystle Grant
Man from Krystle Carrington's past who was contacted in 1982 by Alexis Colby to make trouble for Krystle, using the fact that he was still legally married to Krystle. Had affairs with Fallon Carrington and Alexis. Pushed off a balcony by Neal McVane, who tried to frame Alexis for the murder.

## Martin Gaines
Board member of Denver Carrington.

## Martin Holland
Heart specialist to whom the Carringtons took Kristina Carrington in 1987.

## Marvin Davis
**Spouse:** Barbara Davis
Denver high-roller actively involved in the Carousel Ball charity event.

## Matthew Blaisdel  d. September 1987
**Spouse:** Claudia Johnson
**Child:** Lindsay Blaisdel
Denver Carrington geologist, friend of Steven Carrington, and Krystle Carrington's former lover. Married young, as a teen, in March 1966. Sent to an assignment in the Middle East for a year and a half before learning Krystle was engaged to Blake Carrington, in 1981. Pursued her. Left for

dead in a Peruvian jungle in 1981. Returned to Denver in 1987. Killed by Steven Carrington after taking hostages in the Carrington mansion.

## Maxwell Allen
Reporter at the Denver Chronicle who interviewed Amanda Bedford in 1984 and wrote a huge expose about her being Alexis Colby's illegitimate daughter.

## Maya Kumara
Widow of a dictator killed in a coup, and mistress to Phillip Colby as he posed as Hoyt Parker.

## Melanie
Friend to Krystle Carrington.

## Michael Culhane/ Cullinan
Cunning Carrington chauffeur who was involved with Fallon Carrington in 1981. Fired by Blake Carrington when Blake learned of the affair. Went to New Orleans. Returned to Denver in 1986. Involved with Amanda Carrington.

## Michael Cunningham
Ruthless prosecutor who went after Alexis Colby in the Mark Jennings murder case in 1984.

## Michael Grogan
Phillip Colby's buddy in Vietnam.

## Miles Colby  *b. April 1958 or 1959*
**Parents:** Jason (assumed) & Sable Colby
**Siblings:** Monica Colby, Bliss Colby, Jeff Colby (assumed)
**Spouses:** Fallon Colby, Channing Carter
Hotheaded twin to Monica Colby who met and married the amnesiac Fallon Colby, whom he knew as "Randall." Lost her, fought to regain her, raped her. Given a major share of the company stocks from his father, Jason Colby. At odds with his cousin Jeff Colby, at first. Involved with Fallon again in 1991.

## Miss Lindquist
UFO incident survivor and leader of the UFO survivor support group that Fallon Colby attended in 1987.

### Monica Scott Colby  *b. April 1958 or 1959*
**Parents:** Jason (assumed) & Sable Colby
**Siblings:** Miles Colby, Bliss Colby, Jeff Colby (assumed)
**Child:** Scott Cassidy

Sensible but sensitive and beautiful lawyer. Worked as one of Colby Enterprises' 12 vice-presidents until Dominique Deveraux wooed her away to head up her Los Angeles division of Titania Records. Had an affair with the married Neil Kittredge. Pursued by Wayne Masterson. Reunited with former love Senator Cash Cassidy, only to discover he had adopted the son she had been forced to give up. Moved to Denver in 1989 to be closer to her mother. Good friends with Jeff Colby and was the subject, with him, of a compromising tabloid photo by Adam Carrington.

### Morgan Hess
Corrupt private investigator in bad suits, initially hired by Alexis Carrington to dig into Krystle Carrington's past. Made threats against Blake Carrington in 1982. Tried to frame Alexis in the torment of Claudia Carrington with a tape of the deceased Matthew Blaisdel's voice in 1984. Plotted with Sammy Jo Reece to split Blake and Krystle Carrington apart with compromising photos.

### Mrs. Charles
Nurse who interviewed to be L.B. Colby's nanny in 1982.

### Mrs. Davis
Blake Carrington's defense attorney as Ben Carrington contested Tom Carrington's will.

### Nadine Craig
Obstetrician to Sammy Jo Fallmont.

### Neal McVane
Troublesome but powerful politician who was blackmailed by Alexis Colby. Tried to frame her for the murder of Mark Jennings by dressing up as her and pushing Mark over a balcony.

### Neil Kittredge
**Spouse:** Gail Kittredge
Vice-president at the Los Angeles office of Titania Records. Involved with Monica Colby.

### Nelson
Private investigator hired by Blake Carrington to find out who was sending compromising photos to him and Krystle Carrington.

### Nick Kimball
**Parent:** Ruth Kimball
**Sibling:** Octavia Kimball
Well-reputed drill foreman hired by Blake Carrington in 1986. Son of one of Blake's oil-business colleagues. Graduated cum laude from the Colorado School of Mines. Lover and fiance to Dominique Deveraux.

### Nick (Amerigo Nicholas Francesco) Toscanni
**Siblings:** Maria Teresa (Terry) Toscanni, Gianni (Giancarlo) Maleni (half-brother), Antonia Toscanni
**Nephew:** Joey
Bold and often abrasive psychiatrist who was hired by Blake Carrington to help a suicidal Claudia Blaisdel. Son of Italian immigrants in the lower east side of New York City. Was a neurosurgeon in the military. Lost his wife and baby during childbirth. Has an injured right hand from shrapnel in Vietnam. Later specialized in performance issues in athletes. Had an affair with Fallon Carrington and later pursued Krystle Carrington. Fought with Blake Carrington and left him for dead in the mountains of Skycrest.

### Nicole (Nikki) Simpson DeVilbus Colby
**Spouses:** Peter DeVilbus, Jeff Colby (assumed)
Bored but scheming socialite from Los Angeles who had an affair with Jeff Colby after Fallon Colby disappeared. Married him in a quickie ceremony out of state, which later proved invalid.

### Nikos Livadas  d. 1986
Captain of the Trident, a Colby Enterprises oil tanker. Bribed by Zach Powers in a scheme to bring down Jason Colby.

### Nurse Johnson
Nanny / nurse to Kristina Carrington in 1987.

### Oscar Stone
Down-home businessman whom the Lex-Dex Corp. bought out, after he conned Alexis Colby into a dance and a song at a country bar in 1984.

## Owen Bancroft
Princeton classmate of Steven Carrington whom Steven ran into during a trip to New York in 1984.

## Pete Davis
Communications officer at Air Civil Control in Denver who was involved in the search for the missing plane carrying Blake Carrington and Daniel Reece in 1984.

## Pete McWhorter
Officer in the Harmon Springs Police Department.

## Peter DeVilbus   d. September 1984
**Spouse:** Nicole Simpson
Wealthy international womanizer and boyfriend of Fallon Carrington whom she ran away with when she disappeared in 1985.

## Phil (Phillip) Thorpe
**Spouse:** Evelyn Thorpe
**Child:** Gary Thorpe
Man whose wife died in the fire at LaMirage and who held this against Blake Carrington.

## Philip Spaulding
Denver columnist who wrote scathing pieces about Alexis Colby.

## Phillip Colby   assumed d. 1957
**Parent:** Andrew Colby
**Siblings:** Constance Colby, Cecil Colby, Jason Colby
**Spouse:** Francesca Scott
**Child:** Jeff Colby (assumed)
Black sheep of the Colby clan. Alcoholic often arrested for drunken driving and brawling. Served as a lieutenant in the Army in Saigon, Vietnam. Was kept in a POW camp for 12 years. Assumed the identity of dead friend Hoyt Parker and partook in Parker's illegal arms operations; also took Maya Kumara as a mistress. Returned from a presumed death in 1987, posing as Parker. Suspect in Connie Colby's death.

## Phoenix Chisolm
**Grandparent:** Elsworth Chisolm
Blond, blue-collar woman who, with her grandfather, accused Blake Carrington of the Roger Grimes murder in 1989. Bribed by Adam

Carrington to provide further information. Lived in the Catalina Apartments.

## Polly Trumble
Young blond assistant at the Colby Collection.

## Prasad
Nightclub owner in India who had contact with Connie Colby shortly before she died.

## Prince Michael of Moldavia
**Parent:** King Galen
**Spouse:** Amanda Carrington
Dashing royal young man who entered an arranged marriage with Amanda Carrington as part of a business deal between King Galen and Alexis Colby. Their royal wedding was the "Moldavian Massacre," where several people died. Had an affair with Elena.

## Rashid Ahmed   d. November 1984
**Sibling:** Farouk Ahmed
Dark, dashing oil sheik and occasional lover to Alexis Carrington. Double-crossed Blake Carrington out of the China Sea oil deal in 1984. Shot and killed by Turkish authorities during a botched deal with Adam Carrington.

## Ray Boning
Executive vice-president of Rhinewood Enterprises.

## R.D. Fleming
TV show host in Denver.

## Rebecca Payne
Magazine reporter who antagonized Alexis Colby in 1987.

## Richard Daniels
School friend to Garrett Boydston.

## Richard Winfield
Obstetrician to Kirby Colby.

## Rita Lesley
Washed-out woman with a blue-collar background who resembles Krystle Carrington and plotted with Joel Abrigore to replace her and undermine the Carringtons. Took Krystle's place in the Carrington mansion. Disappeared with Joel after being found out.

## Robert
Waiter at the Carlton Hotel in Denver.

## Roger Grimes
**Parent:** Alfred Grimes
**Spouse:** Emily Grimes
**Child:** Dennis Grimes
Carrington employee who was having an affair with Alexis Carrington in the mid-'60s. Designed an art studio for Alexis on the Carrington grounds. Shot and killed by the child Fallon Carrington after she witnessed him beating her mother Alexis. His body surfaced at the lake owned by Blake Carrington in 1988.

## Roger Langdon
**Spouse:** Francesca Hamilton
British diplomat and lord.

## Rosalind Bedford
**Cousins:** Alexis Morell, Caress Morell
**Spouse:** Hugh Bedford
**Child:** Amanda Bedford (assumed)
English woman who was paid by Alexis Carrington to run her household and who took care of Amanda Bedford.

## Rudy Richards
Detective at the Harmon Springs Police Department. Partner to John Zorelli.

## Sable (Sabella) Scott Colby b. 1939
**Sibling:** Francesca Scott
**Cousins:** Alexis Morell, Caress Morell
**Spouse:** Jason Colby
**Children:** Monica Colby, Miles Colby, Bliss Colby
**Grandchild:** Scott Cassidy
Ruthless, conniving sophisticate who is often jealous of her sister Francesca Scott and wildly protective of her children. Lived in London as a

child, with her "Mummy" after her parents' divorce. Married Jason Colby in the Colby mansion in 1958. Raped when she was 19 and became pregnant with Monica and Miles Colby. Schemed against Constance Colby to protect Miles' shares in Colby Enterprises. Pursued by Zach Powers. Accidentally shot by Jason aboard Zach's yacht. Filed false claims that Jason beat her in an effort to keep him from divorcing her. Fierce rival to Alexis Colby. Had an affair with Dex Dexter and became pregnant by him.

## Sacha Malenkov
Stern and proud former ballet dancer and then instructor to the Rostovs.

## Salvador Ramon
Clerk / official in Mexico consulted by Krystle Carrington as she investigated her supposed divorce from Mark Jennings.

## Sam Dexter
**Child:** Dex Dexter
Businessman at Dexter International, Denver Carrington board member and friend to Blake Carrington. Slept with Alexis Carrington while she was married to Blake. Suffered a heart attack in 1983, and his son took over his seat on the board.

## Sammy Jo (Samantha Josephine) Dean Carrington Reece Fallmont
**Parents:** Daniel Reece & Iris Grant Dean (assumed: Frank Dean)
**Spouses:** Steven Carrington, Clay Fallmont
**Child:** Danny Carrington

Beautiful, wide-eyed but flirtatious brat who came to Denver to stay with her Aunt Krystle Carrington in 1981. Likes junk food. Lived in Memphis after age 7. Shared her assumed father's interest in car racing. Married Steven Carrington in 1982. Left town, then returned later with a surprise – son Danny Carrington. Left town again to pursue a modeling career in New York. Took the last name Reece after learning her true father was Daniel Reece. Inherited his horse stables and became a legitimate businesswoman. Married Clay Fallmont in 1986 when she thought she was pregnant.

*This mid-'80s US magazine cover featured Sammy Jo, Amanda and Dex.*

DYNASTY HIGH

Involved again briefly with Steven in 1987 and became friends with him afterward. Involved with Jeff Colby in 1988. Fought in the mud with Fallon Colby over Jeff. Fell for Tanner McBride. Returned to modeling in 1991. Involved with Arlon Marshall.

## Sarah Curtis
**Spouse:** Boyd Curtis
**Child:** Cathy Curtis
High-school girlfriend of Dex Dexter. Lost her husband and child in a car crash in 1987, and agreed to let her daughter's heart save the life of Kristina Carrington. Became obsessed with Kristina and kidnapped her.

## Sarah Pat Beecham
Young prostitute whom Steven Carrington met when Walter Lankershim took him to a bordello to "cure" him of homosexuality. Later testified in the Ted Dinard murder trial.

## Scott Cassidy  b. 1980
**Grandparent:** Sable Colby
**Parents:** Cash Cassidy & Monica Colby, Adrienne Cassidy (adoptive)
Bright young boy with an interest in space technology.

## Sean McAllister
**Uncle:** Zach Powers
Environmentalist boyfriend to Bliss Colby who spied on the Colbys through Bliss for his uncle, Zach Powers. Holds a master's degree in marine biology from the University of Miami.

## Sean (Aynders) Rowan  d. March 1988
**Parents:** Joseph & Alicia Aynders
**Siblings:** Victoria Aynders, Kirby Aynders
**Spouse:** Alexis Colby
Evil but charming man who rescued Alexis Colby after her car plunged into a river in 1987. An international terrorist wanted for car-bombings and other assorted deeds in various countries, sometimes under the alias Patrick McShane. Set out to destroy Alexis for the pain she had inflicted on his father and sister. Hired by Alexis as the executive vice-president of internal affairs at Colbyco. Involved Leslie Carrington in his Natumbe operation in 1988. Paid Jesse Atkinson to reconcile with Karen Atkinson so Adam and Dana Carrington would not get custody of their surrogate child. Kidnapped the baby. Killed by Dex Dexter in a struggle at Alexis' home.

### Sgt. Benson
Investigator in Kristina Carrington's kidnapping in 1987.

### Sharen
Secretary to Jason Colby.

### Sister Agnes
Assistant to Chen Ling in Singapore.

### Skip Maitland
Star quarterback on Blake's football team in 1987. Sold drugs.

### Spiros Koralis
**Stepfather:** Zach Powers
Chief of the New York office of Powers Shipping. Feels animosity toward his stepfather, Zach Powers.

### Stan McAllister
Coach of Blake Carrington's football team.

### Steven Daniel Carrington  *b. 1958*
**Parents:** Blake & Alexis Carrington
**Siblings:** Adam Carrington, Fallon Carrington, Amanda Carrington, Kristina Carrington
**Spouses:** Sammy Jo Dean, Claudia Blaisdel
**Child:** Danny Carrington
Sensitive, well-read, intelligent, homosexual man who is often the moral conscience of the Carrington family. Almost died of pneumonia at age 5. Favored by his mother Alexis Carrington, who left Denver three days before his seventh birthday. Schooled at Princeton. Often at odds with his father Blake Carrington. Lived with Ted Dinard in New York City before returning to Denver in early 1981. Hovered near death after a pool accident in 1981. Married Sammy Jo Dean in 1982. Presumed dead in a Southeast Asia oil-rig explosion in 1982. Returned to Denver after extensive plastic surgery. Married Claudia Blaisdel in November 1983 amid a custody battle against his father for little Danny. Served as the second-in-command for his mother at Colbyco. Befriended Bart Fallmont. Involved with Luke Fuller. Involved with Sammy Jo again briefly in 1987 and became friends with her afterward. Killed Matthew Blaisdel in 1987 after a hostage situation at the Carrington mansion. Named interim leader of Denver Carrington while Blake ran for governor. Became an environmental activist in Washington, D.C. Involved with Bart.

## Susan Farragut
Registered nurse who served as nanny to L.B. Colby. Knew and loved Nick Toscanni when they were both in New York. Loathes wealthy people such as the Carringtons.

## Sydney Tyler
Doctor who did tests on "Krystle Carrington" (really Rita Lesley) at Blake Carrington's request.

## Sylvia
Doctor who treated Connie Colby after Sable Colby accidentally ran her down with her car.

## Tanner McBride
Handsome young priest whom Sammy Jo Reece fell for.

## Ted (Theodore Franklin) Dinard  d. 1981
**Parents:** Jason & Dorothy Dinard
Homosexual man from North Dakota who was involved with Steven Carrington in New York. Killed by Blake Carrington when he walked in on Ted and Steven in an embrace.

## Terry (Maria Teresa) Toscanni
**Siblings:** Nick Toscanni, Johnny Toscanni

## Timothy Holmes
Colonel in the U.S. Medical Corps who testified that Phillip Colby was sterile at the time he was supposed to have fathered Jeff Colby.

## Tom Bradfield
Editor at the Denver Mirror.

## Tom (Thomas Fitzsimmons) Carrington  d. 1985
**Spouse:** Ellen Lucy Carrington
**Children:** Blake Carrington, Ben Carrington, Dominique Deveraux
**Grandchildren:** Adam Carrington, Fallon Carrington, Steven Carrington, Leslie Carrington, Amanda Carrington, Jackie Deveraux, Kristina Carrington
Carrington patriarch with business in oil, timber and rubber. Drank and had numerous affairs. Had an affair with his maid, producing an illegitimate daughter who was hidden for years from the rest of the

family. Ran a shipping line in the early 1950s and was given a priceless Stahl art collection after transporting some men accused of Nazi war crimes. Partnered with Jason Colby and Sam Dexter. Turned away from both his sons after his wife died in a fire and he held Ben Carrington responsible. Was close to Alexis Carrington while she was married to his son. Left a $500 million estate to Blake, Alexis and Dominique Deveraux.

## Tony Driscoll
Groundskeeper at the Carrington estate who knew it was Alexis Colby who went out shooting on the day Krystle Carrington lost her unborn child to a fall from a horse.

## Tracy Kendall
Beautiful, ambitious Denver Carrington employee who slept her way into her job and had her eye on Blake Carrington in 1984.

## Tyson Lawler
Banker at the Denver-Lawler Bank who issued Blake Carrington a loan to rebuild his company in 1984.

## Vera Nesbit
Former casino worker in Macao whom Ben Carrington talked into stealing casino money for him. Tracked down by Adam Carrington in Australia.

## Veronica Miller
Specialist brought in to help the tiny, premature Kristina Carrington.

## Victor Eckland
Editor at the Denver Mirror.

## Victor Miller
Doctor to Krystle Carrington after she miscarried in late 1981.

## Victoria Aynders
**Parents:** Joseph & Alicia Aynders
**Siblings:** Sean Rowan, Kirby Aynders
Sensible brunette woman who tried to convince Sean Rowan not to avenge their father's suicide.

### Virginia Metheny  *b. 1963*
**Cousin:** Krystle Carrington
Former prostitute. "Baby cousin" to Krystle Carrington who raised herself after her father died. Once involved with Dex Dexter under another identity. Involved with Adam Carrington.

### Vlachos
Greek "taxi driver" who was paid to give false testimony against Jeff Colby in the murder trial of Captain Livadas.

### Volkert
Pawnbroker who bought Krystle Carrington's emerald necklace in 1981.

### Walter Lankershim
Old oil wildcatter, former partner to Matthew Blaisdel and business nemesis to Blake Carrington. Married three times. Likes to play the piano.

### Warnick
Moldavian defense minister involved in the revolution. Held Krystle Carrington captive in 1985.

### Warren Ballard
Famed attorney who defended Alexis Colby when she was accused of murdering Mark Jennings.

### Wayne Masterson
Blind country singer who fell in love with Monica Colby.

### William Handler
Police captain involved in the Roger Grimes murder investigation in 1989.

### William Todd
Attorney for Adam Carrington in the custody dispute over his son.

### Winston Towers
Banker whom Blake Carrington appealed to for a loan in 1986.

### Yuri
Security chief and right-hand man to Prince Michael. Wears an eye patch.

## Zach Powers (Pablo Zacharias)
**Parent:** Salvadore Zacharias
**Nephew:** Sean McAllister
**Stepson:** Spiros Koralis

Smooth, handsome, powerful shipping magnate who pursued Sable Colby and held a vendetta against Jason Colby for his father's suicide. Born in Spain the son of a fisherman, and built his own company by marrying a Greek shipping heiress, who then died in a mysterious boating accident. Renamed her company, Koralis Shipping, to Powers Shipping. Fell in love with the "blushing bride" Sable when as a deckhand he walked in on her dressing aboard the Colby yacht; fired by Jason afterward. Had an affair with Alexis Carrington aboard his yacht in Venezuela. Took care of his sick sister in order to bribe his nephew Sean McAllister into spying on the Colbys through Bliss Colby. Bought the Excelsior hotel from Dominique Deveraux. Tried to undermine several business deals of Jason, including the pipeline deal with Denver Carrington and the IMOS satellite project.

### Behind the scenes

> Ask not what the role can do for you; ask what you can do for the role.

> Because we should always respect other nationalities, I have always tried to play them with dignity.

> True love doesn't happen right away; it's an ever-growing process. It develops after you've gone through many ups and downs, when you've suffered together, cried together, laughed together.

> Hollywood does not write parts for people like me, an elderly gentleman, and when they find out you're crippled, forget about it. No, I'll never work again.

— Ricardo Montalban, from brainyquote.com

# Character Recap:  Marriages and Births

## *Marriages*

Blake Carrington and Alexis Morell, 1950s
Blake Carrington and Krystle Jennings, January 1981, December 1983,
    January 1989
Alexis Carrington and Cecil Colby, October 1982
Alexis Colby and Dex Dexter, December 1984
Alexis Colby and Sean Rowan, November 1987
Fallon Carrington and Jeff Colby, February 1981, March 1986, plus one
    more marriage postshow, between May 1989 and October 1991
Fallon Colby ("Randall") and Miles Colby, November 1985
Adam Carrington and Claudia Carrington, October 1985
Adam Carrington and Dana Waring, May 1987
Steven Carrington and Sammy Jo Dean, January 1982
Steven Carrington and Claudia Blaisdel, November 1983
Amanda Carrington and Prince Michael of Moldavia, May 1985
Jeff Colby and Kirby Aynders, March 1983
Jeff Colby and Nicole Simpson (assumed), January 1985
Jason Colby and Sable Scott, 1958
Phillip Colby and Francesca Scott, 1957
Francesca Colby and Roger Langdon, 1986
Miles Colby and Channing Carter, October 1986
Matthew Blaisdel and Claudia Johnson, March 1966
Krystle Grant and Mark Jennings, 1970s
Sammy Jo Reece and Clay Fallmont, December 1986

## *Births*

L.B. ("Little Blake") (Blake Carrington) Colby, February 1982
Danny (Steven Daniel Jr.) Carrington, 1982
Kristina Carrington, December 1984
Lauren Constance Colby, February 1987

## Episodes

### "Dynasty"

*Season 1 – 1981*

*Three-part premiere: "Oil," January 12, 1981*
The pilot's opening music shows just the major stars' names in yellow over scenes of Denver, with Dale Robertson listed as "special guest star" and Bo Hopkins billed last as Matthew Blaisdel. In subsequent episodes, the opening music evolves to show all of the major stars, with their photos, in order: John Forsythe, Linda Evans (in a black dress, not the white one of later), Pamela Sue Martin, Pamela Bellwood, Al Corley, John James, Wayne Northrop, Katy Kurtzman, "special guest star" Dale Robertson and Bo Hopkins "as Matthew."

Our story begins ... Meet wealthy Blake Carrington, who's about to marry his secretary, Krystle Jennings. Also meet Blake's troubled yet levelheaded son Steven, as he flies home from overseas for the wedding and encounters one of his dad's employees, Matthew Blaisdel, returning from his assignment in the Middle East. Back in Denver, Matthew runs into his old flame – Krystle – at Blake's office. Meanwhile, the wily, sharp-tongued and spoiled daughter Fallon returns from Europe for the nuptials, also, and immediately nails the family chauffeur, Michael. Uneasy about becoming another Carrington "property," Krystle does some soul-searching with Matthew, who sacrificially tells her he no longer cares for her.

The second hour focuses on the not-so-wealthy Blaisdels, as Matthew gets a visit from an old partner, Walter Lankershim, who wants to go wildcatting with him. Matthew wants to get his life in order, though, picking up his daughter Lindsay and tracking down his wife Claudia at a diner, discharged from the sanitarium and not ready to come home. Blake apologizes his way back into Krystle's heart, and wedding plans continue. Walter thinks Blake has sabotaged his oil well. Blake tells Steven it's time to come work for the family business, but when Steven rejects this, Blake tells him he knows Steven is gay.

Claudia wonders if Matthew cheated on her while she was institutionalized. Fallon beats Jeff down in a political argument at the wedding reception, then beats his uncle in a game of pool and flirtation. Michael tries to blackmail Fallon about their affair, but she just threatens him back. Walter crashes the party to accuse Blake of sabotaging his oil well. He's dragged out back and beaten (in a darker Carrington moment, surely!), and Matthew intervenes just in time.

## "The Honeymoon," January 19, 1981
Business brings the happy couple home early from their honeymoon. The car Matthew bought for Claudia scares her. She packs a picnic lunch, though, and drives to Matthew's drill site to surprise him, but meets Steven instead. Steven offers to work for Matthew and "proves" himself by getting into a fight with the other rig workers. Blake almost brushes off Fallon's business idea for luring Matthew and his oil leases. Krystle gets the runaround from the Carrington household staff, until Blake sets them straight. Cecil tells Fallon he'll bail out Blake if she marries Jeff.

## "The Dinner Party," January 26, 1981
Blake invites Matthew and Walter to a dinner party at the Carrington mansion. Fallon tells Krystle a little about how rich people operate. Jeff's straightlaced social consciousness leaves Fallon finding it difficult to hold up her end of the bargain with Cecil *(I mean, come on, he'll hardly even smoke one with her!)*. Claudia finds common ground – and an escape from the lavish dinner party – with Steven in the den. Fallon overhears Matthew declaring his love to Krystle.

## "Fallon's Wedding," February 2, 1981
Ted Dinard is in town, and Steven's not thrilled. Walter wonders if Steven has been leaking information about their operations to Blake. Fallon tells Cecil she'd rather marry him than Jeff. Michael hits on Cecil's secretary, then goes behind Blake's back to try to help him. Cecil gives Krystle some advice on Blake. Steven meets Ted at a restaurant, and Ted wants Steven to come "home." One of Steven's coworkers witnesses this and picks a fight about it at the worksite. Fallon and Jeff tango on a plane on a long lunch hour – then come back from Vegas, hitched.

## "The Chauffeur Tells a Secret," February 16, 1981
Michael tells Fallon he misses her, but she'll have none of it. Claudia tells Dr. Jordan her concerns about Matthew's fidelity. Michael, after pillow talk with Cecil's secretary Jennifer, tells Blake about Cecil's deal with Fallon. Lindsay fights off the advances of a boy from school, who tells her she's going to be as crazy as her mother. Steven goes to dinner at the Blaisdels, and in a quiet moment, he and Claudia kiss.

## "The Bordello," February 23, 1981
Steven's antigay coworker sabotages part of the rig and makes it look like it was Steven's fault. Andrew has Blake transfer key holdings to where his creditors can't get them – to Krystle. Walter takes Steven to a bordello,

## Behind the scenes

*"We thought we would try to do a show that does everything you're not supposed to do on television. Let's write about the extraordinarily rich, that people don't see."*
— Esther Shapiro, about the show, on "Dynasty Reunion: Catfights & Caviar," May 2006

but Steven watches TV with the prostitute instead. Steven appeals to Blake to extend the oil leases of Matthew and Walter, but more of his dad's intolerance is all he gets. Krystle has a friend pawn an expensive necklace then gives the money to Matthew, and they share a near-intimate moment.

### "Krystle's Lie," March 2, 1981
Blake is rabid to know who bailed out Matthew. Lindsay's not happy to find out her parents "had" to get married. Matthew discovers that Ed framed Steven in the rig breakdown – and that Blake paid Ed to do it. A telegram from Ted leaves Steven in a blue funk. Ed tells Claudia about Matthew and Krystle. Fallon picks up Ted in the family jet to try to tell him to stay out of Steven's life. Blake finds Krystle's birth control pills and rapes her in a drunken rage.

### "The Necklace," March 2, 1981
Blake sweet-talks his way back into Krystle's good graces. As Matthew holds out hope beside the oil rig with the crew, Claudia does a night out at a singles bar – then must call Steven to give her a ride home. Michael tells Fallon some tidbits from Jennifer ... about a certain Krystle and a certain sale of jewelry ... Claudia tracks down Krystle at an art gallery and confronts her about Matthew. The Lankershim-Blaisdel No. 1 oil well comes in. Claudia and Steven sleep together.

### "The Beating," March 9, 1981
Jeff and Fallon get into arguments as he returns from overseas. Boosted by his involvement with Claudia, Steven decides to make some changes in his life – working for Blake and moving into his own apartment. Blake finds out that Michael has been sleeping with Fallon, and he hires some thugs to work him over. Lindsay finds out about her mother's affair.

### "The Birthday Party," March 16, 1981
Michael tells Blake about Krystle's pawned emerald necklace. Fallon finds

ladies' lingerie in Steven's new apartment. Fallon slips to Jeff about her deal with Cecil, and Jeff blows it all over the place — including Cecil's birthday party — as he gets wasted with Cecil's new girlfriend. Fallon appeals to Matthew to help Krystle – out of the Carringtons' lives. Ted visits Steven again from New York, aiming to get back into Steven's life. Matthew brings Krystle back her money, but when she goes to the pawnbroker to get her emerald necklace, she learns it's been sold.

### "The Separation," March 23, 1981
Steven tells Claudia he spent the night with Ted. Blake plays cat-and-mouse with Krystle as they visit a buyer for her emerald necklace, then the much-suffering Krystle must endure Joseph's antagonism, as well. Blake meets Ted at Steven's apartment. Ted also meets Claudia at the bookstore, and they have a frank discussion about their tug-of-war over Steven. Fed up, Krystle leaves Blake, saying goodbye to Matthew, as well. Steven leaves a Dear John letter for Ted, prompting Ted to track him down at the Carrington mansion. Blake bursts in as they are hugging and kills Ted in a fit of rage.

### "Blake Goes to Jail," April 13, 1981
Krystle returns, and Blake is arrested for Ted's murder. Court proceedings begin. Steven won't talk to anyone in the family. Jeanette testifies that Blake said, "I'll kill him" when finding out Ted and Steven were in the house. Krystle tells Blake they've got some things to work on between them. A witness to Ted's death, Fallon lies on the stand for her father. Krystle takes Blake's place at his board meeting, keeping the sharks at bay. Steven testifies with the truth.

### "The Testimony," April 20, 1981
Fallon has harsh words for Steven at the courthouse. Back at the Carrington library, tempers erupt. Andrew calls Claudia to the stand against Blake's wishes, and Jake Dunham makes sure Matthew is there just as she admits to her affair with Steven. Matthew then attacks Blake during her testimony. Matthew is jailed, and Claudia runs away with Lindsay. Blake takes the stand. Claudia and Lindsay get into a car crash. And ... in the final moment, into the courtroom walks the one who would change it all ... Alexis Carrington.

*Season 2 – 1981-1982*

### "Enter Alexis," November 4, 1981
*The new opening music shows the stars with the images that would stay with them for the ensuing seasons: Blake, Krystle in a white gown, Fallon*

*in her trademark red sparkle gown, Claudia turning on the lightswitch (!), Steven violently untying his bowtie, Jeff pouring a drink, Joseph, and the so-smooth and smoking Alexis.*
Alexis' testimony captivates as she tells the tale of Roger Grimes and the night 16 years earlier when Blake discovered the two of them together and lost his temper. She alleges Blake bought the silence of a lawyer (Andrew), a servant (Joseph) and herself. Fallon tries a verbal assault of her mother on courtroom break – and finally meets her superior! Blake warns Alexis never to repeat a mysterious "piece of filth" she told him years ago. Claudia awakes in the hospital, but Matthew has taken Lindsay and disappeared. Fallon directs her hostility, once again, toward Krystle.

**"The Verdict," November 11, 1981**
The jury finds Blake guilty of murdering Ted Dinard, with a suspended two-year sentence. Claudia has been put into restraints at the hospital. Blake aims to make changes in his life – especially in his family. Jake tries to get more dirt on Blake from Alexis. Joseph finds Alexis in her old studio on the Carrington grounds, and when he threatens her, she calls him an "impotent voyeur." Steven and Blake seek to reconcile but argue again. Krystle faints – she might be pregnant. Alexis moves into the studio.

**"Alexis' Secret," November 18, 1981**
*The opening music adds James Farentino as Dr. Nicholas Toscanni.*
With an easy, magnificent flair, Joan Collins as Alexis sashays into the Carrington kitchen to reconnect with "old friend" Hilda Gunnerson. She and Krystle then have their first encounter, allowing Alexis to not only assess the changes in the Carrington mansion, but also the worthiness of her new opponent. Andrew picks up Claudia from the hospital and takes her to her home. When Blake checks on Claudia later, though, he has to call Dr. Toscanni to save her from a drug overdose. Nick then takes on Claudia's case – after he meets Krystle. Krystle is adapting to the household: She handily "breaks" the news to Fallon that she's pregnant. After she learns from Andrew that Blake cut Steven out of his will, Alexis appeals to Steven to patch things up with his father. She also tells him Fallon is not Blake's daughter.

**"Fallon's Father," November 25, 1981**
Steven mends his relationship with Fallon. Krystle asserts her command of the household with Alexis. In her continuing campaign to get Steven back into Blake's will, Alexis tells Cecil that Fallon is his daughter and appeals for him to talk to Steven. Krystle consults with Nick on Claudia after her friendly overtures to Claudia are rejected. After another argument with Blake, a drunken Steven hits his head and falls into the pool.

### "Reconciliation," December 2, 1981
*Heather Locklear, representing a brilliant casting move by Aaron Spelling, is added to the opening music.*
Steven wakes up in the hospital, tended by his parents and sister, then goes home to the Carrington mansion. Frank Dean sees Krystle on TV and decides to ship his daughter off to easy street. Blake buys Krystle a snazzy new Rolls. Blake is criticized in the press, and Cecil wants to call in his loan, unless Blake sells him the football team. Heather Locklear as Sammy Jo arrives at the mansion and soon is sliding down the bannister and into a not-so-amused Alexis, who decides to dig a little into Krystle's past.

### "Viva Las Vegas," December 9, 1981
Nick meets with his sister, Terry, who tries to convince him to give up his vendetta against Blake for their kid brother's suicide. Fallon stows away on Blake's plane to Vegas to help him with his meeting with Logan Rhinewood. A storm sends Sammy Jo to Steven's bed for comfort, and Alexis sees her leaving in the morning. Unhappy with how Cecil is treating Blake, Jeff leaves Colbyco. Shortly after Krystle tells Alexis she's pregnant, Alexis secretly spooks Krystle's horse, causing a miscarriage. Blake uses the $9 million he got from Rhinewood's purchase of 45 percent of his football team to pay off his loan to Cecil. Fallon seduces Nick without too much trouble.

### "The Miscarriage," December 16, 1981
Fallon is anxious to learn more about Nick. The doctor tells Blake that Krystle shouldn't get pregnant again. Neither Alexis nor Jeff appreciate Fallon being out all night. Sammy Jo's partying pals talk Steven into a car race. Andrew returns to town to update Blake on his tanker situation overseas – and the mysterious Rashid Ahmed that he needs to reach. Alexis overhears and decides to investigate. Steven can't sleep with Sammy Jo because of Claudia.

### "The Mid-East Meeting," January 6, 1982
Krystle is depressed, and Blake wants her to see Dr. Nick. Jeff suspects Fallon is cheating on him. After Jeff tells Cecil he won't spy on Denver Carrington for him, Cecil bumps into the newly hired Claudia at Blake's offices and promptly asks her out to get some information. Alexis has a rendezvous with her old friend, Rashid Ahmed, in Europe and sets up Blake to fly over for a "meeting." Fallon learns she's pregnant. She also tells Nick that she loves him and wants to marry him. Blake runs into Steven at the club – and Steven is with a prostitute. Jeff takes the phone message about Fallon's abortion appointment.

## "The Psychiatrist," January 13, 1982
Nick puts Fallon in her place when she pulls a jealous fit after Krystle calls him. Jeff investigates his rights over Fallon's pregnancy. Krystle finds out from Frank's letter that Sammy Jo's stay is going to be indefinite. Alexis sets a trap for Blake: He arrives in Italy expecting a meeting with Rashid Ahmed, but instead he gets nothing but temptation from the alluring Alexis. Papparazzi hired by Alexis snap pictures of Blake putting suntan oil on her back and splash it all over the tabloids, which Krystle sees. Steven wins his rematch car race against Sammy Jo's buddy. Alexis seduces Blake into a passionate kiss, while Nick cooks dinner for Krystle and manages to draw her into a kiss.

## "Sammy Jo and Steven Marry," January 20, 1982
Krystle doesn't sleep with Nick. A fortuneteller informs Alexis that she'll marry a man who will die. Fallon makes another lovestruck appeal to Nick. Logan Rhinewood's henchman makes Blake an offer for the rest of his football team. Steven and Sammy Jo elope. Fallon can't go through with the abortion. Blake has to answer to the tabloid story on Alexis to Krystle, then Krystle calls Blake at the house and Alexis answers.

## "The Car Explosion," January 27, 1982
Thinking Fallon has had the abortion, Jeff tells her he's leaving, then tells Blake that he's quitting his job. Fallon baits Krystle about Nick. Alexis manages to drag some mother-daughter quality time out of Fallon. Nick tries to convince Krystle to divorce Blake. Steven and Sammy Jo return with the news of their elopement, and Steven says he wants to be a professional racecar driver. Blake tries to urge Jeff and Fallon to reconcile. Rhinewood's goons try to make changes with Blake's football team. Jeff saves Blake from a car bomb – but Blake is blinded.

## "Blake's Blindness," February 3, 1982
Blake rages about because of his blindness, alienating Joseph and others around him. The family's having a hard time accepting Sammy Jo. Alexis realizes that Nick is Fallon's "other man" and warns her that he's dangerous. Nick presses Krystle for an involvement. Blake sets out to nail Rhinewood for the car bomb and his blindness. Alexis and Fallon plan to scheme against Krystle, whom they think is sleeping with Nick.

## "The Hearing," February 10, 1982
Fallon confronts Nick about Krystle. Alexis sets up an "appointment" with Nick to corner him about Fallon. Blake testifies at the crime commission and begins to get his sight back, and Nick notices then later tells Krystle his suspicions. Sammy Jo charges expensive items to Steven's account –

and bumps into Alexis while she's doing it.  Blake gets a letter of pasted-together text, implying Krystle and Nick are involved.  Blake tells Joseph he can see and swears him to secrecy.

### "The Iago Syndrome," February 17, 1982
Upset that Sammy Jo knows about Fallon's questioned parentage, Alexis confronts Steven.  Blake talks to Nick about Nick's vendetta against him.  Cecil tells Claudia his men have located Lindsay – but Cecil wants Claudia to spy on Blake for him.  Blake tells Krystle that Nick might have been using her against him, and Krystle goes to Nick to confront him about it.  Fallon tells Alexis she regrets their sending the anonymous letter about Nick and Krystle to Blake.  Krystle finds the letter and goes to Blake about it.  Krystle almost gets on a plane back to Dayton, then changes her mind at the last minute after Blake's appeal to her.

### "The Party," February 24, 1982
Fallon decides to throw a party for Steven and Sammy Jo.  Cecil is angry over Blake's desire to adopt Jeff.  Alexis and Cecil make love.  Nick looks for another job, but he doesn't want the neurosurgeon's role offered to him, but then he is desperately needed in surgery.  Jeff walks in on a conversation between Fallon and Nick and surmises that Nick is the "other man."  Krystle overhears the whole exchange.  Blake overhears Krystle telling Nick she's glad she never cheated on Blake with him.  After Sammy Jo causes a scene dancing at the party in a slinky dress, Fallon has it out with her, then Sammy Jo blurts out that Fallon isn't really a Carrington.  Fallon grabs her mother from the party, gets her in the car, and forces her to tell her the truth about her parentage.  The car crashes.

### "The Baby," March 3, 1982
Jeff and Claudia steal away from the party for some quiet talk, and end up having sex.  Claudia sees this as a way to spy for Cecil.  Blake and Krystle enjoy some renewed passion, until Alexis calls him away to Fallon's side at the hospital.  Fallon – and her baby boy – survive, but she's in a blue funk over learning that Blake might not be her father.  Alexis, after finding out that it was Sammy Jo who told Fallon about her questioned parentage, offers Sammy Jo $20,000 to get the heck out of their lives.  Krystle learns it was Alexis who scared her horse and caused her to miscarry and we have ....  **Catfight No. 1:**  In this corner, Krystle in a burgundy pantsuit.  In the other corner, Alexis, in a periwinkle blue silk dress.  Place: Alexis' studio on the Carrington grounds.  Best-er: Krystle Carrington.  Closing quote: "If you want a rematch, just whistle," Krystle says, "if you can."  Alexis later finds out from Morgan Hess that Krystle is still married to some Mark Jennings guy.

### "Mother and Son," March 10, 1982
Fallon's baby boy has a heart problem and needs surgery, and only Nick is able to convince her to see her baby. The surgery is successful, and after she sees her son, she decides she can't let him go to Jeff. Alexis admits to Blake that she believes Cecil is Fallon's father. Jeff catches Claudia snooping through his files, and she explains that Cecil has promised to find her daughter. Claudia decides to resign from Blake's employ. Jeff finds out that Matthew and Lindsay are believed to be lost in a Peruvian jungle, and when Claudia hears the news, she goes for a gun.

### "The Gun," March 24, 1982
A blood test proves Blake is Fallon's father. Claudia confesses to Blake that she's been spying for Cecil, and Blake forgives her. Steven learns that Sammy Jo is working as a nude model in Hollywood. News arrives that the Jeep carrying Matthew and Lindsay has been burned in a Peruvian jungle — apparently with them in it. Claudia resolves to kills Cecil, and Krystle tries to intervene at Claudia's apartment. Just as he arrives there, Nick hears a gunshot.

### "The Fragment," April 7, 1982
Krystle feels sorrowful as Claudia is rushed to the hospital with a gunshot wound, and Nick struggles to bring her back. Blake meets with the mysterious Logan Rhinewood — via video camera. Steven gets a hooker. Blake encounters Cecil at Alexis' studio and calls him a scum for what he did to Claudia. Logan is revealed as Cecil. After surgery, Claudia is fixated on Krystle's affair with her husband, not on her struggle with the gun with Krystle.

### "The Shakedown," April 14, 1982
Steven becomes a target for a con man and is arrested. Claudia is moved to the Carrington mansion. Alexis sends Tony Driscoll, the gardener, off to work for Cecil Colby after she sees Tony talking to Krystle. Claudia deals with her demons. Nick has had enough of Fallon's childishness. Jeff

---

## Behind the Scenes

> Billy Crystal had done a gay character on a show called 'Soap,' but that was a comedy, and so from a dramatic point of view, it was the first time.
> — Al Corley, on the character of Steven, "Dynasty Reunion: Catfights & Caviar," May 2006

and Fallon have a passionate reunion and get frank on how they've both cheated. Blake gets from Tony the truth about the day Krystle lost the baby, then Blake has it out with Alexis for killing his child.

## "The Two Princes," April 28, 1982

Blake visits Steven in jail and leaves him there temporarily. Cecil is trying to hide an illness. Nick manages to talk Claudia out of running off to South America. Nick encounters a nurse he knew in New York, who's now the nanny for the Colby baby. The baby comes home to the Carrington mansion. Nick and Blake tell Claudia the news of the deaths of Matthew and Lindsay, but she tells them how she knew it from the telex on the night of the shooting, plus she reveals to them that it was her who pulled the trigger of the gun that night. Steven gets Alexis to admit she paid off Sammy Jo, then he has it out with his entire family.

## "Cliffs," May 4, 1982

Blake awakens to the sounds of the wedding-reception preparations of Alexis – on his grounds. Claudia sees Little Blake Colby as her replacement for Lindsay. Rashid Ahmed's brother meets with Blake in Rashid's absence. Nick visits Rashid's brother, who tells him Blake could have saved Nick's suicidal brother from the prison in Indonesia. Blake and Krystle go to Skycrest to buy a ranch. Nick goes there and confronts Blake about Ahmed's allegations. They fight in the mountains, then Blake rides off, but is thrown from his horse. Nick realizes this and leaves him for dead. Little Blake is kidnapped. In the throes of passion with Alexis, Cecil has an attack.

### *Season 3 – 1982-1983*

## "The Plea," September 29, 1982

The Carringtons investigate the disappearance of Little Blake. Alexis aims to marry Cecil in the hospital. Krystle searches for Blake in the mountains in a thunderstorm and finally finds him. Susan the nanny is found and questioned on her shady past. Blake goes on TV to appeal for his grandson's safe return, and during the testimonial Alexis tells the story of their firstborn son, Adam, who was kidnapped 25 years earlier, almost to the day. In Billings, Montana, an elderly woman sees the broadcast and reveals to Adam (known as Michael Torrance) who he is.

## "The Roof," October 6, 1982

Blake explains to Krystle how the loss of Adam helped motivate him to build his dynasty. Kate Torrance admits to her "grandson" Michael that she stole him from the Carrington baby carriage, and makes him promise to claim his birthright. Claudia disappears. Farouk Ahmed is questioned in the kidnapping of Little Blake. Jeff visits the ailing Cecil. Signs point to Claudia as the baby's kidnapper, but when she is pursued by the Carringtons and the police at her hotel, she drops the "baby" over the ledge of the roof, and it's revealed to be just a doll she was carrying around! Michael reconciles himself as the long-lost Adam Carrington and heads to Denver.

### "The Wedding," October 20, 1982
Jeff remembers Alfred Grimes' strange behavior, and he and Blake find the baby with Grimes and learn that he was ordered by Nick to kidnap the child. Claudia leaves the Carrington mansion for a sanitarium. Fallon holds a grudge against Nurse Susan, fires her, then tells Blake she wants a more meaningful life. She scopes out his LaMirada hotel, where she spies Michael Torrance. Adam visits Blake and tells him who he is, but walks out after hearing his skepticism. Alexis weds Cecil at the hospital, then he dies.

### "The Will," October 27, 1982
Jeff comforts Alexis at the hospital. Fallon takes control at Blake's "white elephant" hotel. Adam turns his attention toward Alexis. Cecil's will is read, and he leaves Alexis everything – if she has produced an heir. Since she hasn't, Jeff gets half of his possessions, including half-ownership in Colbyco. The reading also reveals to Blake that Cecil was Logan Rhinewood, and Cecil's will says that Alexis was in on the ruse. Blake vows to make her pay for that. Adam visits Alexis, and his revelation touches her heart.

### "The Siblings," November 3, 1982
Alexis pleads with Blake to accept Michael Torrance as Adam. Then, in her new, deluxe, Colby penthouse apartment, Alexis gets a report from Hess on Mark Jennings. Fallon and Michael Torrance flirt at the hotel pool, neither knowing whom the other really is. Blake and Krystle visit the grave of the real Michael Torrance, then speak with Kate's doctor. Alexis sees Fallon talking to Michael and "introduces" them – to their great shock. Fallon is skeptical, but Alexis begins making plans for Adam. Blake softens and tries to hire Adam, but Alexis has beaten him to the punch. Blake and Krystle have Adam over for dinner, and it goes badly. Alexis meets Mark Jennings.

### "Mark," November 10, 1982
Tensions begin between Adam at Colbyco and Jeff at Denver Carrington, as Jeff learns Adam is dealing with the Ahmed brothers. Blake makes new

Dynasty High

overtures toward Adam over lunch, with small talk and a hot new red sportscar, and Adam's refusal meets with a slap in the face later from Fallon. Alexis continues to woo the stubborn Mark Jennings in New York, who's carrying a torch for Krystle. Krystle gets tough with Fallon about Fallon's reservations on Adam, which are hurting Blake. Joseph turns in his resignation to join his daughter in Paris, but Blake stops him and tells him to invite his daughter to the estate. Mark arrives in Denver to offer his services as a tennis pro to Fallon and the newly redesigned LaMirage hotel. Adam steps out of line and fires Gerald Wilson. Jeff decides to rejoin Colbyco.

### "Kirby," November 17, 1982
*The opening includes Gordon Thomson, Kathleen Beller and Geoffrey Scott, but not Al Corley, Pamela Bellwood or James Farentino.*
Adam snoops through a file on Blake's desk. Alexis arranges it so Krystle sees Mark at LaMirage. Kirby arrives at the Carrington mansion and picks right up with her old crush on Jeff. Blake meets with Congressman Neal McVane over shale-oil development. Adam tries to make peace with Fallon. Alexis continues to warn Adam back about his animosity toward Jeff. Krystle accuses Fallon of trying to make trouble for her by hiring Mark. Adam plans to renovate Jeff's new office at Colbyco – with some poison paint.

### "LaMirage," November 24, 1982
Krystle learns that Blake did not know of Mark Jennings' hiring as the LaMirage tennis pro. Amid their happy reunion, Fallon hires Kirby as the baby's nanny. Fallon receives a letter from Steven – from Hong Kong. Alexis and Krystle try on the same outfit at the costume shop. Fallon hosts a Roaring '20s opening for LaMirage. Fallon's French pal Pierre recognizes Kirby as a party girl he met in Monte Carlo. Fallon then makes a spectacle of herself in the pool with Mark. Blake is uneasy as he spies Neal McVane dealing with Alexis – upstairs in the hotel – but he straightens out McVane on their "agreement," thereby cutting Alexis out of a deal. Mark breaks the news to Krystle that they're still married.

### "Acapulco," December 1, 1982
Blake heads to Washington with Neal McVane as Krystle worries about Mark's revelation. When she meets with Mark, he tells her Alexis was the one who clued him on to the invalid divorce. Jeff begins to feel the effects of his new office décor. Steven is in Indonesia. Krystle's trip to Mexico finds no evidence of her "divorce." Blake asks Adam to keep Alexis out of Denver Carrington's affairs. Blake meets Krystle in Mexico, then starts the process for her real divorce. The oil rig that Steven is on explodes.

## "The Locket," December 8, 1982
Blake hears of the oil-rig explosion and resolves to go find Steven himself. Fallon and Alexis feel their own deep grief over Steven being missing — and each takes it out on Krystle! Krystle tells Mark personally that she's proceeding with the divorce. Adam keeps hitting on Kirby, and she's fairly repulsed by that. Jeff gets more irate and snippy at his office. Sammy Jo's dad comes skulking around the Carrington mansion, and Krystle accuses him of gold-digging in Steven's assumed death. In Bali, Blake and Alexis dig into the details about Steven and the explosion. Frank Dean threatens Krystle, and Mark roughs him up.

## "The Search," December 15, 1982
Mark pays off Frank Dean and gets him out of town. Blake and Alexis speak to the foreman of the oil rig Steven was on. In his paint-fume stupor, Jeff confuses Kirby with Fallon and kisses her, causing her to run off – and into the arms of Adam. Refusing to give up, even as Steven's belongings surface, Blake decides to contact a psychic. Adam woos Kirby with dinner and champagne at the penthouse, then he rapes her. Meanwhile, Jeff passes out but is OK later. The psychic comes to Denver to get some vibes off Steven's old room. Jeff apologizes to Kirby for his behavior, and they both know how much he really loves Fallon.

## "Samantha," December 29, 1982
Krystle has her reservations about the psychic. Blake gets jealous of Krystle's dealings with Mark. Alexis presses on with the memorial service for Steven. Mark accuses Alexis of "screwing up" his life, then tells her he's leaving Denver. They then sleep together! The psychic tells Blake he's giving up on Steven. Krystle and Fallon actually share a concerned moment over Blake. Blake gets Steven's jacket, returned from the oil-rig wreckage, and the psychic gets a reading from it. Sammy Jo – now calling herself "Samantha" – returns to Denver with a surprise just for Blake: Steven Daniel Carrington Jr. The baby is welcomed with open arms, and Blake believes this is the "reading" that the psychic got about Steven.

## "Danny," January 5, 1983
*Heather Locklear is added back to the show's opening.*
Sammy Jo goes after her "pound of flesh" with the Carringtons for not accepting her before. She implies to Krystle that the family will have to buy little Danny from her. Blake answers with a stern stance that they won't buy Danny but they will offer her some money to help her in New York. Alexis asks Mark not to leave town – in her own special way. Kirby tells her father she wants a better life. Jeff is walking around in a haze.

Alexis tries to throw money at Sammy Jo to get Danny for herself, and they take turns calling each other "tramp." Sammy Jo tells Krystle she wants her and Blake to adopt Danny. In Singapore, a man in bandages wakes up from a coma.

## "Madness," January 12, 1983
Jeff gets irritable around the nursery, and both Kirby and Krystle are concerned. Then he taunts Fallon at LaMirage and raises her concern. Meanwhile, Adam works on further loosening Jeff's grip on reality by playing him against Blake. Alexis blows a gasket when Krystle tells her about the adoption of little Danny. The injured man in Singapore claims his name is Ben Reynolds. Mark gives Alexis an expensive piece of jewelry. Jeff tries to strangle Fallon. Alexis tells Jeff she wants a more active role in Colbyco. Alexis then tells Adam she's moving into Jeff's office, and Adam tells Alexis about the poison paint. When he doesn't get her buy-in for his plot against Jeff, he threatens to make it look like it was her idea.

## "Two Flights to Haiti," January 26, 1983
Alexis comes out swinging, verbally, after Adam's threat, determined not to let him gain power over her. Blake confronts Jeff about his attack of Fallon. Fallon heads to Haiti to get a divorce. Adam asks Kirby to be a translator for his business dealings. Adam gets Jeff to sign over his son's shares of Denver Carrington. Alexis feels regrets about the effects on Jeff. Increasingly jealous over the time Fallon spends with Mark, Jeff marches onto the tennis courts at LaMirage and challenges Mark to a match. After the longest volley in history (!), Jeff finally collapses. Mark surprises Fallon when he shows up in Port-au-Prince.

## "The Mirror," February 4, 1983
Alexis worries about the tests being run on Jeff in the hospital. Joseph doesn't want Kirby working as a nanny. In Haiti, Mark laments to Fallon how tough life is when you're so handsome. The Torrances' family doctor Jonas Edwards drops in on Adam and mentions Adam's past "breakdown" with drugs. Kirby makes a big confession of love to Jeff in the hospital, but he falls asleep. The bandages come off the man in Singapore – who's young and blond and reminiscent of ... *hmmm* .... Blake warns Gerald Wilson that Alexis better not harm Jeff. Alexis taunts Blake with the shares she and Adam scammed away from Jeff, threatening to merge Denver Carrington with Colbyco, but then Blake gets the call from the hospital that neurotoxins were found in Jeff's system.

## "Battle Lines," February 16, 1983
Blake puts Andrew on the case of stopping Alexis from taking over Denver

> ## Behind the scenes
>
> "As I play Fallon, I can see she has a method to her madness. She's strong-willed and she has her own reasons for doing what she does."
>
> — Pamela Sue Martin

Carrington. Really coming into her fashionable own in furs and other finery, Alexis waltzes into the hospital to whisk Jeff away to a Swiss spa, but she's stopped by Blake. Jeff comes home to the mansion instead, where he struggles to remember the events leading up to his collapse. Kirby repeats her love confession to Jeff, only this time he's awake, and they have sex. Krystle sees Mark and Fallon kissing. Krystle hears from Sammy Jo that she's signed the adoption papers. Dan Cassidy arrives in Singapore to check out this "Ben Reynolds" – then realizes it's not Ben Reynolds. He calls Blake.

### "Reunion in Singapore," February 25, 1983
*Jack Coleman is added to the opening.*
Everyone wants to go with Blake to Singapore: Krystle, Fallon, Alexis. Neal refuses to be influenced by Alexis, so she hires Hess to dig up dirt on him. Motherhood has really changed Fallon – she continues her soft words for Krystle, then works to smooth the waters between herself and Jeff. Jeff tells Alexis and Adam he wants control of his shares back. Alexis realizes Mark has something going on with Fallon. On a driving business trip, Adam pretends the car is broken down to lure Kirby into a seedy motel. Jeff comes to her rescue, just as Adam attacks her again, then afterward Jeff asks Kirby to marry him. Blake sees Steven – and knows that he is his son – and while Steven tries to walk away, Blake tells Steven he has a child.

### "Fathers and Sons," March 3, 1983
Steven's family members – Blake in person and others via phone in Denver – finally convince him to come home. Jeff and Kirby elope to Reno. Krystle and Alexis take a timeout from their Cold War as Krystle shares the happy news about Steven. The family gets their first emotional look at Steven and his new face. Steven has a little talk with Alexis about her buying off Sammy Jo, and she tells him Blake bought Danny for Krystle. Mark comes on to Fallon full-force. Steven has it out with Blake then decides to go to New York to find Sammy Jo.

### "The Downstairs Bride," March 9, 1983
*Heather Locklear appears in the opening for this episode.*
In New York, Sammy Jo finds out Steven is alive – from the cover of the National Enquirer (which, incidentally, also bears a whopping big photo of the cast of "Dallas" with the enticing headline, "Sneak Peak")! Alexis tells Adam to make friends with Steven, pronto, but Adam bungles it by telling Steven he's better off without Sammy Jo. Fallon welcomes back Jeff and Kirby with remorse. Alexis also finds the new marriage disturbing. Steven sees Sammy Jo in New York, and she tells him she wants nothing to do with him or their child.

### "The Vote," March 16, 1983
Steven tells Fallon he's moving into an apartment with his new baby. At Alexis' special board meeting, Blake's old friends vote against him and for the merger with Colbyco. Krystle tries to calm the waters between Blake and Steven. While delivering a report on McVane's affair with a teen girl, Hess gets nervous about a man he sees from Alexis' balcony. After seeing Mark kissing Fallon, Alexis tells Fallon he's a "male tramp." Steven sees a lawyer to get a divorce. Steven and Adam continue their rocky relations. When Blake calls a meeting with Alexis, she sets it up at her penthouse, in a slinky ensemble, but this brings only Blake's repulsion.

### "The Dinner," March 30, 1983
*Pamela Bellwood appears in the opening for this episode.*
Blake has terse words in the nursery for the visiting Steven, who now lives at LaMirage and works at Colbyco. Chronicle reporter Claire Maynard taunts Steven with questions about Claudia. Kirby is increasingly sensitive about Jeff's interaction with Fallon. Alexis takes on Krystle after Krystle visits Steven at the office. Blake cuts a deal with the inventor of a shale-oil process, leaving Alexis out in the cold. Steven visits Claudia at the sanitarium, and she tells him he's treating her like she's going to "shatter." Alexis tells Mark she wants him out of Fallon's life, and when he refuses, she sets it up so Fallon sees the two of them together. On a trip to the field, Steven makes it clear to Adam that oil rigs are his turf.

### "The Threat," April 13, 1983
Blake and Krystle try to talk through a fight they had as the newspaper arrives, splashed with the scandal about McVane. After Krystle's sorrowful goodbye, little Danny goes with Steven to live at his apartment. McVane accuses Blake of digging up the dirt on him, but Blake points him in the right direction – Alexis. Kirby learns she's pregnant. Steven's lawyer Chris tells him that he's also gay. Sick of Alexis' schemes, Fallon tells her she regrets helping her torment Krystle. Alexis then confronts

Krystle at the lily pond on the Carrington grounds and we have …
**Catfight No. 2:** In this corner, Krystle in a blue satin robe. In the other corner, Alexis, in a black-and-white patterned, blousy dress, with black-and-white wide-brimmed hat. Best-er: Krystle Carrington, who got in a couple solid punches and crawled out of the pond first (so Blake could yell at her, unfortunately). Opening quote: "You miserable bitch!" Krystle says as she pushes Alexis into the pond, black patent-leather purse and all. Humiliated by Blake's reprimand, Krystle then packs and heads for LaMirage. Blake tries unsuccessfully to woo her back. McVane sneaks into Alexis' office and attacks her, but Blake rushes in just in time to save her.

### "The Cabin," April 20, 1983
Steven tells Fallon that Chris has moved into his apartment. After Adam criticizes Steven's personal life to his face once again, Alexis tells Adam she's rewriting her will to disinherit him until his behavior improves. Steven visits Claudia again. Hess tells Alexis he needs cash, and when she refuses to loan it, he threatens her. In Denver for a convention, Dr. Edwards has a run-in with Adam, then unknowingly gives Fallon a key piece of info about one of Adam's previous cases – involving poison chemicals. Mark also threatens Alexis. McVane broods about Alexis. Joseph even threatens Alexis after she taunts him about some knowledge she has about Kirby's mother. Blake drops by Steven's apartment – and meets Chris. Kirby learns she's three months along, meaning the baby must be Adam's. Alexis draws Krystle to Steven's cabin in the ruse of a meeting with Steven, but really tries to buy her out of Blake's life with a $1-million check. While they talk, though, a mysterious male figure sets fire to the cabin and traps them inside!

### *Season 4 – 1983-1984*

### "The Arrest," September 28, 1983
Mark rescues Krystle and Alexis from the cabin. Steven tells an enraged Blake to stay away from his apartment. Blake rushes to Krystle's side at the hospital. Alexis suspects Adam of setting the fire. Kirby is increasingly agitated about the baby. The police question Blake about the fire. Jeff has Alexis inform Adam that Jeff will be running Colbyco until Alexis is out of the hospital. Fallon asks Adam about the chemical-poisoning case, and he lies to cover himself. Then Dr. Edwards recants his story to her. Kirby takes out an unruly horse and deliberately gets thrown from it. Mark is arrested in the fire investigation.

## "The Bungalow," October 5, 1983
Fallon asks Krystle to comfort Kirby, who admits to Krystle that she doesn't want the baby. Blake visits Hess to see if he was the one who set the fire. The missing Joseph returns. Blake tries to determine if McVane set the fire. Meanwhile, Mark is charged with arson and attempted murder – but Blake posts his bail. Alexis' attempted murderer tries to smother her with a pillow at the hospital. She returns home with frazzled nerves and hair that's been shortened from the cabin blaze. Joseph places a troubling phone call to Blake, and just as Blake and Jeff find him at his wife's old house, Joseph shoots himself.

## "The Note," October 19, 1983
*Pamela Bellwood is added back to the show's opening; Lee Bergere is taken out.*
The police find a note from Joseph confessing to the cabin fire, and telling of his hatred for Alexis. Blake confronts Alexis about her threat to tell Kirby the secret about her mother. Blake then comforts Kirby and tells her she'll always be part of the family. Now a free man, Mark thanks Krystle for believing in him. Claudia leaves the sanitarium and checks into LaMirage, and she and Steven have sex. Alexis asks Mark to be her bodyguard, which he flatly refuses. Claudia encourages Steven to reunite with Blake. Kirby admits to Krystle that she deliberately tried to miscarry, and that the baby is Adam's. Adam decides to go back to Billings. Blake aims to proceed with a custody suit against Steven, and the two have a physical scuffle.

## "The Hearing, Part 1," October 26, 1983
*Heather Locklear appears in the show's opening.*
Blake suits up for a court battle over Danny, and Sammy Jo sees the tabloid news about it in New York. Claudia goes to work for Fallon at LaMirage. In the nursery, Kirby gets enraged and tries to choke Alexis because of Joseph's suicide. Steven alienates the court-appointed social worker. Blake convinces Adam to stay in Denver, so Adam starts working for Denver Carrington – and living at the Carrington mansion. Blake loses his cool in the courtroom. Krystle and Alexis both testify on Steven's behalf. Sammy Jo calls Blake, offering to help him secure custody of Danny.

## "The Hearing, Part 2," November 2, 1983
Alexis goes home to find her penthouse ransacked. She then tries to convince Adam to move back in. Fallon testifies to Steven's paternal love at the hearing. Sammy Jo enters the court with a flourish – and a dress and hat that seem to be a pale imitation of Alexis' style — and makes

BILLIE RAE BATES

allegations of gay promiscuity about Steven.  Fallon takes Jeff along in her investigation in Billings.  On the stand, Steven refuses to say whether or not Chris Deegan is his lover.   Jeff and Fallon sleep together in Montana.  At Sammy Jo's hotel room, Claudia tells Sammy Jo to retract her lies on the stand, leading us to ... **Catfight No. 3:** In this corner, we have Claudia, in a semicasual, low-cut sweater and slacks in neutral shades.  In the other corner, it's Sammy Jo, in a red and white short bathrobe.  It's a simple catfight, but meaningful nonetheless: WHACK, goes Claudia to Sammy Jo.  Stunned silence ... studying, studying .... then, WHACK goes Sammy Jo to Claudia.  Another stunned silence ... studying, studying ... then, finally, WHACK goes Claudia to Sammy Jo another time.  That'll do it, because Claudia then heads out the door of the hotel room.  *Meow!*

## "Tender Comrades," November 9, 1983
Sammy Jo lashes out at Krystle when Krystle asks her if she lied on the stand.  Fallon and Jeff agree to forget their night of sex in Montana.  Claudia and Steven elope to Reno as part of Claudia's plan to help Steven win custody of Danny.  Adam decides to head off Fallon at the pass by framing Alexis for Jeff's chemical poisoning.  Steven and Claudia arrive in court just in time, and the lawsuit is dismissed, in light of Steven's new wife.  Acting on the advice of Andrew to treat Krystle more like a partner than a possession, Blake asks Krystle to be his chief of public relations.  Fallon and Jeff tell Blake that Adam poisoned Jeff, but Blake doesn't want to believe it just yet.

## "Tracy," November 16, 1983
*Deborah Adair is added to the opening.*
Tracy Kendall, the assistant to Blake's public relations chief, is pushed out of the running for the chief's job as word spreads that Blake has appointed Krystle to the post.  Mark stops by Krystle's room at LaMirage and tries to rape her.  Adam tells Blake that Alexis poisoned Jeff.  When Blake investigates with the paint company, he finds the papers that Adam planted – signed by Alexis.  Andrew then grills Adam about Alexis' involvement in the poisoning.  Jeff and Kirby grow further apart.  Blake faces off with Alexis on the chemical poisoning and demands that she return Jeff's signed-away company shares, thereby forcing an end to her attempt to merge Colbyco and Denver Carrington.

## "Dex," November 23, 1983
*Michael Nader is added to the opening.*
Tracy Kendall really resents working for Krystle.  Jeff marches into Alexis' office, accuses her of trying to kill him, and doesn't leave until she signs his shares back over to him.  Blake woos Krystle over dinner at the

restaurant they first went to. In light of his betrayal, Alexis tells Adam he's on his own, as far as she's concerned. Mark agrees to be Alexis' bodyguard. Dex Dexter sweeps onto the scene to take over his father's place on the Denver Carrington board, and he lets Blake know he means business. Alexis flies to Billings and talks with Dr. Edwards, who tells her that Adam's judgment is impaired by the drugs he took in his youth. Dex breezes into Alexis' office unannounced for their "unfinished business" – he takes her into his arms for a kiss, then proposes a business deal, which she turns down.

## "Peter DeVilbus," November 30, 1983
*Helmut Berger is added to the opening.*
Jeff comes on to Fallon, then Adam antagonizes her. Alexis puts a negative spin on the failed merger in the press. Jeff cuts Alexis a deal – his 50 percent of Colbyco for her 47 percent of Denver Carrington. Alexis is concerned about the "image" Claudia is projecting as Steven's wife. Jeff goes back to work for Blake. Adam entices Tracy in a kiss. Peter DeVilbus, handsome millionaire playboy, woos Fallon at the racetrack and at the hotel he owns. What she doesn't know is that he's a crackhead who's in debt. Jeff finds out Kirby is further along than he thought, and she admits that Adam raped her.

## "The Proposal," December 7, 1983
Dex continues to pour on the charm with Alexis, and she continues to fend him off. Jeff accuses Kirby of wanting her sexual involvement with Adam, but then he tries to throw Adam over the edge of a Denver Carrington building project. Krystle fires off her own PR to counter Alexis' negative spin. Kirby almost flies out of Denver, and though she doesn't take the plane, she still tells Jeff she's divorcing him. Alexis finally cuts a deal with Dex – then, as he tries to get her into the sack, she delivers the classic line, "Nobody takes me to the cleaners and to bed on the same day, Mr. Dexter." Blake proposes to Krystle, and she says yes.

## "The Carousel," December 21, 1983
Everybody's in bed at the beginning of this episode: Dex and Alexis, Fallon and Peter, Blake and Krystle. Having been told about the baby by Jeff, Adam keeps wanting to talk to Kirby, but she'll have nothing to do with him. Dex forms the Lex-Dex Corp. in honor of his new partnership with Alexis. Blake agrees to buy half-interest in Peter's prize horse, Allegre, which arrives at Blake's farm. At Denver's illustrious Carousel Ball, the Carringtons bump into Henry Kissinger, and former President Gerald Ford and his wife Betty. Blake announces to the crowd that he and Krystle are engaged. Steven shakes his father's hand – a big step. Alexis tells Adam

she cancelled the merger to protect him. Jeff witnesses an outburst by Peter, then worries about Fallon.

## "The Wedding," December 28, 1983

Alexis warns Fallon that Peter is not right for her, but Fallon tells her to butt out. Peter puts the moves on Claudia. The Carrington estate is transformed for a wedding once again, and this time Fallon leaves the sugar couple *on* the cake. Alexis decides to gift Steven with some Colbyco stock for his birthday. Alexis then gets testy with Claudia when she won't reschedule a party for Steven that conflicts with her own. Adam tells Kirby he'll fight for the right to be a father to his child. Blake and Krystle remarry, as Alexis and Dex have a little afternoon delight in her office. Alexis then makes plans to go to Rio – where Blake and Krystle will be honeymooning.

## "The Ring," January 4, 1984

Mark tussles with Dex when Dex stops by Alexis' penthouse. Adam pleads with Kirby to marry him. A strange man keeps greeting little Danny by name at the park where Mrs. Gordon takes him. Dex gets the cold shoulder from Steven. Dex charms Alexis with an extravagant sapphire necklace. Kirby signs the divorce papers. Blake and Krystle return from their honeymoon. Mrs. Gordon calls Claudia away from work because the park stranger has followed her and little Danny home. Claudia then moves the child to the Carrington mansion for safety, which angers Alexis. Kirby's wedding ring has to be cut off her finger because her body is developing rapid swelling.

## "Lancelot," January 11, 1984

Kirby is diagnosed with pre-eclampsia. Jeff tells Blake he's divorcing Kirby. Jeff is increasingly concerned about Fallon's thrill-seeking – flying with Peter in his plane and partying with him. Krystle seeks her doctor's help in assessing her chances for having a child. Kirby collapses. Tracy maneuvers Krystle out of an important meeting so she can go instead. Kirby tells Jeff she's going to marry Adam, then Adam admits the rape to Blake, who tells him he should be "horsewhipped." Meanwhile, Allegre is horsenapped, just as Krystle receives a strange phone call telling her to go check on the animal. Then Claudia receives some mysterious violets with a note using the nickname Matthew used to have for her.

## "Seizure," January 18, 1984

Adam keeps a vigil at Kirby's bedside, telling her he's the only one who truly loves her, then reaching out with an apology for Jeff. Kirby then suffers another attack and is hospitalized. Allegre's disappearance is investigated, and amid the press furor, Peter announces on TV that Fallon is going to marry him.  Blake is uneasy about this.  Alexis and Dex go to extreme measures to woo a potential client, Oscar Stone – and the dancing in skintight brown leather pants is one thing ... but Alexis *singing*?  Whoa.  Claudia slaps Peter after he advances on her again.  Blake and Peter get a ransom note for Allegre.  Kirby's condition worsens.

### "A Little Girl," February 1, 1984
Blake voices his concerns about Peter to Fallon, then Alexis tells Fallon about a scandal from Peter's past.  Jeff tells Peter not to take Fallon flying, and they end up in a fistfight.  Peter pays the ransom of $2 million in diamonds, against Blake's wishes, and Allegre is returned.  Tracy reports to Blake what she heard from one of her PR contacts – that Lex-Dex bought out Oscar Stone.  McVane tries to recruit Mark to sell out Alexis, but Mark refuses.  Steven comforts a distraught Adam at the hospital.  Claudia gets another delivery of violets and suspects that Matthew, and perhaps Lindsay, are still alive.  Blake threatens to toss Dex off his board for his involvement with Alexis and Oscar Stone, and Dex turns his suspicions to Tracy as Blake's informant.  In a weak moment, Adam admits to Blake that it was he that poisoned Jeff, not Alexis.  To save Kirby's life, the baby (a girl) is lost.

### "The Accident," February 22, 1984
Kirby is devastated to learn she lost the baby.  Claudia tells Fallon that Peter hit on her.  Tracy sleeps with an old contact for a little corporate information exchange.  After Tony makes a puzzling comment, Jeff and Blake dig deeper into the events surrounding Allegre's horsenapping.  Adam and Blake talk over Adam's role in Jeff's poisoning, then Blake apologizes to Alexis for accusing her of poisoning Jeff.  Alexis tells Fallon that Peter dumped a foreign princess because she was pregnant, then Jeff tells Fallon that he believes Peter had Allegre horsenapped to collect Blake's cash.  Fallon then learns that Peter has skipped town.  A drunk driver strikes the distraught Fallon as she rails out of LaMirage.

### "The Vigil," February 29, 1984
Adam sticks to his desire to marry Kirby, and she accepts.  Fallon is comatose.  Blake is determined to track down Peter, rushing to the airport to attack the man, just as Peter is detained by security for the drugs in his attache case.  Claudia visits Matthew's mother in her investigation of the mysterious violets.  Alexis tries to talk Adam out of marrying Kirby, and when he won't listen, she decides to investigate Kirby's mother.  Tracy sleeps her way into another deal:  getting Blake a job as party chairman, and herself the job as his PR chief.  Adam asks for Jeff's forgiveness for

the poisoning. McVane is only too happy to tell Alexis about Blake's party seat. Fallon wakes up, but she doesn't have the feeling in her legs.

### "Steps," March 7, 1984
Fallon's doctor thinks her paralysis might be psychosomatic. Alexis tries to get Kirby out of Adam's life by offering her a job in Paris. When Kirby refuses, Alexis tells her that her mother is not dead – she's been locked up in a facility for the criminally insane, for murder. Fallon does walk again – to save Little Blake when he totters close to the edge of the pool. Claudia receives another mysterious package, this time with a photo that Matthew took of her years ago.

### "The Voice, Part 1," March 14, 1984
When Krystle nearly faints in her office, Tracy blurts out in front of Blake that Krystle might be pregnant. Claudia runs off to Peru to investigate the supposed deaths of Matthew and Lindsay. The doctor confirms that Krystle is pregnant, and Blake lavishes her with gifts. Blake goes to Hong Kong to negotiate a big business deal with the China Sea oil leases, and he learns that Rashid Ahmed is in on the deal. In Peru, just as one of Matthew's former classmates is coming on to her, Steven steps in and "saves" Claudia. The two of them then see the Jeep crash site, and Claudia is convinced Matthew and Lindsay are dead. Blake senses that Tracy is coming on to him at the hotel in Hong Kong. Fallon is getting strange headaches. Back in Denver, Claudia receives a strange phone call, and it's Matthew's voice on the line!

### "The Voice, Part 2," March 21, 1984
Having learned about Blake's dealings with Ahmed through Adam's answered phone call in her office, Alexis sets out to intervene. Meanwhile, Blake and Ahmed close the China Sea oil deal. Blake confronts Tracy's reporter informant about his antics. Tracy then outwardly comes on to Blake, and he fires her. Steven

*TV Guide featured a great-many "Dynasty" covers over the years.*

spots Dex with violets in Alexis' office. Kirby visits her mother's grave in North Dakota. Alexis heads to Hong Kong to "reconnect" with Rashid Ahmed, not telling the monogamy-minded Dex where she's going. Claudia receives another call, this time from Dex.

## "The Voice, Part 3," March 28, 1984
Kirby goes to the police department and reads Joseph's suicide note. Dex follows Alexis to Hong Kong and finds her with Rashid Ahmed. He erupts in anger, and the two have a knockdown, drag-out fight, after he tells her she is "a slut with the morals of a dog." Kirby looks into buying a gun, now that she knows Alexis was the source of her father's torment. Blake alienates the reporter for a financial magazine. Krystle takes Claudia's next mysterious phone call, and this "Matthew" is beginning to sound like a broken record – or a recording. Fallon becomes disoriented and surmises it's from the skull fracture she suffered in her accident. Krystle and Claudia visit Mother Blaisdel, who finally admits that she sold the tape of Matthew's voice to a stranger. Blake suspects Alexis, and visits Morgan Hess, who does, indeed have the tape of Matthew's voice, but tells Blake it wasn't Alexis. Dex beds Tracy then proposes that she work for Alexis, and report back to him.

## "The Birthday," April 4, 1984
Krystle finds Tracy in her office and promptly has words – and a swift slap – for her. Steven grouses to both Alexis and Adam that Adam stole his work, and his glory, on the China Sea deal. Fallon's doctor orders a brain scan, and it shows that she's perfectly healthy. The Carringtons throw an elaborate, circus-themed party for Little Blake's second birthday. Krystle is delighted to tell Alexis that she's pregnant, and Alexis slips by saying, "Talk to me when you've been through four," but then covers herself by saying that she miscarried after Steven. Jeff gives Fallon his grandmother's engagement ring, and she accepts. Kirby trains for her new gun. The news comes across that allegations of arms sales surround Blake's $100-million deal of the oil leases with Ahmed. Blake turns his suspicions to Alexis.

## "The Check," April 11, 1984
*Heather Locklear appears in the show's opening.*
Mark sees Blake having it out with Alexis over the Ahmed deal, and Mark later uses his knowledge to blackmail some cash out of Alexis. Fallon breaks the news of her engagement to Kirby. Krystle tries to handle the financial reporter that Blake had miffed. McVane comes snooping around, but Mark won't give him any information on Alexis. Officials in Hong Kong try to track down Ahmed for Blake, who worries that he can't

recover his $100 million. Kirby secrets Alexis away to Joseph's old house, but just as she is about to pull her gun, a neighbor knocks on the door. Tracy flatters Alexis into giving her a job. Mark says a cryptic goodbye to Krystle. In New York, Sammy Jo gets slapped around by her cosmetics-company sugar daddy. Claudia worries about the trial against Morgan Hess.

### "The Engagement," April 18, 1984
*Heather Locklear appears in the show's opening.*
Gordon Wales' hatchet job of Blake in the new issue of World Finance magazine has everyone talking, while Blake struggles to get an extension on his $100-million loan from the bankers. Alexis tells Adam she thinks Kirby is a little off-kilter these days. Miffed by the order that all Lex-Dex business must go through Steven, Dex knocks on Alexis' door again – and gets thrown out. Sammy Jo barges in for a visit with Danny. Alexis assigns Tracy to extract info from Blake's banker. At the LaMirage engagement party for Fallon and Jeff, Fallon soundly puts crasher Sammy Jo in her place. Mark tries to blackmail Alexis into sexual favors, but she orders him out, then heads off to the engagement party, first encountering McVane near her departing limo. Tracy gets upset over Dex's "obsession" with Alexis. A police sergeant arrives at the party to tell Alexis that Mark has died from a fall off her penthouse balcony.

### "New Lady in Town," May 2, 1984
*Diahann Carroll is added to the show's opening; Geoffrey Scott is dropped.*
Krystle finds it hard to believe that Mark committed suicide. Andrew suggests that Blake mortgage the mansion to cover his debt. In a flash of red leather, Sammy Jo moves into the mansion to be with Danny. Tracy tells all to Alexis about Dex. Dominique Deveraux checks into LaMirage and starts digging for info on the Carringtons. Blake goes to Alexis with his shale-oil process to offer, and she throws it in his face. The police question Alexis on her involvement with Mark. Steven finds out Sammy Jo has been lying about her modeling contract, and when he confronts her, she says she wants Danny back. Dominique makes a rather threatening visit to Alexis, content to remain a well-heeled mystery to her.

### "The Nightmare," May 9, 1984
Alexis recognizes Dominique as a well-known singer. Sammy Jo drops in on Hess, and it's revealed that she was the one who had him torment Claudia with the violets and the tape of Matthew. Kirby pulls a gun on Alexis, but Alexis talks her down. Kirby then decides to go back to Paris. Sammy Jo and Adam kiss in the workout room. Dex buys Blake's football

team for $10 million. Dominique's visit to Blake goes about as badly as her visit to Alexis, but after he walks out of the room, she says that she is a Carrington. Overhearing her catty comment, Krystle "slings mud" at Alexis at the spa. Plagued by her mysterious headaches on the stormy night of her wedding, Fallon escapes out the window and drives off in her car. The police arrest Alexis for the "murder" of Mark.

## Season 5 – 1984-1985

### "Disappearance," September 26, 1984
*Pamela Sue Martin, Kathleen Beller and Deborah Adair are dropped from the show's opening; Billy Dee Williams is added.*
Fallon's car has crashed, and she is missing. Alexis' bail is set at $2 million, and Dex and Steven post it. Alexis then hires Adam to defend her. Dominique's husband Brady tracks her down in Denver. Blake struggles to deal not only with Fallon's disappearance but the loss of his empire. Steven finds a bookkeeping glitch at Colbyco that shows Alexis' involvement in Rashid Ahmed's double-cross of Blake. Steven kicks Sammy Jo out of the mansion. Steven then tells Blake about Alexis' payoff of Ahmed, and Blake gets motivated to rebuild his company and to find Fallon. Sammy Jo runs off with her son.

### "The Mortgage," October 10, 1984
Steven holds Adam responsible for Sammy Jo's taking off with Danny. The investigation into Fallon's disappearance turns up nothing but a lot of crank calls. Alexis descends like a vulture on the banker who receives the Carrington mansion as Blake's collateral. Steven decides to stay at Colbyco long enough for Alexis to make it through the Mark Jennings murder trial. Krystle sells a bunch of her belongings and hands Blake a check for $4.5 million. Jeff gets a call to ID a body at the morgue, but it's not Fallon. Dominique won't tell Brady why she insists on staying in Denver. Blake goes about buying up his old holdings – then finds out Alexis is the one who holds his mortgage. Jeff meets a trucker who says he gave Fallon a ride to Portland, Oregon.

### "Fallon," October 17, 1984
*Billy Dee Williams and Heather Locklear are taken out of the opening.*
Jeff's follow-up in Portland turns cold, as the man he speaks to is evidently lying for Fallon. Blake travels to Venezuela to do business with an old associate, Billy Waite. Adam gets drunk, upset that Kirby won't return his calls in Paris. In the frustration over keeping her scandalous past out of the trial, Alexis fires her attorney Warren Ballard, leaving Adam to defend her alone. Dex and Alexis share another "reunion." Sammy Jo calls

BILLIE RAE BATES

Steven to set up a meeting in Los Angeles.  Alexis visits Billy Waite to once again ruin Blake's business dealings.  Dominique investigates Blake's business status.  Alexis is charged with leaving the U.S. to avoid prosecution.  Jeff is told Fallon stayed in a monastery, but that she's dead.

## "The Rescue," October 24, 1984
*Heather Locklear appears in the opening.*
Jeff and Blake follow another lead on Fallon to Seattle, where they learn she evidently died in a plane crash with Peter DeVilbus.  The family grieves.  A memorial service is held back in Denver, and Jeff blurts out at the service that Fallon is a "bitch" for running off with Peter.  Billy Waite turns down Blake's loan.  Sammy Jo meets Steven in Los Angeles and demands $30,000 a month for life in exchange for Danny.  Adam later sneaks into Sammy Jo's motel room, ties her up and takes Danny home to Denver – as part of a plan that Blake devised.  Dominique visits her Aunt Bessie in northern Colorado to look through her mother's old things.  Krystle is forced to let the mansion staff go.  Dominique visits Blake and tells them they share a daddy.

## "The Trial," October 31, 1984
At the Denver Detention Center, Alexis has champagne and caviar delivered to her cell.  Steven tells Krystle he saw Mark Jennings' killer on Alexis' terrace.  Dominique shows Blake her mother's postcards from Tom Carrington, but he's reserving judgment.  Case #84-CR-3026-23, the People of the State of Colorado vs. Alexis Colby, begins.  Dominique tries to befriend Krystle.  Jeff angers a blond floozy in bed by calling her Fallon.  A woman who lives across the street from Alexis' penthouse testifies to seeing someone on the terrace with Mark.  Dex tells Alexis he loves her.  Blake is called to testify against Alexis, but Adam turns his testimony around to help her.  The prosecution calls Steven to the stand.

## "The Verdict," November 7, 1984
Jeff is really going on a "floozy" binge.  Steven testifies that he saw Alexis on her terrace as Mark Jennings fell to his death.  Alexis is devastated and tells Steven she disowns him.  Dominique offers to buy 51 percent of Denver Carrington, but Blake talks her down to 40 percent.  He's then able to pay off the mortgage with Alexis.  Krystle testifies for the defense.  Alexis insists on taking the stand, and when Adam objects, she fires him and defends herself.  She only damages her case further as the prosecution produces the cape that Steven saw on her terrace.  Blake invites a grimy business associate to stay at the mansion, and the man makes a pass at Krystle.  Steven and Dex duke it out on Alexis' terrace.  The jury finds Alexis guilty of first-degree murder.

### "Amanda," November 14, 1984
*Catherine Oxenberg is added to the show's opening; Billy Dee Williams also appears.*
A young blond female wants to visit Alexis in jail, then changes her mind. Dex digs into Mark's life. Steven wheels and deals with Hal Lombard – in direct competition with his father, but the two talk honestly about it. Dominique tells Brady she bailed Blake out to then "snatch away his crown." Adam and Dex see Alexis' mysterious visitor at her penthouse. Brady and Dominique aren't being open with each other. Krystle gets upset when Hal Lombard appears in her house again. Adam and Dex find snapshots that show Alexis' terrace when Mark was killed – and Neal McVane in a wig and Alexis' cape! They confront McVane, who then confesses. Alexis' mysterious female visitor drops by again, and calls her "mother."

### "The Secret," November 21, 1984
Amanda continues to confront Alexis about Alexis' hiding the fact that she's the girl's mother – even from Amanda herself. Steven and Alexis reconcile. Amanda splashes her story of illegitimacy all over the front page of the Chronicle, earning a "You bitch!" slap from Mummy. Alexis calls her cousin Rosalind Bedford in London and threatens her to keep her mouth shut about Amanda's father. Claudia tells Steven she's "tired of being an afterthought" in his life. Blake asks Dominique to track down Rashid Ahmed. Tension grows between Blake and Krystle. Peter DeVilbus' widow Nicole sparks Jeff's interest. Steven works with a new male PR rep, Luke Fuller, while Claudia is approached by a handsome gallery owner, Dean Caldwell.

### "Domestic Intrigue," November 28, 1984
Blake digs around to find out who Amanda's father is. Jeff sleeps with Nicole. Dominique locates Rashid Ahmed in Turkey and tries to convince him to sign a statement clearing Blake of the South China Sea oil-lease scandal. Amanda has dinner at the Carrington mansion, even arguing with Steven, much like Fallon once did. Krystle is increasingly dismayed about Blake's business practices. Steven sees Dean Caldwell hitting on Claudia. Sensing a plot by Blake, Ahmed calls Alexis for help, but she gives him a big kiss-off. Adam infiltrates Ahmed's villa and blackmails him into signing the statement for Blake, but Ahmed then tries to escape and is killed by the Turkish authorities. When Krystle learns a man has been killed by one of Blake's deals, she has it out with him – then falls down the mansion staircase.

BILLIE RAE BATES

## Behind the scenes

> *It touched a nerve at a time when people wanted to be glamorous, when people wanted to be powerful, and when people wanted to see people that were like that suffer.*
> — Pamela Bellwood, about the show, on "Dynasty Reunion: Catfights & Caviar," May 2006

### "Kristina," December 5, 1984

*Diahann Carroll does not appear in the show's opening.*
Krystle is forced into early labor. Jeff and Claudia each see some questionable behavior in Nicole. Krystle has a girl, who's not breathing as she's born. The paramedics – then the hospital staff – keep her alive, but she has respiratory distress syndrome. Alexis worries about Blake's investigating Amanda. Amanda comes on to Dex, but he calls her bluff. On a business trip, Steven is uncomfortable with Luke Fuller's attentiveness to him. Krystle names her daughter after a strong female friend. Dean Caldwell lures Claudia into a kiss. Jeff finds Nicole's photo from her "husband" Peter DeVilbus. The doctor tells Blake and Krystle that their baby girl needs massive blood transfusions.

### "Swept Away," December 12, 1984

Jeff checks further into Nicole's story, which involves a map to a treasure in Bolivia. She thinks Peter gave Fallon half of the map. Amanda continues to strike a mutual chord with Blake. Kristina takes the transfusions well. Blake sets in motion his clearance in the Ahmed alleged "arms deal." Blake pieces together the events surrounding Amanda's conception. Alexis wants Amanda to return to the Sorbonne to continue her education. When that fails, Alexis suggests a getaway for the two of them and Dex. Claudia is uneasy as Luke Fuller drops off a file for Steven at the mansion. Alexis stiffs Dex and Amanda as they leave for the trip. Alexis is only concerned with getting Amanda out of Denver because Blake is insisting on having her take a blood test. But on this getaway in New Mexico, Dex and Amanda give in to some pretty hot passion. Blake handles a press conference on the Ahmed situation. Jeff holds out hope that Fallon was not the woman with Peter in his plane crash. Alexis arrives at the getaway – and accepts Dex's marriage proposal.

## "That Holiday Spirit," December 19, 1984
*"Special guest star" Rock Hudson appears in the show's opening.*
Blake decides to buy Allegre back for Krystle, and the owner is Delta Rho Stables and the powerful Daniel Reece. Blake asks Amanda to come back to Denver from London to take a blood test. Daniel recognizes Krystle from his past then offers Allegre to Blake exclusively, pulling the horse off the auction. The nuptials of Dex and Alexis leave Amanda hurt and angry. Claudia confesses to Steven that she slept with Dean Caldwell. Amanda finally drags the truth out of Rosalind, that Blake is her father. Blake tells Dominique that his father denied sleeping with her mother. Amanda flies right home to see Blake. At Christmas, Blake announces to the family that Amanda is his daughter. A gift from Daniel sparks an argument for Krystle and Blake.

## "The Avenger," January 2, 1985
*Billy Dee Williams appears in the show's opening.*
Claudia packs up and moves into LaMirage. Alexis still denies to Amanda that Blake is her father. When Krystle confronts Daniel about his gift, they're called away to a horse who's about to give birth. Seeing Dominique dejected over Blake's refusal to acknowledge her as his sister, Brady tells Blake they are now enemies. Alexis offers Dominique a handsome profit for Dominique's Denver Carrington shares. Krystle sees another side of Daniel – he didn't walk out on her sister as she had thought. Krystle then tells Steven that Daniel is Sammy Jo's father – a fact no one else but she and Iris has ever known. Alexis throws her offer at Brady, who denies her as Dominique did. At a party in his honor, Daniel monopolizes Krystle's time. Dominique tells Blake she's suing him over the mortgage she helped pay, then Blake gets a call from Sumatra, Indonesia, that his father has had a heart attack. Krystle decides to explore a "dream" of going into business – with Daniel.

## "The Will," January 9, 1985
Steven apologizes to Claudia for charging into her room at LaMirage and trying to force himself on her. Blake holds a grudge against his father for mistreating his mother. He arrives in Sumatra – and introduces his father to Dominique. After they find the other half of the treasure map in Fallon's safe at LaMirage, Nicole realizes that Jeff will never let go of his love for Fallon. Dex keeps telling Amanda that their night together meant nothing. Adam and Claudia go on a business trip and end up smooching. Tom finally, after much prodding, admits that Dominique is his daughter – and even leaves her one-third of his estate, with the other equal shares going to Blake and Alexis, who was also there at Tom's bedside.

### "The Treasure," January 16, 1985
On her drive home from Delta Rho Stables, Krystle is nearly run off the road. As Jeff and Nicole search for their foreign treasure, Jeff is convinced they're right behind Fallon herself. Blake apologizes to Dominique for not believing her claims before. Blake and Daniel have a tense talk at the mansion, as Blake senses Daniel has an interest in "Krystie." This filters over to Krystle, who has a talk with Blake. Alexis visits Daniel to tell him to stay out of Dex's life; he sees right through her motives, though, when she brings up Krystle. Alexis detects a few vibes from Dex toward Amanda. Jeff and Nicole discover their coveted statue – then a mysterious female pulls a gun on them. Blake officially welcomes Dominique into the family with a formal dinner.

### "Foreign Relations," January 23, 1985
*Ali MacGraw is added to the show's opening.*
Krystle goes horse-shopping with Daniel – and gets the cold shoulder from Blake. Jeff and Nicole come back from Bolivia announcing that they're married. Dex returns to Alexis after their few-days fight. Adam starts a fight with Steven in the workout room. Claudia breaks it up, then Steven heads right into Luke Fuller's arms. Daniel tries to lure Dex onto another foreign mission with him. Wrapped up in Blake's negotiations over the South China Sea oil leases is the internationally known, and atrociously acted, Lady Ashley Mitchell. She wouldn't mind wrapping herself around Blake. A photographer captures Krystle and Daniel frolicking in the hay at the stables. Meanwhile, Ashley steals a kiss from Blake.

### "Triangles," January 30, 1985
*Billy Dee Williams appears in the show's opening.*
Krystle continues to defend to Blake her need to accomplish something in business on her own. Fed up with being around Alexis and Dex, Amanda packs up and heads to the Carrington mansion. One of Krystle's colts gets sick. Steven tries to break it off with Luke, and Claudia interrupts their goodbye embrace. Dominique tells Brady they can use the money she inherited from her father to save both of their companies. But Alexis' Colbyco is trying to take over Dominique's company. Brady tells Dominique they're through. Krystle sees an affectionate photo of Blake signed by Ashley. Meanwhile, Alexis arranges it so Ashley will be in Acapulco when Blake is.

### "The Ball," February 6, 1985
*Michael Praed is added to the show's opening.*
In Acapulco, Alexis wants a piece of Blake's South China Sea oil leases, up for bid. Claudia meets with Luke to tell him to get out of Steven's life.

Jeff doesn't appreciate it when Nicole tries on Fallon's "sacred" red sparkle dinner dress. Krystle is hurt that Blake went to Acapulco without her, and there, Blake is mailed a photo of Krystle and Daniel. Amanda attracts the attention of the suave prince of Moldavia. Jeff nicknames L.B., who'll have nothing to do with Nicole. Ashley, of course, hits on Blake in Acapulco. Meanwhile, back at the ranch(!), Krystle and Daniel share the famous kiss that would worry viewers everywhere when the news hits that Rock Hudson has AIDS.

### "Circumstantial Evidence," February 13, 1985
Daniel confesses his love to Krystle, but she tells him she loves Blake. Amanda's standoffish attitude about Prince Michael is met by Alexis' matchmaking. Krystle receives a photo of Blake dancing with Ashley, and Blake gets more photos of Krystle and Daniel. Dex has a fight with Alexis and changes his mind about the mercenary trip with Daniel. Alexis cuts a deal with Blake and his South China Sea oil leases. Prince Michael manages to bed Amanda, then tells her he's engaged to a duchess. Daniel says goodbye to Krystle to leave on his mission. Blake gets home and shows Krystle one of the photos he received.

### "The Collapse," February 20, 1985
Dominique answers Alexis' takeover attempt with one of her own on Colbyco. Claudia and Adam sleep together, bringing her tally to three men of the Carrington household! Krystle confronts Alexis as a suspect in the mysterious photos. Dominique gets divorce papers from Brady. Adam and Jeff get into a fistfight after Jeff hears Adam coming on to Claudia over the phone. Alexis is enraged that Jeff has married Peter DeVilbus' widow. Krystle pays a visit to Ashley in her pursuit of the mysterious photo-sender. Brady steps in and blocks Alexis' takeover attack on Dominique. Krystle shows Blake her own mystery photos. Dominique's coughing fits get worse; she even collapses on stage.

### "Life and Death," February 27, 1985
Blake insists on the best care for his sister at the hospital, then ruffles a few feathers in the family when he tells everyone else to go home. Alexis tells Jeff that his marriage to Nicole wasn't valid, and Jeff goes to Nicole with the allegation, which she admits. Dex returns from overseas, deathly sick of malaria. Luke tells Steven he's having a hard time letting go of him. Blake sees the two of them together then asks Steven about it later. Steven says he can't fight who he is anymore. In his delirium, Dex cries out Amanda's name to Alexis. Alexis keeps mum, but then puts in a call to Prince Michael's daddy the king to get her daughter taken care of.

### "Parental Consent," March 6, 1985
At the hospital, Dex recovers but keeps his secret adventure from Alexis, who's really only concerned about his relation to Amanda. Dominique, meanwhile, fears she has lost her career. Jeff lavishes flowers on Ashley. Alexis travels to King Galen to try to wed off Amanda to Prince Michael. After wrestling with it, Steven tells Claudia he's going to make a go of it with Luke. Dominique tells Krystle she better patch things up with Blake before Ashley scoops him up. A deal falls through for LaMirage when Claudia won't sleep with a company rep. Adam uses the incident to draw Claudia's trust. Alexis returns to Denver, Prince Michael in tow.

### "Photo Finish," March 13, 1985
*Heather Locklear appears in the show's opening.*
Amanda gives Michael the royal brush-off. When Daniel comes up missing, Dex reveals to Krystle the Paraguay adventure they were on. Michael proposes to Amanda, and she smells a rat – or a "Mummy." She confronts Alexis. Blake has a family dinner, making a point to invite Luke in an effort to accept Steven's lifestyle. Amanda tells Dex that he's the one she loves, but he tells her to marry Michael. Dex and Alexis – then Dex and Michael – square off over the issue. Amanda finally accepts Michael's proposal, under the condition that it be a marriage in name only. Blake has his reservations about Michael. In New York, Sammy Jo is upset that all of her anonymous photos, facilitated by Morgan Hess, haven't split up Blake and Krystle. She then spots a Krystle look-alike at the bar. Fed up with the Ashley situation, Krystle leaves the mansion with Kristina.

### "The Crash," March 20, 1985
Alexis asks Luke to return to work at Colbyco. Dex tells Krystle that Daniel is in a prison camp. Claudia decides to file for divorce in Mexico. Blake grills Michael about Amanda; he won't give the wedding his blessing. Adam follows Claudia to Mexico. Dex breaks Daniel out of the prison camp. Daniel has an emotional reunion with Krystle in Denver. Ashley and Blake do what they can to bring Dominique out of her funk, throwing her a surprise party. An angry Blake follows Daniel to the airport to confront him about Krystle. He gets onto Daniel's plane and won't leave until the issue is resolved. The plane takes off, the two fight, the pilot is knocked out and the plane heads for a crash.

### "Reconciliation," March 27, 1985
The plane crashes, and Blake drags the weak Daniel away from the plane just as it explodes. The air patrol authorities hold off the search for the night, so Jeff hires a helicopter pilot and ventures out to search for Blake.

DYNASTY HIGH

Meanwhile, in the shelter of a cabin, Daniel tells Blake that when they get back to safety he intends to do all he can to win Krystle. Finally, Jeff spots them and rescues them. Alexis asks Blake to call Prince Michael and convince him to "unbreak" the engagement. Blake and Krystle reunite. Krystle tells Daniel about his daughter, Sammy Jo. Adam overhears Blake telling Jeff he's going to leave him control of Denver Carrington in his revised will.

## "Sammy Jo," April 3, 1985

Amanda tells her mother that nothing happened between her and Dex and that she loves Michael. Resigning herself to the fact that Blake loves Krystle too much for her to split them up, Ashley turns her attention to Jeff. Adam changes the date on a cable from Jeff, screwing up a drilling start, so that he can come to the rescue and make Jeff look incompetent. Krystle takes Daniel to New York to meet Sammy Jo, and Sammy Jo, of course, puts her worst face forward. Alexis sees Ashley talking to Dex and warns her off, forthwith. Alexis and Dex then have a fiery reunion. Daniel manages to tame the wild Sammy Jo. Jeff and Ashley sleep together. Jeff then sees a woman in one of Ashley's photos that he thinks is Fallon. Daniel makes Krystle promise that she'll take care of Sammy Jo if he doesn't come back from his newest mission.

## "Kidnapped," April 10, 1985

Jeff is obsessed over Ashley's photo of the woman who looks like Fallon. Prince Michael's right-hand man, Yuri, plots behind his back, then Amanda is kidnapped. After she is returned, everyone in the family fusses over her safety. Adam sees Steven and Claudia getting along as friends and threatens Steven to stay away from Claudia. Steven invites Luke to the wedding in Moldavia. Michael and Amanda leave for Moldavia. The painting of Fallon on the wall bears a new face, and Jeff's flashbacks show a new actress (Emma Samms, who's only named in the show's closing credits). In Los Angeles, meanwhile, Fallon is at the police department, stricken with amnesia.

## "The Heiress," May 8, 1985

Dex comes to Krystle with the news that Daniel has been killed in Libya. Just arriving in Moldavia, Alexis and Amanda meet the troublesome Duchess Elena, former fiancee of Michael. Sammy Jo moves right in on Daniel's estate. Elena tells Amanda that Michael is still sleeping with her. Sammy Jo stops by the mansion to threaten Steven over custody of Danny. Claudia approaches Blake about drawing up a contract for her work at LaMirage, and he tells her he's thinking about selling the hotel. Galen is jealous of Dex. Daniel leaves his estate to Sammy Jo, but he names Krystle the executor. Jeff asks Ashley to marry him. Elena strips in front of Michael, just in time for Amanda to walk in. Sammy Jo sees dollar signs in Rita's resemblance to Krystle.

### "Royal Wedding," May 15, 1985
*Emma Samms, in Fallon's famous red sparkle dress, is added to the show's opening.*
As the rest of the family arrives in Moldavia, Amanda is refusing to go through with the wedding. Blake runs interference between Amanda and Michael. Dex sees an affectionate moment between Alexis and King Galen and decides he's outta there. Alexis and Galen turn up the heat on Elena, forcing her to come clean with Amanda about the scene Amanda walked in on. Steven, then Blake, witness Adam and Claudia getting cozy. Michael and Dex come to blows, and Amanda breaks it up. Ashley can't say yes to Jeff's marriage proposal. On his way out of the palace, Dex witnesses some shenanigans by Yuri and is struck and taken out of the way. As the wedding march plays, soldiers close in on the palace, and Dex struggles with the rope that binds him. Just as the couple is pronounced united, bullets spray the scene, leaving a pile of bodies in the "Moldavian Massacre."

## *Season 6 – 1985-1986*

### "The Aftermath," September 25, 1985
*Heather Locklear and Joan Collins have new photos in the show's opening; Maxwell Caulfield is added. Ali MacGraw is taken off.*
The dust clears, and the revolution is afoot in Moldavia. The bodies include Ashley, Luke and King Galen. Soldiers have taken away Alexis in a cloud of mystery. The new minister, Warnick, tries to coerce a deal with Denver Carrington by "detaining" Krystle, also. In New York, Sammy Jo lets Rita in on her plan to get Daniel Reece's money away from Krystle. Ashley wrote Jeff a goodbye letter that she planned to give him after the wedding. Krystle is placed in a cell and subjected to Yuri's advances. In Los Angeles, Fallon, now going by Randall Adams, seeks out Miles Colby after seeing his last name in the newspaper. Warnick hits on Dominique. Krystle sees the weak body of Galen, not dead as Yuri is telling everyone.

### "The Homecoming," October 2, 1985
*"Special guest star" George Hamilton is added to the show's opening.*
Alexis is added to Krystle's cell, and then they're both freed when Blake makes a counterthreat against Warnick and Co. The wedding party is then flown back to Denver, but Michael is without his country and his reign. Adam tries to convince Claudia to marry him. The whole family

attends Luke's funeral. Rita's loser boyfriend Joel drops by Sammy Jo's apartment. Michael lays down the law with Amanda when she shares some thoughts on affairs of state. In Los Angeles, Miles charms the mysterious Randall. Meanwhile, Jeff's obsession with the alleged photo of Fallon is eating away at him, Blake says. When Sammy Jo comes home from a fruitless trip to Denver, Joel tells her he has the answer to her troubles.

### "The Californians," October 9, 1985
*The show's opening includes "special appearances by" Charlton Heston, Maxwell Caulfield and Barbara Stanwyck.*
Jeff plans a California trip to search for Fallon, while Blake calls back the psychic he hired when Steven was missing. Alexis wants Dex to rescue Galen in Moldavia. Jason Colby phones up a nonplussed Blake about a new deal. Then Jason's doctor tells him he's dying. Jason's sister Connie opposes Jason's pipeline plan with Blake. Jason flies to Denver to pitch the project to Blake, telling him Blake can only use his tankers to get the oil out of the South China Sea. Alexis decides to put corporate and political pressure on to free Galen from the revolutionaries. Joel talks Rita into plastic surgery. Randall remembers a boy being in danger near the water (the time she saved L.B. from drowning at the Carrington pool). Connie beckons Jeff to California for a big change in his life.

### "The Man," October 16, 1985
Jason pressures Blake further on the pipeline deal. Claudia tells Steven she's leaving and that Adam and her are over because Adam pulls her in a direction she doesn't like. Alexis appeals to Blake for help with saving Galen. She overhears a message from Jason to Blake and decides to cut a deal of her own, but Jason's not interested. Connie tells Jeff she's giving him her $500 million in Colby holdings. Jonathan Lake continues to hit on Dominique. Krystle drops in on Sammy Jo in New York. Adam follows Claudia to San Francisco to profess his love. Surgery and hair coloring make Rita's transformation complete. Amanda feels like one of Michael's subjects. Krystle spots Joel in Denver and remembers seeing him at Sammy Jo's apartment. Joel tells Rita the plan has changed – they're now going after Blake's fortune.

### "The Gown," October 30, 1985
The next phase of Rita's training occurs at Delta Rho with Joel and Sammy Jo. Dex wants to have more of Alexis – and less of her talk about Galen. Alexis gets a visit from a nun who bears a message about Galen. Jeff tells Blake he's now Jason's partner, and that he's moving to California. Since Blake now has an ally at Colby Enterprises, he agrees to the pipeline deal

with Jason. Michael sees a doublecross in the note Alexis received about Galen. A man follows Adam and Claudia in San Francisco, and it's revealed to be the minister Adam hired to marry them! A music box shakes up Randall's memories. Krystle pops in unexpectedly at Delta Rho, and comes face-to-face with Rita. Joel then knocks her out, and moves up the plan for Rita to take her place.

## "Titans," November 13, 1985 – special two-hour episode

Jason is determined to "devour the rest of his life like a steak." Blake tells Jeff he's dedicating a hospital wing to Fallon, which upsets Jeff, who believes Fallon is alive. After being hit on the head, Krystle awakens blindfolded and bound. Bliss disagrees with her daddy's pipeline project. Settling into the mansion, Rita worries about having to sleep with Blake. Sable touches talons again with her cousin, Alexis. Dex and Alexis depart on their rescue mission to Moldavia. After Michael tries to force himself on her, Amanda wants a divorce. Monica has to really press Miles to go to the big splashy pipeline party at the Carrington household in Denver. Dex is stopped at the Moldavian border, though Alexis in her nun attire gets through. Adam breaks the news to Blake about his marriage to Claudia. Blake tells him he's changing his will to leave Adam $1 until Adam proves himself to Blake again and stops lying. Blake appoints Michael as chairman of LaMirage. Alexis meets up with Elena, who says her father caused the revolution but who says she wants to help Galen. At the party, Claudia and Steven have it out. Dominique reconnects with "old friend" Garrett Boydston. Alexis reaches out to God at a Moldavian church. Krystle's escape attempts fail. As Miles and Randall arrive for the party, Randall panics at the sight of the house and rushes back to the car. Jeff sees this from a mansion window.

## "The Decision," November 20, 1985

*The show's opening includes Maxwell Caulfield and Ken Howard.*
Rita struggles to fill Krystle's shoes, while Krystle must deal with Joel's lies and manipulations. A distraught Jeff is determined to search for Fallon. Weakened in a grimy prison, Dex manages to escape and find Galen. Steven suspects that Sammy Jo, whom he keeps seeing whispering in "Krystle"'s ear, is up to something. Garrett pushes his memories – and passion – on Dominique, who resists. Miles and Randall stay at a hotel on the road from Denver, and they eventually make love. L.B. is uneasy about "Krystle." Jeff realizes Fallon must have been with Miles Colby the night of the party. Rita continues to avoid intimacy with Blake, fearing this will give away her secret.

## "The Proposal," November 27, 1985
Alexis and Dex return to the U.S. with Galen. Michael gives Dex a begrudging thank-you – and a warning to stay away from Amanda. Blake gives Alexis the news that he has seen Fallon at the Colby mansion in California. Joel poses as Krystle's doctor to get into the mansion. Dominique tells Blake someone is buying up shares in her recording company. Sammy Jo bristles at the sight of Claudia spending time with Danny. L.B. walks in on Rita and Joel kissing. Claudia learns that she inherited the oil well that Walter Lankershim shared with Matthew. She moves back into the mansion with Adam. Alexis tells Amanda to get her act together with Michael. Now on the mend with the best medical care, Galen professes his love for Alexis.

## "The Close Call," December 4, 1985
*John James is dropped from the show's opening.*
Blake is beginning to wonder why Krystle is acting so weird. Dominique gives Garrett the major cold shoulder. Claudia learns that Blake now owns the oil well she supposedly inherited, and he won't do anything to give it to her. As Galen is prepped for surgery, both Dex and Amanda fight for their marriages while at the hospital. Joel binds and gags Krystle as Blake visits Delta Rho to buy his wife a horse. Krystle breaks free and is able to pry a knothole out of the boarded-up window – and see Blake outside! She realizes she's been in the attic at Delta Rho. Alexis wants to move Galen into the penthouse, but Dex refuses.

## "The Quarrels," December 11, 1985
Dex tries to talk Alexis out of her banking – and housing – deal with Galen. But Galen has his own deal brewing, and he instructs Michael to stay married to Amanda. Blake faces an injunction on his pipeline. Alexis sees Krystle yelling at L.B. and lays into her, then reports the incident to Blake. Amanda and Michael share some passionate bonding, but talk of LaMirage and starting a family turns the reunion sour. Joel lures the weary Krystle into a hot bath. Sammy Jo brings Danny to Delta Rho for an outing, and an angry Steven follows them there. Krystle sees Steven, but Joel muffles her cries for help. To fight off Blake's bedroom advances, Rita runs down the hall and locks herself in another room.

## "The Roadhouse," December 18, 1985
Sammy Jo urges Joel to push forward with the plan to get her inheritance. Settling into his new surrounds, Galen cautions Michael not to trust Dex. Rita is impressed by Blake's gifts and show of love. Jonathan entices Dominique to dinner. Joel tells Krystle he's taking her out for "a night on the town," and if she tries any funny business, Kristina's life will be in

danger. Claudia appeals to Steven in her quest to get her inherited well. Adam goes up against Bart Fallmont on the pipeline injunction, then Steven appeals to him as well. On their "night out" at a seedy roadhouse, Krystle and Joel see Dex and Alexis, but Krystle's silent pleas for help go unnoticed by Alexis. Krystle sees her double with Blake on the TV news and has an emotional breakdown.

## "The Solution," December 25, 1985

Blake wants "Krystle" to see a psychiatrist. A magazine expose implies that Alexis is helping Galen so that she can become queen of Moldavia. Blake tells "Krystle" he sees her as a stranger. L.B. tells Alexis about seeing "Krystle" and her "doctor" in bed. Garrett happens upon Dominique lunching with Jonathan. Joel tells Krystle he wants to spend his life with her. Alexis brings up to "Krystle" the roadhouse incident of the other night, and Rita confronts Joel about his night out with Krystle. After Alexis spills the beans to Blake, he confronts "Krystle" about her alleged affair with her "doctor." Rita then goes to Joel, who has a plan to poison Blake with heart medication. Claudia is upset to learn that Adam is not at all helping her get the oil well Walter Lankershim left to her.

## "Suspicions," January 8, 1986

Blake starts to feel the effects of the poison. Bart Fallmont taunts the Carrington brothers about blocking the pipeline deal. Joel strings Krystle along with promises of trips. Amanda sees Elena in Denver and learns she's been working with Michael on the counterrevolution. Alexis is evasive when Dex says she got a mysterious phone call. Steven sees Bart railing on the Carringtons on TV, and he goes to the gym and starts a fight with Bart. In Venezuela, Alexis' sister Caress is released from prison, and she's been writing a tell-all book about Alexis. Alexis pokes around the mansion to find out more about "Krystle" and her "doctor." Blake gets sicker and leaves Adam to run the office. Sammy Jo finds the bottle of medication outside Blake's bedroom door and confronts Rita about it.

## "The Alarm," January 15, 1986

Caress digs around for information about Alexis for her book. Getting no answers from Joel, Sammy Jo takes the medication bottle to a lab for analysis and learns what was in it. Blake goes home sick again, leaving Dominique at the company helm this time. While Blake is in a dizzy haze, Adam has him sign power of attorney over to him. Elena interrupts the quiet dinner of Michael and Amanda, and Amanda has it out with her. Rita continues to feed the poison to the increasingly sick Blake. Sammy Jo goes to Steven for help. Rita allows the weak Blake to fall down the stairs just before Steven and Sammy Jo arrive.

## "The Vigil," January 22, 1986

Blake is rushed to the hospital. Krystle senses something is wrong with Blake. Galen keeps asking Alexis for money for the counterrevolution. Joel poses as a doctor in the hospital to get to Sammy Jo before she squeals. Jonathan sees Garrett comforting Dominique at the hospital. Galen is no longer paralyzed, though it's his secret. Dex is frustrated, once again, that Alexis is so distraught over Blake. The doctor reports that Blake is going to make it. Joel pushes up his plot to skip town with Krystle. In Oklahoma, Claudia finds a document signed by Adam, denying her request for the title of the oil well. Blake wakes up and tells Rita he knows she's not Krystle. Rita then runs back to Delta Rho and finds Joel gone. She checks on Krystle, and it's ... **Catfight No. 4:** In this corner, we have the real Krystle, in a slimming black dress with red belt. In the other corner, it's the fake Krystle, in a powder blue dress and elegant jewelry. Much rolling around on the attic floor ensues. "I'll kill you," the real Krystle says. She throws a lot of good punches. The fake Krystle resorts to biting. Finally, Sammy Jo rushes in and knocks the fake Krystle out. Just as the two are trying to escape the ranch, Joel appears.

## "The Accident," January 29, 1986

Sammy Jo gets Krystle out of Delta Rho by pretending that Krystle is Rita. Krystle then rushes to the hospital and is reunited with Blake. Rita realizes Joel had planned to run off with Krystle. As they argue, their car goes over a cliff. Garrett and Dominique sleep together. Alexis grills Sammy Jo about Joel's imprisonment of Krystle. Sammy Jo apologizes to Krystle, and Krystle says she won't press charges against her as long as she testifies against Rita and Joel. Claudia gives Adam a big kiss-off. Dex tries to expose Galen's trickery, and it backfires. Dominique gets a surprise visit — from her daughter, Jackie. Alexis goes to the National Informer tabloid to pitch a steamy tale about Krystle's captivity.

## "Souvenirs," February 5, 1986

*Emma Samms, Maxwell Caulfield and "special guest star" Ricardo Montalban are included in the show's opening; Kate O'Mara is added.* Blake and Krystle try to rest and recoup. Fallon drops in for a visit. Taunting questions from Alexis send Krystle into a tizzy about her impersonator. Caress is cutting a deal for her book. Miles follows Fallon to Denver and tries to apologize for raping her. Alexis calls Zach Powers when she hears Caress has been released. Krystle is shaken up after an obnoxious reporter poses as a nanny to get into the mansion. When he finds Alexis trying on Galen's crown jewels, Dex again attacks Galen. Zach visits Blake to offer his fleet for Blake's shipping deal with Jason. Dex tries to drink away his sorrows, and he and Amanda end up in the sack again.

## "The Divorce," February 12, 1986
Learning that Rita stole about $1 million from the family accounts, Blake is even more determined to find the vanished Rita and Joel. Alexis walks in on Dex and Amanda in bed. She tells Blake, who questions Amanda. Blake then punches Dex. Krystle accuses Alexis of sending the nanny-disguised reporter into the mansion. Caress tries to dig info on Alexis out of Steven. Subtle sparks fly between Bart and Steven. An ill Dr. Edwards visits Adam to tell him Claudia is in Billings asking questions about him. Caress makes herself at home in Alexis' penthouse, and bumps into Dex. Garrett is struck by a meeting with Dominique's lovely young daughter, and he tells Dominique he wants to know more. Alexis gets a divorce in the Virgin Islands. She then hears Galen telling someone on the phone about how he has her fooled, and she boots him out forthwith.

## "The Dismissal," February 19, 1986
Amanda grovels to Alexis, who has disowned her. Amanda then appeals to Dex, who tells her he still loves Alexis. It's all-out war for Alexis, though, as she tries to buy Dex out of their Lex-Dex corporation. With Galen headed for exile in Lisbon, Michael wants to stay in Denver and make it work with Amanda. Bart overhears Steven telling Adam to back off his digging around for "skeletons" in Bart's closet. Caress grills Adam about Alexis. Sammy Jo tries to hire Morgan Hess to find Rita and Joel. Alexis realizes it's always been Blake she has loved. Caress finally visits Alexis. Dex and Amanda get right back into their affair. Alexis comes on to Blake, and his refusals give her an idea for revenge — his brother, Ben.

## "Ben," February 26, 1986
*Christopher Cazenove is added to the show's opening.*
Caress tries to get information out of Blake Her questions about his brother Ben make Blake reminisce. Blake tells Amanda that Dex is too worldly for her. Still officially in the closet, Bart admits to Steven that he has feelings for him. Sammy Jo tells Blake she's leaving, and he convinces her to stay. Someone is buying up a lot of Denver Carrington stock. Blake tells Krystle about Alexis' pass at him. Later, at a dedication of the joint Colbyco / Denver Carrington wildlife park, an infuriated Krystle confronts Alexis and it's ... **Catfight No. 5:** It's a sort of "mini" catfight, but it registers, nonetheless. Krystle and Alexis accidentally skid down a hill in the wildlife park, and they land smack-dab in a mudpit. Alexis screams, "You stupid bitch!" No real blows are exchanged. But they're drenched in mud, a sight that no-doubt the producers felt the viewers would love. Alexis visits Ben in the Australian outback and offers him $125 million to help her ruin Blake. When Alexis returns to Denver with Ben, they're greeted by Caress at the penthouse.

## Behind the scenes

> *Once in the puddle, covered in mud and screaming at each other, our makeup people came into their own, appearing to get enormous enjoyment from smothering Linda and me from top to toe in thick gooey mud. ... It tasted like horse dung. We had to scrub ourselves for hours to get it off.*
> — Joan Collins, in her autobiography, "Second Act," describing the catfight in the mud

### "Masquerade," March 5, 1986
*Ted McGinley is added to the show's opening.*
Caress doesn't want to leave Alexis' penthouse — she tells Alexis that Alexis owes her for the time she spent in prison. Steven's assignment on the Denver Carrington board irks Adam. Blake invites the Fallmont family over for dinner. Sammy Jo slides down the bannister for the third time, this time bumping into the late-arriving Clay Fallmont. Alexis discovers Caress' writing project about her. Alexis plans a costume benefit for the joint Colbyco / Denver Carrington project without Blake's knowledge. Dominique doesn't appreciate Garrett's investigation of Jackie through her boarding school. Steven dukes it out with Adam over the tabloid story on Bart's gay orientation. Clay hits on Amanda. During Blake's important speech at the benefit, Ben reveals himself. Blake boots him out.

### "The Subpoenas," March 12, 1986
Dex tells Amanda he's leaving town for some business — without her — and that he doesn't love her. Alexis doesn't take kindly to Ben's brusque doubt about their plan to ruin Blake. Steven and Adam fight again in the workout room over a tabloid story "outing" Bart. Alexis secretly buys Caress' publishing company. Buck and Blake have a heart-to-heart about dealing with their sons' gayness. Claudia returns to town, but then packs her bags to move into LaMirage. Jackie investigates her birth records. Dominique gets subpoenaed in Ben's contesting of Tom Carrington's will. Alexis won't accept Amanda's apologies over Dex. Blake gets subpoenaed. He then has a confrontation with Ben over his mother's grave, accusing Ben of killing her.

### "The Trial, Part 1," March 19, 1986
The Carrington brothers duke it out in court over Tom Carrington's estate. Ben claims on the stand that he didn't kill their mother — Blake did. Alexis delivers the blow to Caress that she now owns the rights to her "piece of

filth" book. Claudia takes the stand and tells how Blake denied her oil-well inheritance. Steven takes the stand and must recount the Ted Dinard ordeal. When Blake testifies, he refutes Ben's version of their mother's death. Dex fires a foreman at Lex-Dex, who later starts a fight with him at a bar. Alexis lies on the stand that Blake was drunk and in bed with her when the fire started that killed his mother.

### "The Trial, Part 2," March 26, 1986
Blake pushes to find the woman who was with Ben on the day their mother died. Bart is OK with his newspaper "outing," determined now to live his life freely. This hurts Buck deeply. Franklin agrees to tell the truth on the stand for Blake. Jackie disappears, calling Dominique from payphones as she tries to deal with the mystery and lies about her real father. Caress tells Alexis that she — not Blake — was with her on the day of Ellen Carrington's death. Dex employs Clay Fallmont for his drilling project, then Dex almost gets killed by his disgruntled ex-foreman, though Blake pulls him out of the way of the falling equipment. Claudia comes on to Adam. Franklin falters on the stand, and the judge decides in Ben's favor. Then, Ben meets with Emily Fallmont — his companion on the day Ellen Carrington died.

### "The Vote," April 2, 1986
Blake has a $41-million court-ordered bill hanging over his head, along with dropping stock prices. Alexis seeks to buy into his company and his boardroom. Amanda continues to give Clay the cold shoulder, though he finds some companionship with Sammy Jo and Danny. Dominique appeals to Garrett about Jackie's disappearance, then finally admits to him that Jackie is his daughter. Ben wants to cement his partnership with Alexis in a more personal way, though she brushes him off. Amanda is distraught over hurting Alexis, and Krystle speaks to Alexis on her behalf, but to no avail. Claudia steals an incriminating document from Adam's office to even the odds between them. Blake and Alexis verbally attack each other to reporter Gordon Wales. On his board, Blake proposes a hostile takeover of Colbyco; Steven casts the deciding vote, in favor.

### "The Warning," April 9, 1986
Blake gets turned down for a loan. Both Alexis and Caress try to pry out of Ben the name of the woman he was with when his mother died. Then Caress sees him meeting with Emily Fallmont, and she sets up her own meeting with Emily to trick her into admitting the affair. Clay chases down a distraught Amanda, jumping into her car with her, and the car runs off the road. Clay lies to police and says he was driving to save Amanda jail time. Dex confronts Alexis over business, and they share a

passionate kiss. Blake puts up his South China Sea oil leases to raise cash. Krystle speaks to Ben, who shows her his full hatred toward Blake. Ben has one of Blake's business partners offer him money for one of Denver Carrington's holdings.

### "The Cry," April 16, 1986
A reporter overhears Amanda's remorse over the car-crash cover-up with Clay. Blake gets another refusal from a money broker, amid worries over his tarnished reputation from the trial. The broker then deals with Alexis. Caress tells Blake about Emily and Ben. Blake goes to Emily, who 'fesses up. Garrett and Dominique find Jackie, who's upset with Dominique when she learns her mother has hidden the fact that Garrett is her father. Silently representing Alexis, Farouk Ahmed offers Blake a $1-billion loan, with the South China Sea oil leases as collateral. Claudia coerces Adam to sign over control of her inherited oil well with his ill-gotten power-of-attorney for Blake. Alexis is irate with Amanda when the reporter tells her about the car-crash cover-up. Amanda tries to overdose on pills.

### "The Rescue," April 30, 1986
Alexis and Blake are each concerned about Amanda's withdrawn behavior. Dominique and Garrett get engaged. Alexis rushes in to find Amanda passed out. Dex recognizes Ben from somewhere. Caress cons Ben for 10 percent of his court settlement for her silence, but when he meets her later to deliver, he's got a surprise: He's arranged for her to serve the rest of her sentence in Caracas. Steven tries to get into Adam's files. Claudia says goodbye to Danny then has harsh words for Krystle. Amanda comes home from the hospital. Alexis' Hong Kong contact is double-dealing with Ben. Amanda and Alexis reconcile.

### "The Triple-Cross," May 14, 1986
*Kate O'Mara is dropped from the show's intro.*
Adam worries about the debt Blake is incurring in his vendetta against Alexis. Dex remembers Ben from China and warns Alexis about him. Blake is summoned to Hong Kong over "discrepancies" in royalties from his oil leases. Steven tells Blake that Adam won't let him into his files, and Blake grants him access, which makes Adam nervous. Amanda and Sammy Jo clash over Clay, then Sammy Jo moves in on Clay with an intimate dinner. Ben follows Alexis to Hong Kong, professing love for her, but really dealing behind her back. He shows Caress' manuscript to the Japanese minister, and both Alexis and Blake lose the leases — to Ben. Claudia goes on a buying binge, charging it up to Adam.

## "The Vendetta," May 21, 1986
Ben gives Alexis half of his new oil leases so they can "chew up Blake together." Claudia accuses Blake of siphoning off her well to make it look dry, and she shows him Adam's dirty power-of-attorney paper. When Alexis' plane lands from Hong Kong, Blake meets her at the airport with Caress' "Sister Dearest" manuscript, offering copies to the hovering press. In prison, Caress tries to get a letter to Blake. Blake learns that Alexis was behind Farouk Ahmed's loan. Dominique offers Alexis her holdings to bail out Blake. Ben and Dex duke it out. Jackie hears Garrett's school chum saying Garrett was never married. Alexis later coaxes this juicy tidbit out of Jackie and uses it to upset Dominique at the engagement party. Sammy Jo sees Amanda kissing Clay, asks him to go get drinks, then confronts Amanda, and we have ... **Catfight No. 6:** In this corner, it's Amanda in a gunmetal lame' full-length dress with slightly flared shoulders and a peekabo neckline, her hair pulled back. In the other corner, it's the smashingly cool Sammy Jo in a full-length, appropriately slinky, red sequin gown with halter neckline, her hair big and puffed around her face. *Meow!* Amanda reaches out to shove Sammy Jo, and they both fall into the LaMirage pool. Shocked and drenched, they rise up out of the water and Sammy Jo insults Amanda and turns to leave. Amanda pulls her back into the water, and much thrashing ensues. Meanwhile, Claudia manages to set fire to her room — and to the greater LaMirage — while lighting candles and thinking of how much she hates the Carringtons. Blake and Krystle return home to see that Alexis has packed their belongings and moved into the mansion, claiming ownership as she calls in her loan. Blake proceeds to choke her.

## *Season 7 – 1986-1987*

## "The Victory," September 24, 1986
*Emma Samms is included in the show's opening for a flashback during the episode; Jack Coleman, Michael Nader, Diahann Carroll and Joan Collins all have new photo treatments; Karen Cellini and Wayne Northrop are added while Catherine Oxenberg is gone.*
We open the seventh season with Blake choking Alexis, then Krystle stops him. Blake and Krystle must then take their things and check into a hotel. Blake learns that LaMirage is burning. Amanda is rescued by the former Carrington chauffeur, Michael. As Alexis settles into the mansion, Ben presses for a relationship. Jackie is badly burned, and Dominique breaks the news to her that she's not going to marry Garrett. The fire has killed Claudia. Ben gets a mystery call from a woman from his past. Amanda asks Blake for a job. Amanda introduces Blake to the man who rescued

her, and Blake realizes who he is. Alexis buys the Mirror newspaper to wage a special attack on Blake.

### "Sideswiped," October 1, 1986
Blake learns that Alexis bought the Denver Mirror, as she prints screaming headlines claiming he set the fire at LaMirage. Dex offers to buy the paper from Alexis to save her from her vicious vendetta. Steven tells Adam he's resigning from Colbyco and that they should band together to help Blake. Adam runs to Alexis to tell him Steven has resigned, and that he has stepped down from Denver Carrington. Alexis promptly hires him. Krystle and Amanda go to work for Blake in public relations. Dex offers to bail out Blake, and Alexis sees this. Alexis officially lays claim to Denver Carrington, forcing Blake to vacate his offices. Sammy Jo presses Clay for an introduction to his mother. Phil Thorpe, the angry man who's wife died in the LaMirage fire, runs Blake's car off the road, and Krystle is badly hurt.

### "Focus," October 15, 1986
Thorpe keeps threatening Blake, as Krystle tries to recover at the hospital. Blake threatens to kill Alexis if anything else happens to Krystle. Michael sees a man from his past, Gary Tilden, who has an offer for Dominique. Sammy Jo thinks Clay is ashamed of her. Blake calls a press conference to exonerate himself from the LaMirage fire and to announce his new "Carrington Ventures." Steven tells Alexis that he and Danny are moving out of the mansion. Ben tries to convince Dex to stay clear of Alexis. Dominique sells Titania Records to Zach Powers and gives Blake the cash, and Blake uses the $50 million to pay off his debt to Colbyco. Thorpe holds Krystle at gunpoint at the hotel, and she manages to talk him down.

### "Reward," October 22, 1986
Blake fires his LaMirage manager, Jay Bradley, after learning he hired a questionable employee. Michael romances Amanda. Blake is inspired by a piece of property from his mother, and he hires a key drill foreman, Nick Kimball, and a worker crew to help him build his dream. Ice melts between Dex and Steven. Alexis sets a contest between Ben and the newly hired-back Adam. Sparks fly when Nick meets Dominique. Alexis hires Gordon Wales for the Mirror. Ben fires Blake's former assistant, Dana, who won't squeal on Blake. Adam then hires her, and we learn she's someone who has a particular interest in Adam. Sammy Jo, and her "gift horse," make a nice impression on Emily. After Ben's conniving with Bradley, Blake is arrested for arson.

**"The Arraignment," November 5, 1986**
Alexis realizes Ben has been feeding incriminating lies to the authorities about Blake and the LaMirage fire, and she demands a truthful case from him. Alexis tells Blake she'll help him out of his charges — if he leaves Denver. Ben and Adam butt heads at Colbyco, and Adam sees Ben receiving repeated mysterious phone calls from Australia — calls he refuses to answer. After listening to Jackie's account of the fire, Krystle and Dominique suspect Claudia's room was where the blaze started. Steven is very suspicious of Michael's attention toward Amanda. Ben breaks down at the sight of his mother's photo. Blake's case is dismissed in light of the investigation of Claudia's room. In a tense dinner at the Fallmonts, Sammy Jo defends the Carringtons to Buck. Alexis makes an angry visit to Dex in the field, and a storm strands her there. She and Dex end up in the sack. Adam intercepts a letter for Blake at the Denver Carrington offices, a letter that Ben requested be routed to him first. Adam delivers it to Blake, and it's Caress' letter from prison.

**"Romance," November 12, 1986**
Alexis and Dex make declarations and promises in their love nest. Blake and Krystle visit the prison in Caracas, but the officials deny that Caress is there. Alexis turns down Dex's marriage proposal, and he accuses her of being power-hungry. Steven investigates Michael's recent past. Blake sees Michael kissing Amanda and fires him. Fallon and Jeff visit, Jeff telling Alexis they don't particularly care for the way she's attacked Blake, and Fallon telling Amanda to stay away from Michael. As Ben once again verbally attacks Dex, Alexis boots Ben out of the mansion. Nick hits on Dominique, who's been convinced by Tilden to return to the recording studio. Blake recruits Dex to bust Caress out of prison.

**"The Mission," November 19, 1986**
As Alexis wonders where Dex went, Ben keeps trying to profess love for her, but she's not fooled. Sammy Jo tells Krystle she's pregnant with Clay's child. Adam beds Dana, who tells him she has had a crush on him since high school and even moved to Denver to be close to him. Adam then manages to get from her information on Blake's natural gas venture with his mother's land. Blake loses his financial backing then must talk Nick Kimball into staying on with the project. Dex and Clay get Caress out of the prison and safely back to the U.S. Blake then takes her story to the assistant district attorney, who's not interested in prosecuting. Michael keeps up the romance with Amanda, then calls in a marker — from Zach Powers.

## "The Choice," November 26, 1986
*Ricardo Montalban appears as "special guest star" in the show's opening.* Caress drops in on Alexis and Ben, and Alexis wants to make amends for Ben's treachery in putting her back in prison. Dana tells Adam she won't let him use her again. Michael has Zach front a business deal with Blake on the natural-gas project. Michael beds Amanda. Caress confronts Zach and tries to get some cash out of him for putting her in prison five years ago. Sammy Jo tells Clay she's pregnant. Emily begs Caress not to tell about her affair with Ben. Alexis tries to cut her own deal with Zach. A shooter tries to kill Caress. Amanda tells Blake she's moving in with Michael.

## "The Secret," December 3, 1986
Caress begins extorting cash out of Emily. Clay tells Sammy Jo to get an abortion. After talking to Blake about Amanda, Alexis begins investigating Michael. A therapist tells Steven that Danny is troubled. Blake tries to appeal to Ben to build his own dreams. Sammy Jo tells Clay she's having the baby with or without him. Adam reignites the fire with Dana. Emily appeals to Blake about Caress' threats, and Blake confronts Caress and gets her to back off. A fight with the drunk Buck propels Clay into an elopement with Sammy Jo. Alexis airs Michael's dirty laundry in front of Amanda at dinner. Emily tells Buck about her affair with Ben, and his angry suspicions about Clay's parentage send her running away upset, and she's hit by a car.

## "The Letter," December 10, 1986
Clay and Sammy Jo marry in Vegas. Emily dies in the hospital. Blake gets the letter Emily left for him at the hotel's front desk, confessing she was the one with Ben on the day Ellen Carrington died. A distraught Buck berates both Sammy Jo and Clay when he learns of their elopement. Sammy Jo uses her new name to threaten Steven over custody of Danny, though Alexis then has a few choice threats of her own. Nick resents Dominique ordering him around on Blake's crater project. Alexis switches gears on Michael, flattering him to gain information on his deal with Blake. Nick makes a pass at Dominique. Dex warns Amanda about Michael. Caress goes to Australia. Michael comes clean to Blake about being his silent partner, confessing love for Amanda, but it makes Blake all the more determined to regain his losses — and use Emily's letter.

## "The Ball," December 17, 1986
Blake's threats give Alexis pause, as Michael considers selling his shares of the crater project to Alexis. Nick sees Tilden menacing Dominique and intervenes. Alexis loves up to Dex to learn more about Blake's project.

When Michael won't sell his shares to him, Blake puts the crater project on hold. The doctor tells Sammy Jo she has a false pregnancy. Blake visits the drunk who testified against him at the trial. Adam tells Dana he loves her. At Alexis' illustrious black-and-white ball at the mansion, Dex and Amanda get an eyeful of Michael and Alexis' conniving. Amanda tells Alexis to stay away from Michael. And Blake lowers the boom on Alexis and Ben, armed with Emily's letter and affidavits from a couple others to back it up. Alexis is forced to sign back over Denver Carrington and the mansion.

**"Fear," December 31, 1986**
Alexis puts her own media spin on her losses. When Alexis tries to get rid of Ben, he threatens to tell the district attorney about her perjury at the trial. Danny's therapist Claire hits on Steven — until he tells her he's gay. The staff at the mansion welcome back the Carringtons. Alexis moves into their former residence, the Carlton, and gets consolation from Dex. Dana decides to stay on at Denver Carrington and work for Blake again instead of following Adam to Colbyco. Alexis has a music reviewer trash Dominique in the Mirror, and when Dominique visits her at the Carlton to demand a retraction, we get ... **Catfight No. 7:** It's a flash of silk shirts and slacks. In this corner, Alexis is adorned in blue shell and long overshirt with white slacks. In the other corner, her foe this time is Dominique, a first-timer in the Catfight Count. She's dressed in black slacks and a black-and-white patterned blouse. The first slap comes from Dominique. Shin-kicks follow. Alexis yells, "You bitch!" Things are thrown, things break, a tabletop is overturned, and Alexis' pooch whimpers nearby then finally runs for it. There's much rolling around on the floor of Alexis' suite. Finally Adam rushes in and breaks it up. It's a draw, with each one threatening the other afterward. Alexis sends Adam to Australia to dig into Ben's mysterious phone calls of a few weeks back.

**"The Rig," January 7, 1987**
*Terri Garber is added to the show's opening.*
Blake takes Ben and Alexis to Hong Kong to sort out ownership of the South China Sea oil leases. Krystle warns Ben not to hurt Blake anymore. Ben tells Blake about his wife and child. Adam then has a chance encounter with Ben's daughter, Leslie, in Australia. Sammy Jo worries about losing Clay over her false pregnancy. Adam tracks down Ben's mystery caller, a casino worker named Vera. Alexis then uses this knowledge to get Ben to back off his threats of her. Amanda is upset over Michael's business dealings. Dex gives Sammy Jo encouragement about Clay. When Blake, Ben and Alexis visit the offshore oil rig, there's

an explosion. Ben must then choose whether or not to help Blake to safety.

## "A Love Remembered, Part 1," January 14, 1987
Blake thinks he's back in 1964 because of injuries from the explosion, and Alexis doesn't miss a beat, assuming her former role as his wife and scheming to get the South China Sea oil leases back from him. Krystle arrives in Hong Kong and sees Ben but can't find Blake. Then Dex arrives and joins forces with her, while Alexis continues to relive the old times with Blake. Sammy Jo gets pushed by a horse, and the doctor tells Clay she isn't pregnant.

## "A Love Remembered, Part 2," January 21, 1987
Alexis continues her fantasy world with the amnesiac Blake, no longer even caring about the oil leases. Sammy Jo finds a listening ear in Steven. Krystle and Dex learn that Alexis checked Blake out of the hospital in Singapore — as his wife. Sammy Jo asks Clay for an annulment. Tilden tries to shake down Dominique, hiring a couple thugs to ransack her new recording studio, but Nick comes to her rescue. Krystle finally finds Alexis, then Blake, but Blake doesn't remember her. She walks out, then Alexis 'fesses up with Blake, admitting that Krystle was his wife. In a moment of emotional anguish, Blake remembers Krystle and runs after her.

## "The Portrait," January 28, 1987
Alexis and Dex have their own explosion over Alexis' time spent with Blake. Sammy Jo and Steven spend time together as a family. Blake thanks Ben for saving his life and convinces him to return with them to Denver. Alexis visits Blake at the mansion and once again speaks honestly with him about why she lied in Singapore. Amanda runs off to London.

## Behind the scenes

> From the beginning the plan was for the show to grow and change through personal and business confrontations. As long as dangerous business rivals, former husbands, lost children, poor or forgotten relatives continued to emerge, some pretenders, some real, all wanting to cross the moat to the Carrington castle, the dynasty — and 'Dynasty' — would flourish.
>
> — Esther Shapiro, *"The Authorized Biography of the Carringtons"*

Leslie arrives in Denver and meets up again with her new pal, cousin Adam. She then gets reacquainted with a former love who did her wrong, Michael. Steven and Clay fight over Sammy Jo. Leslie finds her father and accuses him of abandoning her and her mother, who just died a couple months ago.

## "The Birthday," February 4, 1987

Clay tries to reconcile, but Sammy Jo still makes him sign the annulment papers. Blake convinces Leslie to give her father another chance. Adam proposes to Dana, and Alexis, still swooning over her time spent with the amnesiac Blake, is actually happy for him and wants to have the wedding in the mansion. Dominique has another argument with Nick and commiserates with Dex, though it doesn't get physical. Just before her third birthday party, Kristina has trouble breathing and is admitted to the hospital for testing.

## "The Test," February 11, 1987

*John James is included in the show's opening.*
Kristina flatlines, but she is brought back. The family learns she has congestive heart failure. Michael talks Alexis into investing in his business deal — and he's looking for a more personal relationship with her, too, though she resists. Dana tells Adam she wants to elope. Ben begins to melt the ice with Leslie. Sammy Jo and Steven talk about being together for the sake of Danny, and Clay later warns Sammy Jo against getting back with Steven. Blake asks Ben to help Steven cover for him at the office while he tends to Kristina at the hospital. Alexis visits Jeff in Los Angeles, and Michael follows her there. Kristina has a heart catheterization, then the doctor says she has acute viral myocardosis and needs a heart transplant.

## "The Mothers," February 25, 1987

*Cassie Yates is added to the show's opening.*
Dex invites Dominique to the Dexter Ranch in Wyoming. Blake and Krystle go with Kristina to a California hospital to wait for a suitable heart. Blake and Krystle make a televised appeal for help in finding the heart, and Blake even enlists the help of Alexis' newspaper in getting the word out. McVane is released from prison. A car crash shatters the lives of friends of Dex, but their little girl ends up providing the heart for Kristina. McVane turns up in Adam's hotel room and tells him he has proof Adam is not really the kidnapped Carrington child.

## "The Surgery," March 4, 1987
*Leann Hunley is added to the show's opening.*
Sarah Curtis changes her mind about the heart donation, but Dex manages to talk her back into it. Adam receives a baby bootie with his name on it from McVane. Kristina comes through the surgery well. Adam learns more about his kidnapping from Alexis, and it seems to agree with McVane's story. Leslie has an unfriendly encounter with Clay on the road, then learns that she's working for him at Dex's company. Alexis grills Dana over lunch. Adam visits Dr. Edwards in Billings and can't get an answer out of him about who he really is. McVane blackmails Adam into giving him corporate insider information.

## "The Intruder," March 11, 1987
Kristina returns home to the well wishes of a host of family and friends. Dirk Maurier hits on Alexis. Sarah struggles with the death of her daughter. McVane shakes down Adam for an invite to Maurier's society party. Dr. Edwards drops in on Adam again and tells him to tell the Carringtons he's not really their son. Blake tells Adam he's put him back into his will. Krystle rescues the suicidal Sarah. Alexis is appalled when McVane shows up at Maurier's party — from Adam's invite. McVane approaches Michael in a scheme against Alexis. Ben doesn't much like Leslie dating Clay Fallmont.

## "The Shower," March 18, 1987
Adam has nightmares over his questioned parentage, as well as fights with Dana. Alexis confronts Adam over McVane's appearance at Maurier's party. Dana presses Dr. Edwards for more information on Adam. Adam gets into McVane's hotel room, but he gets nowhere in his struggle to end the blackmail. Driving recklessly, Adam is pulled over. Blake and Krystle are increasingly fed up with Kristina's nanny and discharge her. The women host a surprise bridal shower for Dana. Drunk, angry and paranoid, Adam shows up later and calls off the wedding.

## "The Dress," March 25, 1987
Dana has difficulty with the broken engagement. McVane wants a piece of the action with Alexis' current takeover interest. Adam realizes he's being followed, though he doesn't know it's Blake's doing. Steven and Sammy Jo share a night of passion, but Steven has regrets. Clay and Leslie have an ugly encounter with Buck. Blake senses an attachment by Sarah to Kristina. Ben and Buck have an angry confrontation, though Ben just wants Buck to let their kids live their own lives. Sarah decides to leave the mansion, but Krystle talks her into staying.

## "Valez," April 1, 1987

Sammy Jo is heartbroken when Steven tells her he just can't be with her. Maurier realizes Alexis is still hung up over Dex. Blake tells Adam he's the one who's having him followed. Dex warns Alexis about Maurier. Dominique senses Sarah's obsession about Kristina. Sarah tells Krystle she's leaving. Clay and Sammy Jo make peace, allowing Clay to move on, with Leslie, whom he then sleeps with. Steven takes a spill that hurts Danny's favorite horse, Valez, and is wracked with guilt. Sarah abducts Kristina.

## "The Sublet," April 8, 1987

McVane browbeats Adam into telling him about Alexis' takeover attempt with Maurier, then McVane celebrates with Michael later. Police search for Kristina and Sarah while Blake and Krystle try to hold it together. Sarah has Kristina at a secret apartment across town and is calling her Cathy. Adam gets drunk and picks a fight at a local boxing ring, then gets hauled in by the police. Kristina refuses to take her medication and gets sick. Now that his oil wells have hit, Nick is wealthy, and he whisks Dominique to San Francisco and asks her to marry him. Alexis bails Adam out of jail. Krystle finally finds Kristina and Sarah.

## "The Confession," April 22, 1987

Stock plunges for the company that Alexis and Maurier took over. Gordon Wales then pokes around the story — and around Adam. Adam comes clean with Alexis and Blake. Leslie tells Clay that Buck tried to bribe her to leave town. Sarah is institutionalized. Steven goes to Billings to look for Adam, and finally finds him at Kate Torrance's grave. Danny wants to run away. Adam returns to Dana. Jackie returns from her time spent with Garrett in New York, and she tells her mother Garrett still loves her. Just as Adam and Dana prepare to elope, Blake and Alexis convince him that they love him whether he's a Carrington or not. Maurier gets a visit from his nephew, Gavin. Adam tells McVane his blackmail is through, and that he filed a complaint with the police.

## "The Affair," April 29, 1987

Buck tells Blake that Clay is Ben's son, then Blake goes to Ben with the idea. Ben is incensed, so then Blake goes to Clay with the claim. Clay goes to Ben, accuses him of lying and punches him. Sarah, in the institution, thinks her daughter is alive. Krystle takes her to Wyoming to see Cathy's grave. Jackie tells Nick to stay away from Dominique. Clay tells Leslie about Buck's allegation. Leslie then goes to Ben and tells him she hates him. Gavin Maurier woos Alexis in a night of motorcycle riding, burgers and arcade games. As the mansion gets prepared for Adam and Dana's wedding, a mysterious workman leaves Krystle puzzled.

**"Shadow Play," May 6, 1987**
Steven must explain to Danny why he's leaving town for a while. Krystle sees a man on the Carrington grounds during the night. The blood test shows that either Ben or Buck can be Clay's father, and Clay says goodbye to Leslie. Ben tells Leslie he's leaving, too. Buck then congratulates himself that he lied to everyone about Clay's parentage. Blake and Alexis serve Adam with a formal adoption decree on his wedding day. Dana and Adam wed. Dominique tells Nick she loves him. Dex tells Gavin to stay away from Alexis. Alexis and Dex then fight, and Alexis rushes off in agitation, taking one of the caterer's cars and driving off a bridge. Men with guns rush into the mansion and take it over, and in walks Matthew Blaisdel, who says he's there to get what belongs to him: Krystle.

### *Season 8 – 1987-1988*

**"The Siege, Part 1," September 23, 1987**
*The show features a brand-new opening, with dual photos of each star. John James and Emma Samms are added back in. James Healey and Bo Hopkins (as a special guest star) are added, while Diahann Carroll, Ted McGinley and Christopher Cazenove are taken out.*
Alexis is pulled out of the water by a handsome stranger. Blake and Krystle each try to reason with Matthew, who's holding the whole mansion hostage. Blake formulates a plan and convinces Matthew he's getting a company jet to fly him and Krystle back to Peru. Fallon is missing in California; the sheriff finds only her car in the desert. Jeff later finds her. Alexis tracks down her rescuer. Dex tries to flee the mansion and is shot in the back. During the car ride to the company jet, Blake gets away from his captor and brings the police back to the mansion — but it's empty.

**"The Siege, Part 2," September 30, 1987**
The police find Dex on the mansion grounds, and he recovers at the hospital. Fallon also recovers at a hospital in California, but she struggles to remember where she's been. Matthew and his men take the hostages to his old well site. Dana and Adam continue to honeymoon in Hawaii, oblivious to what's going on in Denver. Adam talks children, and this makes Dana uneasy. Leslie tries to break away but is stopped by Matthew. Gerard confesses to Jeanette that he loves her. Matthew presses Krystle to tell him it's always been him for her. Police surround the hostage site, and shooting ensues. Fallon remembers the UFO that abducted her. Matthew finally lets the hostages go, except Krystle, then

Blake, who has rushed in to save her. Steven intervenes and is forced to kill Matthew.

**"The Aftermath," October 7, 1987**
Steven has difficulty with the fact that he killed Matthew. Jeff and Fallon visit the Carringtons in Denver. Leslie introduces herself to Fallon and gets a brushoff, but her later encounter with Jeff is much more friendly. Alexis has Morgan Hess investigating her mysterious rescuer. Fallon tells Jeff what she recalls of her disappearance, and he has a hard time stomaching the UFO story. Blake is approached about running for governor and eventually lets the family know, during a fancy dinner party, that he has decided to run. Steven tells Sammy Jo he will move back into Delta Rho — but into his own private bedroom. Alexis accidentally overhears a phone call between Dana and her doctor.

**"The Announcement," October 14, 1987**
Blake asks Steven to be his campaign manager, but Steven turns down the job. Leslie overhears Jeff and Fallon arguing over her spaceship tale. Alexis tries her best to charm her rescuer, Sean Rowan, but he has more devious interests in her. Fallon relays her story to Steven. Blake extends the offer of being his campaign manager to Jeff. Sean accepts Alexis' offer for room and board in one of her suites at the Carlton, though he doesn't appreciate her changing his wardrobe without asking. Still, he beds her. Blake has a press conference to announce his run for governor, which irks Alexis, who was dumped from the ticket when she got into her car wreck. Dana's doctor tells her she can't conceive, and Adam overhears.

**"The Surrogate, Part 1," October 28, 1987**
Fallon decides to move back to Denver, and Jeff is upset that she didn't consult him first. Alexis eyes timberland for a paper mill, but Blake has it scoped out for a wildlife preserve. Dana visits Dr. Edwards to discuss a truth about her past that they share. Steven breaks up a fight between two of the players on Blake's football team. Sean discovers Alexis is having him followed. He then takes her up on an offer of a job at Colbyco. Dex and Leslie have been growing closer. Dana visits an adoption agency. Steven buys Blake's football team, and his star quarterback, Josh, becomes attracted to Sammy Jo.

**"The Surrogate, Part 2," November 4, 1987**
Dana consults with an agent about surrogate parenting, then she must convince Adam of the merits of the idea. Alexis tries to counsel Leslie away from Dex, hiring her on at Colbyco. Dana and Adam meet with a

## Behind the scenes

> *The priest intoned solemnly, 'Alexis, do you take this man to be your lawful hus-' and was interrupted by a tremendous roar like an express train. All the pots above us shook as did the walls of the adobe hut. ... 'Earthquake! ... it's the big one!' someone screamed. ... Everyone ran for their lives.*
> — Joan Collins, in her autobiography, "Second Act," on filming the overseas marriage of Alexis and Sean — in L.A.!

prospective surrogate mother, Karen. Jeff gives Fallon the cold shoulder at Blake's campaign office, then takes Leslie up on her offer for dinner. Karen is inseminated, and Dana is feeling uneasy about Adam's liking of Karen. Josh hits on Sammy Jo, but she's unimpressed by this jerky jock, until she sees his more human side.

### "The Primary," November 18, 1987

Blake learns that the timberland he wants might be sold to Alexis, so he visits the owner to appeal to him. Fallon wants to learn more about her extra-terrestrial experience, but Jeff wants no part of it. Karen's insemination was successful. Sean takes Alexis on an exotic trip, and the two wind up getting married. Both Dex and Fallon take note of the closeness of Jeff and Leslie. Blake gets the timberland after all. Josh grows more enamored with Sammy Jo.

### "The Testing," November 25, 1987

Jeff tells Blake and Krystle about Fallon's UFO story. Leslie rejects Dex's apologies over his rudeness, and she tells him about Alexis' elopement. Dex and Alexis then share kind words. Josh tells Sammy Jo he's falling in love with her. Fallon is enraged with Jeff after her father consoles her over her UFO "delusion." Adam senses that Blake is testing his children for the reins of Denver Carrington, which he'll have to step down from if he becomes governor. Fallon calls Jeff on his New York trip, and Leslie answers the phone. Josh has been scoring cocaine. Sean takes his sister Victoria to the house where their father — Joseph Aynders — committed suicide. Blake announces to his children that he's chosen Steven to run the company.

### "The Setup," December 2, 1987

Josh's coke supplier gets arrested, and the press is all over it. Alexis coaxes Dana into telling her about her botched abortion as a teen. Alexis then goes to Blake and tells him in an effort to rally against Dana. Though they slept together on the business trip, Jeff tells Leslie he wants to make his marriage work. Fallon is wise to their involvement, though, and tells Jeff she wants a separation. Sean tracks Dana's high-school friend and then goes back to Dana with the knowledge that Adam was the one who made her pregnant as a teen. Alexis goes digging at the whorehouse where Blake found the madam who testified against Ben, and she comes back with a video she has a devious use for.

### "The Fair," December 9, 1987

Josh quits the team, then later has second thoughts, and even asks Sammy Jo to marry him. Blake is upset when Fallon tells him she's divorcing Jeff. Alexis borrows a PR film of Blake touring a facility — she's got a trick up her sleeve. Sean begins blackmailing Dana, pressing her for the minutes of the Denver Carrington board meeting. Alexis throws a costume ball with lots of fun and games. Josh crashes the affair, high as a kite, and makes a fool of himself. Alexis and Krystle do a tug-of-war game over a pit of mud, with Krystle making the winning pull. Leslie and Fallon have a catty verbal exchange in the powder room. And Alexis, during the showing of the PR film, mixes in the clips of Blake visiting the whorehouse — which was his investigation into Ben's whereabouts when their mother was killed, but is packaged as Blake visiting prostitutes.

### "The New Moguls," December 23, 1987

Blake and Krystle battle the backlash of the bordello video. Alexis tries to talk Fallon out of the divorce. Josh comes to Sammy Jo with an apology and just makes things worse. Then, his pusher tells Steven that Josh is a cokehead. Steven then confronts Josh. Krystle visits the madam to find out more about the video. Steven pursues a deal that his siblings don't like, and when Dex goes to West Africa to drop in on an old associate and check out the deal, he finds a connection to Sean. Krystle and Blake disprove the video on TV. Sammy Jo finds Josh overdosed at his apartment.

### "The Spoiler," December 30, 1987

Sammy Jo and Steven try to sort out Josh's death, with Sammy Jo feeling very guilty. Jeff offers her a listening ear. Chris Deegan visits Steven. A frank talk from Steven prompts the football team to volunteer for drug testing, stemming the controversy surrounding Josh's death. Dana delivers the board minutes to Sean but tells him his blackmailing is over. Alexis lashes out at both Sammy Jo and Blake when she learns that Steven has moved out of Delta Rho without Danny. Fallon serves Jeff with divorce papers. Sean seduces Leslie without too much trouble. Sammy Jo and Jeff take a ski trip with their sons.  Alexis announces her own candidacy for governor.

## "The Interview," January 6, 1988
Alexis asks Sean to run Colbyco while she's running for governor.  Blake appeals to Alexis to withdraw from the campaign, reminding her of their time in Singapore, which only makes her more determined.  Sammy Jo and Jeff enjoy their time together on the ski trip.  Fallon goes blond in her newfound independence.  Jeff tells her he's moving out of the mansion.  Sean has Blake stranded without his limo so that he will miss the TV gubernatorial debate.  Krystle covers for Blake during the debate, though, soundly thrashing Alexis on the air and slapping her a good one off-camera.  Dana tells Adam about the abortion, and that it was his child.  Adam then cries on Karen's shoulder.

## "Images," January 13, 1988
Krystle does some investigation of Alexis by talking with Cecil Colby's former lawyer and doctor — and even the priest that married Cecil and Alexis.  Leslie follows Sean to the grave of Joseph Aynders, then later blackmails him with her newfound knowledge, scoring a job as an executive assistant as a result.  Alexis hires an imagemaker.  Adam and Dana reunite, and Dana tells him about Sean's blackmail.  Adam then confronts Sean.  Fallon and Dex fly to Natumbe to check out the business deal, and a drunken Fallon is photographed with Dex.

## "The Rifle," January 20, 1988
Blake doesn't want to use the dirt Krystle has gathered on Alexis.  Thoroughly hung over, Fallon is not overjoyed to see her photo in the tabloids.  Alexis tries to hire Cecil's old lawyer Gerald for Colbyco, then is upset to learn he told Krystle about the circumstances of Cecil's death and Alexis' wedding.  Gerald then goes to Krystle and gives her a copy of Cecil's old will.  Fallon, Adam and Steven finally agree on the Natumbe deal, and Sean's plot for revenge draws closer.  Leslie comes on to Dex, who resists her charms.  Alexis tells Sean she might withdraw from the campaign.  During a debate on live TV, Sean secretly shoots Alexis from the rafters.

## "The Bracelet," January 27, 1988
Alexis recovers at the hospital and tells Sean she's going back to Colbyco and leaving the campaign.  She then changes her mind when Gordon Wales tells her public sympathy has lifted her to frontrunner in the race.  Karen's ex tells her they're still married, and that he still loves her.  Jeff offers to bail Sammy Jo out of a financial difficulty, which upsets Steven.

Sammy Jo gets attacked by a weirdo at campaign headquarters, and Jeff comes to the rescue. Dex shows Alexis a photo he found among Sean's things of Sean and Harry Thresher. Alexis then finds Leslie's bracelet at her own bedside.

### "The Warning," February 3, 1988
Krystle is increasingly concerned about Blake's safety. Karen collapses, then Jesse rushes in to the mansion to see her. Alexis asks Blake to withdraw from the race and run as her lieutenant governor instead. Sean threatens Leslie to be more cooperative with him. The Carrington siblings are nervous over large purchases of their stock. Adam bribes Jesse to go away. It's then revealed that Sean has hired Jesse to cause trouble for Adam. Jesse tells Karen about Adam's bribery, which angers her. Leslie asks Dex for her old job back, nervous about Alexis and Sean. Jeff reveals himself as the Carrington stock purchaser, demanding a seat of oversight in the pipeline deal. Jesse tries to shake loose of Sean's evil plot.

### "Adam's Son," February 10, 1988
Alexis plays cat-and-mouse with Leslie over the bracelet she found. Jeff forces the Carrington siblings to hire Dex back onto the pipeline project. Blake shows his disappointment at that. Jeff then resigns as Blake's campaign manager. Karen goes into labor, and Adam's child is born, right after a fistfight between Adam and Jesse. Leslie wants to resign from Colbyco. She tells Dex she knows a dangerous secret about Sean. Dex then goes to Alexis and tells her that Sean's father is Joseph Aynders. Jeff and Sammy Jo grow closer. Karen tells Adam and Dana that she's keeping the baby.

### "The Scandal," March 2, 1988
Alexis takes the news about Sean to Blake, who makes plans with Dex to investigate the deal in Natumbe. Jeff and Sammy Jo sleep together. Sean learns of Blake and Dex's trip. Adam presses McVane for the name of the prisoner who gave him info about Adam's kidnapping. Adam then visits the prisoner, who admits to lying to McVane, and who says that Adam is, indeed, the baby he kidnapped from the Carringtons. Hess digs up for Alexis a secret life Sean has led as an international terrorist. Sean arrives in Natumbe and threatens Harry Thresher to not run out on the deal. Blake and Dex find illegal arms aboard a tanker. Sean locks Blake and Dex inside, then sets explosives. They escape just in time. They believe Sean to be dead, but he is shown swimming away.

### "The Trial," March 9, 1988
Dex consoles Alexis over the Sean situation. Hess tells Alexis that Sean

hired Jesse Atkinson, and she has him get proof. The custody battle for Adam's son begins. Blake's name is drawn into the Natumbe arms scandal. Leslie moves out of Dex's place to move into Jeff's since he's now divorced, but Jeff stops her. Alexis brings evidence of Sean's hiring of Jesse to the custody hearing. Jeff and Blake make peace, and Jeff comes back as his campaign manager. Steven and Fallon go to Natumbe and clear Blake's name. Dana says in court that she cannot go on with the custody dispute, and that the baby belongs with Karen. This causes Adam to leave her. Krystle is getting mysterious headaches. Authorities find Thresher's body, and there's evidence that Sean killed him, but there's no sign of Sean's body.

### "The Proposal," March 16, 1988
Adam pleads with Karen to agree to joint custody and to move into the mansion. Alexis fires Leslie and gives her severance pay — the bracelet she found at her bedside. Jeff asks Sammy Jo to marry him. Steven hears about this and confronts Sammy Jo. Sean sneaks into Alexis' home with a gun, but before he can reveal himself, Dex arrives. Leslie begs Alexis to forgive her. Dex and Alexis have a passionate reconciliation. Steven tells Fallon about their exes' engagement, and this upsets her. At first Blake leads in the campaign, but his lead slips. Adam's baby son disappears from the hospital.

### "Colorado Roulette," March 30, 1988
Sean has kidnapped Adam's son, and he then draws Leslie into his scheme. She calls the Carringtons to try to tell them where Sean has taken her and the baby, but Sean cuts her off. The call is still traced, though, and Adam and Steven find the cabin hideaway. Adam and Sean duke it out, and Adam and Steven end up saving Adam's son. Rayford wins the governor's seat. Krystle's dizzy spells and headaches prompt Blake to contact a doctor. Fallon and Sammy Jo have a tense talk about Jeff. Fallon then goes to Jeff to have it out, and they end up having sex. Steven decides to leave Denver. Karen gets custody of the baby. Sean gets into Alexis' apartment with a gun, then Dex bursts in. The two struggle with the gun, and it goes off. Sammy Jo arrives at Jeff's apartment to tell him that she'll marry him, unaware that Fallon is there. Blake discovers that Krystle has ransacked their bedroom and disappeared.

### *Season 9 – 1988-1989*

### "Broken Krystle," November 3, 1988
*Jack Coleman, Terri Garber and James Healey are gone from the show's intro; the rest of the cast get new photos.*

Sean is dead, Dex is OK, Fallon makes it out of Jeff's place before Sammy Jo sees her, but then she returns through the front door to taunt both Jeff and Sammy Jo. Blake chases after Krystle but misses her. He asks Jeff to call for a hush-hush search for her by the police. Dana and Adam talk it out, but Dana says goodbye to him. Alexis and Dex revel in their newfound togetherness. Jeff and Sammy Jo do their own search for Krystle at a lake Blake owns — and they find a body there.

## "A Touch of Sable," November 10, 1988
The body of the man at the lake is examined, and Jeff and Sammy Jo find Krystle's diary there, too. Adam finds Steven's goodbye letter to Blake and burns it. Krystle's car is found, having been stolen by a drunk. Sable spots Alexis in Los Angeles and hires a detective to investigate what she's up to. Later, she and her date, Hamilton Stone, run into Alexis and Dex. The cats claw a bit, and Alexis sees Hamilton as her angle for her tanker situation in Natumbe. Blake gets a call from Krystle's cousin, saying Krystle is with her in Dayton. When he gets there, Blake tells Virginia about Krystle's horse-riding accident a few years earlier and the health problems it caused. Virginia tells Blake that Krystle talked about killing someone.

## "She's Back," December 1, 1988
*Stephanie Beacham is featured in the show's intro.*
In Dayton, Krystle doesn't remember her trip to the lake or her flight from Denver. Adam employs Steven's assistant, Claire. The Atkinsons have left town, but Adam tells his lawyer to try to bribe Jesse. While Alexis is away, Sable plays — with Dex. The family realizes that Steven left goodbye letters to them, and Adam is accused of taking them. Sgt. John Zorelli stops by the house with questions that upset Krystle. She realizes the family has been keeping things from her and insists on going to the morgue to see the body from the lake. She doesn't recognize it, but Blake secretly does.

## "Body Trouble," December 8, 1988
Adam is angered by Jeff's involvement at Denver Carrington, plus he vows to get Dana back. Sammy Jo doesn't appreciate that Jeff will be working closely with Fallon. Sparks fly between Fallon and Zorelli. In Los Angeles, Krystle is upset to learn of her further injuries from the horse-riding accident years ago — injuries that Blake kept from her. Fallon goes to the morgue with Zorelli and finds something familiar about the body. Sable finds Blake and Krystle in L.A. and presses one of the doctors for information. Krystle wigs out at a dinner party at the mansion, throwing plates all over the place. Zorelli then shows up to say that the body from

the lake has been dead for 20 to 25 years.

## "Alexis in Blunderland," December 15, 1988
Fallon is haunted by the body from the lake — both in her waking and sleeping hours. Sammy Jo sees Jeff kissing Fallon, and when she confronts him, he inadvertently admits to sleeping with Fallon, too. Sammy Jo then goes to the Carrington stables to have it out with Fallon, and we have ... **Catfight No. 8:** In this corner, it's Sammy Jo in tight pants and a white, waist-length jacket. In the other corner, it's Fallon in a dark riding habit. Just as soon as Fallon can call out her name, Sammy Jo whacks her into the nearby watering trough. Sammy Jo thrashes Fallon around in the water, then they both roll out onto the mud next to the trough. Classic line, by Sammy Jo: "Eat mud!" They argue about Jeff the whole time, but in the midst of their argument, they both realize that neither one of them actually wants Jeff! They laugh the whole thing off! Alexis moves to sell the Carlton hotel. Her junk bonds, arranged by Sean, have come up dry. Adam beds Steven's former assistant, Claire. Fallon sees Blake poking around in the basement and decides to go looking there, herself.

## "Every Picture Tells a Story," December 22, 1988
Virginia visits Blake in California, then goes to Denver with Blake and Krystle to stay at the mansion. In the basement, Fallon discovers the photo of Blake with the man whose body was found at the lake. She goes to Zorelli to see the body again and secretly compares the photo to it. Zorelli captures this on film. Despite her troubled health, Krystle tells Blake she's determined to live. Jeff helps Dex uncover the depth of swindling by Sean and Fritz Heath in Alexis' company. Alexis then learns that Sable is the secret buyer of the Carlton, and Sable gives her 30 days to move out. Alexis takes this out on Dex, who arranged the sale. Adam fires Claire. Fallon shows Jeff the photo of Blake and the man from the lake, and Sable sees it and recognizes the man. Fallon then takes the photo to Alexis, who gets upset. Sable, meanwhile, tells Blake that Fallon is showing the photo around. Alexis then confronts Blake, saying that she is going to make him pay — for killing Roger Grimes.

## "The Last Hurrah," January 5, 1989
Alexis is so concerned about the Roger Grimes finding that she barely notices Dex having dinner with Joanna. Dex then starts up an affair with Joanna. Zorelli questions Alexis about the body at the lake. Krystle is inspired to do charity work after seeing a would-be pursenapper living on the streets. Virginia shocks Krystle and Sammy Jo by kicking the crap out of a drug-dealer. Dr. Hampton tells Krystle that only surgery can save her.

Sable tells Krystle that the body at the lake was Alexis' lover, Roger Grimes. Krystle confronts Alexis and tells her to stop accusing Blake of murder.

### "The Wedding," January 12, 1989
Virginia tells Krystle about her life on the streets. Krystle decides to accept Blake's proposal to remarry, but she also convinces him to sign some papers for her living will, should she not survive her surgery. Krystle sees a man she thinks she recognizes from a "dream" about the lake. It turns out he's a diver employed by Sable. Sable is making lots of friends at the mansion. Krystle also makes every effort to ensure Virginia is welcomed there. Dex talks to Blake about the body from the lake — and the other secrets it could uncover. Virginia recognizes Dex, though he finds nothing familiar about her. Blake and Krystle remarry by candlelight, then head straight to Switzerland for her surgery.

### "Ginger Snaps," January 26, 1989
Virginia becomes obsessed with Dex. Krystle lapses into a coma after the operation. Blake returns to Denver, distraught. Dex makes a connection between Fritz Heath and Joanna and questions her on it. Sammy Jo hears strange noises at Delta Rho and is knocked out when she investigates in the barn. Zorelli is told to drop the Roger Grimes investigation, but he doesn't. Jeff tells Sable she better stay away from Blake, now that Krystle seems to be out of the picture. Virginia tells Dex that she knew him before, when she went by the name "Ginger."

### "Delta Woe," February 2, 1989
Fallon catches flak from both Adam and Blake for being with Zorelli for the night. Jeff and Sammy Jo enjoy a reunion. Sable tells Blake that Jason also had dealings with Roger Grimes. Virginia throws a tantrum at Dex in front of the family. Sable visits Gibson after realizing he was the one prowling around Delta Rho. Both Sable and Dex are following Heath, and teasing each other in the process. Sammy Jo encounters another stranger at the stables, and the place catches fire.

### "Cadavers to Chance," February 9, 1989
Jeff rescues Sammy Jo from the burning barn. Adam overhears Dex talking to Virginia. At the hospital, Sammy Jo thinks she recognizes her assailant. Back from Natumbe, Alexis works to claim Dex back — wondering if he has something going on with Sable. Adam snoops in Virginia's room. Blake and Dex are working together to protect the secret of the valuable "collection" tied in with Roger Grimes' murder. Adam taunts Virginia with her childhood secrets, making her think Dex told him

— and that he told Alexis, too.  He then comes on to Virginia, and they sleep together.  Sable buys Alexis' tankers for 10 cents on the dollar.

## "All Hands on Dex," February 16, 1989
*Linda Evans is dropped from the show's intro.*
Alexis angrily confronts Hamilton Stone over betraying her to Sable.  She then hires soldier of fortune Cray Boyd to seize back her tankers.  Zorelli fights to get back on the Roger Grimes murder investigation.  Adam and Jeff get into a brawl at the office.  The incarcerated and frustrated Gibson tells Blake that Sable hired him.  Blake then confronts Sable, and in walks Alexis.  Adam humiliates Virginia by treating her like the hooker she used to be.  Sable has Joanna buy a gambling marker — and thereby leverage for her fight against Alexis.

## "Virginia Reels," February 23, 1989
Sable pays Fritz Heath a visit at the tables to let him know she has bought his gambling marker.  She then tries to blackmail him into giving her secrets about Alexis.  Sammy Jo intervenes with hospital administrators for one of Tanner McBride's cases.  Sable tells Blake and Dex that she hired Gibson to dive for an unknown "collection" treasure to get back at Jason.  Virginia confronts Dex about Adam's knowledge of her past, and he tells her that Adam won't hurt her anymore.  Dex then charges into the office and attacks Adam over it.  Gibson tells Blake he was at Delta Rho to investigate an unnamed treasure.  Fallon finds in Zorelli's apartment a photo from surveillance of her peeking through the files in her office — with the photo of Blake and Roger Grimes together.  Adam makes a deliberate acquaintance of Joanna.  Virginia leaves, with apologies to Blake.  Heath goes to Sable with evidence against Alexis — and a gunpoint for $5 million.

## "House of the Falling Sun," March 2, 1989
When Alexis drops in to check on his progress in Paris, Cray has her bound and gagged.  Blake finds out from Dex that Adam taunted Virginia.  Blake angrily confronts Adam, slapping him to make him fall down the staircase.  After an argument over the phone with Alexis, Dex finds himself with a distraught Sable, and they sleep together.  Alexis and Cray spend the evening teasing each other.  Zorelli tries to find out why Fallon has been avoiding him.  Alexis and Cray sleep together.  Sable and Dex continue their own affair.

## "The Son Also Rises," March 16, 1989
*Tracy Scoggins is added to the show's intro.*
Adam realizes that Joanna has been behind Sable's attacks on Alexis, so

he offers Joanna a job at Colbyco. When Blake limits his access to the files at Denver Carrington, Adam walks out. Tanner cooks dinner for Sammy Jo and Fallon. Monica drops in to visit Mom, who has Dex in a towel in her suite. Sable asks Monica to move to Denver and work with her. Monica reacquaints herself with "big brother" Jeff. Zorelli tracks down Fallon at Delta Rho and realizes she left because she saw the photo of herself from his surveillance camera. Alexis puts an ad in the paper asking for information on the Grimes case.

### "Grimes and Punishment," March 23, 1989
Sammy Jo tells Fallon to make peace with Blake. Zorelli gets his gun back at work. Sammy Jo makes a donation to Tanner's work then tells him she wants to get involved. An associate of Tanner's later asks him if Sammy Jo knows he's "married." Alexis gloats to Sable that she has sunk the tankers Sable bought out from under her. Alexis then gets the cold shoulder from Dex, who admits to sleeping with Sable. Fallon cries on Zorelli's shoulder after an argument with Blake when Blake saw the surveillance photo of her with the Grimes photo. Adam and Alexis meet with an informant in the Grimes case, who claims that Blake killed Grimes.

### "Sins of the Fathers," March 30, 1989
Fallon tells Zorelli she had a nightmare about Roger Grimes having a snake tattoo on his back. Adam privately bribes Phoenix Chisolm, who tells him that other construction workers disappeared at the time of Grimes. Adam spies a strangely cozy moment between siblings Jeff and Monica. Sable finds Alexis burning papers down in the storage room at the Carlton, and she spies a peculiar painting Alexis says Grimes gave her. Sable then goes to Blake and tells him she knows "the collection" is a set of valuable paintings once hoarded by Hitler. Fallon asks Alexis if she ever had contact with Grimes in her childhood. On the way to a benefit for their new youth center, Tanner tells Sammy Jo he's a priest. Blake tells Dex and Sable he thinks his father killed Grimes when Grimes discovered his Nazi art treasure. Dex dives at the lake and tells Blake and Jeff that the vault's seal has been blown.

### "Tale of the Tape," April 13, 1989
Blake, Dex and Jeff surmise that the collection was removed from the vault years ago, right after Tom Carrington stored it. Alexis appeals to Captain Handler to reopen the Grimes case, pointing him in the direction of Chisolm. Tanner tells Sammy Jo he took a leave of absence from the priesthood to gauge how people would react to his work if he wasn't a priest. Zorelli's gentle prodding of Fallon for information leads him to Dominique's uncle Charles Matthews, who might have information that

Tom Carrington left with Dominique's mother. Blake receives a divorce decree. Sable and Monica barge into Alexis' office and seize her files with a court order. Adam keeps snitching to Blake about Alexis' moves, even telling him about Chisolm. Blake then visits Chisolm and bribes him, as an unseen person listens in. After Blake leaves to get the bribery money, Adam and Phoenix return to the apartment and find Chisolm dead.

**"No Bones About It," April 20, 1989**
Fingers point to Blake in Chisolm's death. Sable checks out Alexis' painting at the gallery she sent it to for appraisal. Charles and Jane Matthews bring Blake the box of items Tom Carrington gave to Dominique's mother. Blake tells Fallon that Zorelli visited the Matthews, and Fallon then angrily confronts Zorelli for using her for information for the case. Adam has a photographer capture Monica and Jeff in a close moment. Phoenix pulls a gun on Adam, blaming him for her grandfather's death, though he is able to talk her down. Blake, Dex and Jeff dig around in the basement after finding a lead among Tom Carrington's things. They find a secret room behind a brick wall — and there's a skeleton inside.

**"Here Comes the Sun," April 27, 1989**
Zorelli comes to the mansion and tells Fallon he's quitting the force for her. Blake comes up from the basement but is able to lie about why he was down there. Adam has the photo of Jeff and Monica doctored up. Sable tells Monica she's pregnant. Jeff and Monica see their photo in a tabloid. Jeff is then photographed accosting the tabloid's editor. Zorelli and Fallon go to Alexis' old cottage, and Fallon gets strange vibes there and even thinks she sees Roger Grimes outside the window. Blake visits Phoenix, who won't talk to him. Jeff and Dex visit Roger Grimes' widow and learn that they also have a son. It's revealed that the son, Dennis, has been working with Captain Handler to get the art collection.

**"Blasts From the Past," May 4, 1989**
The Matthews tell Blake an awful secret. Zorelli and Fallon discover a bug in his loft but don't know it was placed there by Dennis Grimes and Captain Handler. Sable discovers Adam's role in the tabloid photo and points Jeff in his direction. Jeff attacks Adam in the Carlton bar. Alexis then marches in and tells everyone that the tabloid photo wasn't depicting incest — since Monica is not really Jason's daughter. Of course, then we have ... **Catfight No. 9:** In both corners, it's slim and smart suits — Alexis in black and white with ruffles at the neck, and Sable in red and black. There are so many verbal slings it's hard to tell who said what. Much clawing and rolling around on the sofas ensues. Monica tries to break it

up, so appropriately dressed in her workout attire. Sable is on top most of the time. Sammy Jo "confesses" to Tanner that she's in love with him but won't interfere with his priesthood. Zorelli and Rudy pull a ruse at the station to try to find out who planted the bug in his loft. Sable tells Dex about the pregnancy but that she's raising the child alone since he'll always be in love with Alexis. Sable tells Blake that Monica and Miles were the products of a rape. Captain Handler tries to blackmail Blake into giving him the collection. At the cottage, Fallon remembers seeing a fight between Alexis and Roger — then she remembers killing Roger herself!

### *Finale:* "Cache 22," May 11, 1989

Alexis and Blake untangle the details of Tom Carrington's cover-up of the fact that Fallon shot Roger Grimes. Dex, Jeff and Zorelli put their heads together and realize Handler has been behind some illicit activities in pursuit of the collection. Jeff and Zorelli search Handler's house. After Fallon recognizes a melody Kristina has been humming, she has Kristina lead her to the music box it came from — down a mine shaft in the pumphouse on the Carrington grounds. Dennis Grimes follows them there and takes them hostage. Dex attempts to make up with Alexis and fails. Fallon breaks away from Dennis and shoots him, but then part of the mine shaft begins to cave in. Tanner tells Sammy Jo that he feels the same way about her, and they kiss. Handler brings a dozen men and a search warrant to the mansion. Blake turns the tables and forces him to tell him where his daughters are. As they are trying to leave the mansion, Zorelli rushes in, shooting ensues, and both Blake and Handler are hit. Meanwhile, Fallon wakes up amid the mine shaft debris and tries to lead Kristina out, just as Dennis' body stirs. As Alexis and Sable sign papers to end Sable's lawsuit against her, an enraged Dex bursts onto the scene and announces Sable's pregnancy. Adam and Dex begin to fight, and Alexis and Dex go over the balcony railing of the Carlton.

### Behind the scenes

" Once it was over, I gained 25 pounds in two years — and it was fun. I just ate and drank everything I wasn't supposed to! "

— Linda Evans, in the UK's *Sunday Mirror,* 2006

# "Dynasty: The Reunion"

**Airing on ABC, October 20 and 21, 1991**
*The intro to the miniseries features the photos and names much like the last episode of the show: We see John Forsythe, Linda Evans, John James, Heather Locklear and Emma Samms all with familiar photos, along with Kathleen Beller, Al Corley, Maxwell Caulfield, Michael Brandon, Robin Sachs (as Adam), Jeroen Krabbe and Joan Collins.*

Blake is in prison. Krystle has just come out of her coma in Switzerland. A nurse senses something is wrong at the clinic and sneaks Krystle out of there. She arrives at the mansion and finds a huge auction in progress. Blake gets a pardon from prison and goes to Washington to sell his conspiracy theory on a consortium buying up parts of America. He stays with Steven, who's an environmental activist there. Fallon is living in California, hanging out with Miles and divorcing Jeff for the third time. Krystle arrives there and is reunited with Kristina. Sammy Jo, having lost Delta Rho, is modelling again, under the employ of Arlon Marshall. When Jeff goes to Switzerland to check on Krystle, he is kidnapped and interrogated by a mysterious man we see to be Jeremy Van Dorn, with whom Alexis is pursuing a business deal. Alexis strikes into the fashion world with Arlon Marshall. Adam bumps into Kirby in Switzerland. Krystle, who was brainwashed in Switzerland, places a mysterious phone call, receives a gun from a strange man, and we learn she has been programmed to kill Blake when they make love. Alexis takes over at Arlon Marshall's company, promoting his wife to CEO. Kirby is upset to learn that Adam plotted to make Blake lose his company while in prison. Adam still manages to recruit her to help him and Miles find Jeff. They eventually break him free of the Switzerland clinic. Krystle points a gun at Blake, but his love for her wins out and brings her out of her hypnotic spell. Adam is reconciled with Blake, and he then testifies to his malfeasance. Krystle goes to confront Alexis in her Fashion Fury offices, and we have ... **Catfight No. 10:** In one corner, it's Alexis, in yellow jacket with wide lapel and black skirt with black hosiery and a shimmering silver anklet. In the other corner, it's Krystle, with mauve jacket and black skirt in strange cut slats over her hips, a black fabric flower standing out at the top of her jacket, and black hosiery, as well. There are slaps and angry words *(as usual — I mean, what would we expect from the reunion movie?)*, and they roll around amid mannequins and feather boas in the fashion studio. The skirts on both females hike way up, as far as they can go! Good thing they are both wearing opaque black hosiery! Adam proposes to Kirby, who accepts. Sammy Jo slides down the bannister one last time, this time to the cheers of her son and several of the Carringtons.

The Carringtons then reunite for home movies at the mansion. Alexis and Jeremy Van Dorn arrive, then leave, and Jeremy reveals his sinister side to Alexis, whom he ties up and leaves in a room on the estate that is filling with poisonous gas. Miles relinquishes Fallon to Jeff. Jeremy is apprehended on the Carrington grounds, but the "police" who are taking him away are really his accomplices.

## "Dynasty II: The Colbys"

### Season 1 – 1985-1986

**Premiere: "The Celebration," November 20, 1985**
*The opening music introduces the show as "Dynasty II: The Colbys" (which continues for the first few episodes, then drops to the title, "The Colbys"). Stars pictured in the opening music, in order of appearance: Charlton Heston, John James, Katharine Ross, Emma Samms, Maxwell Caulfield, Stephanie Beacham, Tracy Scoggins, Joseph Campanella, Claire Yarlett, "special guest" Ricardo Montalban, Ken Howard and Barbara Stanwyck. The opening of the first few episodes also features "With special appearances by" these "Dynasty" stars: John Forsythe, Diahann Carroll, Gordon Thomson and Jack Coleman.*
Jason holds a press conference on the pipeline deal in the San Miguel Harbor. Sable fumes later that Connie gave "half the Colby empire" in shares to their nephew, Jeff. Back in Denver, Jeff looks at pictures of the missing-and-presumed-dead Fallon, now in the image of Emma Samms. Meanwhile, the amnesiac Fallon, who's taken the name Randall, is with Miles and is having nightmares about her cloudy past. Jeff arrives in Los Angeles, and Jason immediately gives him an assignment, but Jeff tells Jason he won't be ordered around by him. Connie flies off to be with her secret boyfriend, Hutch. Jason hears rumors about his deal in China and takes his suspicions to rival Zach Powers. Jeff tells Monica he believes he saw Fallon with Miles in Denver. Bliss tells Jason that she and her "friend" Sean believe his pipeline deal is bad for the environment. Miles makes a grand entrance at the family dinner party with his new bride, Randall.

**"Conspiracy of Silence," November 27, 1985**
The Colbys reel from the entrance of Miles and his new wife – the amnesiac Fallon. Francesca arrives from London to a tense reunion with

her bitter son Jeff. Blake rushes to California to see Fallon, but she still does not remember who she is, or who he is. Zach Powers sweeps into the Colby Collection art gallery to meet Sable.

### "Moment of Truth," November 28, 1985
Jason gets news of a terminal illness in one moment, then says the Thanksgiving blessing to the family in the next. Jason gives Miles 10 percent of Colby Enterprises. Sable tries to run Jeff off, but Connie intervenes. Jason meets Sean McAllister, the marine-biologist boyfriend of Bliss, whom Jason suspects is threatening his pipeline project. Frankie, discouraged by Jeff's chilliness, wants to return to London, but Jason pleads with her to stay. Jason gets the news that his "illness" was really a computer error.

### "Family Album," December 5, 1985
Zach proposes to supply supertankers to Jason for shipping Denver Carrington oil out of the South China Sea. Sable consults her lawyer to try to stop Connie from giving her shares to Jeff. Miles and Jeff continue going at each other's throats. Dominique visits to investigate what she believes is Jason's takeover attempt of her company. Blake comes to California with L.B., whom Fallon doesn't recognize. After Monica discovers Garrett Boydston is the one buying up Dominique's company stocks, Dominique recruits her to Titania Records. L.B. shows Fallon a photo album under his dad's bed, and when she sees the photos of herself as Fallon, she wigs out and runs out.

### "Shadow of the Past," December 12, 1985
Adam visits Zach for Blake, to sort out the supertanker situation. Fallon looks to Dr. Paris for help. Bliss feels out of place in the Colby family. Sable gives Miles a pep talk regarding Fallon. Sable begins her plan to make Connie look incompetent, but Frankie gets caught in the crossfire as she has a riding accident with the horse that Sable uncinched. The accident draws Jeff to Frankie. Under hypnosis with Dr. Paris, Fallon remembers a rape scene on the night of her wedding. Jason resents Adam going behind his back to Zach. Fallon recognizes Adam as her rapist.

### "A House Divided," December 19, 1985
Jeff and Adam have a knockdown, drag-out fight. Dr. Paris helps Fallon remember that Adam didn't rape her – that her wedding-night disappearance resulted from her own unacceptable, subconscious attraction to Adam! Jason signs the contract for Zach to provide supertankers for his excess oil. Jason tells Frankie he's having problems

with his marriage. Sean tells "Uncle Zach" that he wants out of the scheme to get insider info from Bliss. Fallon is wracked with guilt over the pain her disappearance caused her family. Hutch returns the $200,000 Connie deposited into his bank account, and when the banker calls the Colby mansion, Sable becomes aware of Connie's secret life. Miles blows up at Fallon after seeing her hug Jeff.

### "The Reunion," December 26, 1985
Miles witnesses an interlude between his father and Frankie. Connie reaches out to Fallon, who's pushing Miles away. Monica rubs Neil the wrong way at Titania. Monica meets Hutch and tries to strong-arm him, resulting in his anger that Connie withheld information about herself to him. Garrett visits Dominique at the office and mentions a jealousy of Jonathan Lake. Fallon has a proper reunion with Blake and L.B. Miles tells Fallon he'll let her choose between Jeff and him. Connie receives the summons to court as Sable's plot against her deepens.

### "Fallen Idol," January 2, 1986
Jason tells Frankie he plans to divorce Sable. Nikos Livadas creates an oil spill in San Miguel Harbor, implicating Colby Enterprises. Miles shows great concern over his parents' marriage, even asking Sable to drop the case against Connie. Monica verbally volleys with a smart-mouth, blind country singer in a bar, then seeks to sign him to her record label. Frankie returns to London, not wanting to cause trouble for Sable and Jason. Miles walks out on his dad after confronting him over Frankie.

### "The Letter," January 9, 1986
Adam arrives with letters Connie was seeking from Cecil Colby's belongings, including one that helps her case: a letter she wrote to Cecil shortly after Jeff was born, explaining that she would one day give Jeff her own Colby shares. In London, Frankie accepts Roger Langdon's marriage proposal. Sable gets outbid at Sotheby's in New York on a Matisse she wanted for the Colby Collection. Monica has dinner with Neil to try to smooth over their working relationship. Back in New York, Zach woos Sable over dinner, champagne, stories of their first encounter when as a deckhand he walked in on her dressing aboard the Colby yacht – plus the Matisse he outbid her on. She refuses the gift. Connie sees a letter Adam showed to Jeff, from Phillip to Cecil, saying Phillip didn't believe Francesca's baby was his. Sable accidentally hits Connie with her car. Sable then finds the letter about Jeff's parentage.

### "The Turning Point," January 16, 1986
Jeff confides in Fallon over Phillip's letter on his parentage. Connie

recuperates.  Jason tells Sable he wants a divorce.  Zach has the Matisse delivered to the Colby Collection, but Sable rejects his advances once again.  Sean proposes to Bliss, then tells Zach of his plans, then goes to Jason and not only tells Jason his plans but also tells him of his connection to Zach.  Monica and Neil cozy up in San Francisco.  Miles tells Sable that Frankie is the reason for Jason's leaving her, then Sable tries to save her marriage by telling Jason that Frankie has cheated on other men in her life (a reference to Phillip's letter).

### "Thursday's Child," January 30, 1986
Sable shows Phillip's letter to Jason.  Zach offers to bail out Jason from the pipeline mess.  With Connie feeling down, Monica makes an appeal to Hutch, who then visits Connie.  Jason tries to address Miles' frustration on the job.  Jason tells Bliss about the Sean-Zach connection.  Livadas is murdered.  Monica is touched by the video shoot of Wayne's new single.  In the midst of annulment talk, Miles rapes Fallon.  Sable tries to convince Fallon to stay with Miles by telling her about Jeff's questioned parentage.  Sable confronts Zach for using her family, but gets more than she bargained for.  Jason flies to Rome to ask Frankie if Jeff is his son.

### "The Pact," February 6, 1986
Frankie denies Jeff is Jason's son.  Dominique lets it slip to Monica that Neil is married.  Sable plans her attack on Jeff's company holdings, starting at a talk with Jeff, then working her way over to Fallon, then offering to drop the whole thing to Jason if he drops the divorce.  He takes her up on the offer.  Fallon proceeds with the annulment from Miles.  Garrett thinks Dominique is hiding something – or someone.  Meanwhile, Dominique opens her new club with a full array of Colbys – and Wayne Masterson as entertainment.  L.B. is diagnosed with bacterial meningitis.

### "Fallon's Choice," February 13, 1986
Fallon and Jeff keep vigil over L.B., growing closer in the ordeal.  Bill Mahoney is found dead in the San Miguel Harbor, and Miles is questioned.  Sean takes Bliss to see his ill mother.  Jeff and Fallon get engaged, and Miles takes Fallon on a scare ride in retaliation.  Sable slickly hands off Phillip's letter to Miles, who's determined to use it.  Connie decides to return to Colby Enterprises.  Roger is named vice consul in Los Angeles.

### "The Trial," February 20, 1986
Summons are served for the court date regarding Jeff's company holdings.  Jason tries to talk Miles out of the lawsuit.  Wayne tells Monica that Neil is about to doublecross her, so she fires Neil.  The Lord and Lady

Langdon arrive in California, and Sable has it out with Frankie at the welcome reception. Feeling empty, Bliss runs back to Sean. The court proceedings begin.

## "Burden of Proof," February 27, 1986

Frankie's in a hotspot, now that Col. Holmes testified that Phillip was sterile. Just as she is about to be forced to tell who else she had slept with at the time, Jason rises and proclaims that Jeff is his son. Afterward, Frankie finds disgust from her son and comfort from Roger, while Jason finds Sable pointing a shotgun at him. Zach tracks Sable to the Colby Collection and offers her some "comfort." Miles gets increasingly violent, finding Jeff and Fallon at the beachhouse and duking it out with Jeff, who falls over a cliff.

## "My Father's House," March 6, 1986

Jeff is not injured in the fall. Jason and Sable plan to divorce. Frankie tries to reconcile with Sable, then they have it out again. Sable still can't sleep with Zach, who even offers to use some favors to get Roger transferred away from California. Sable still spends the night in Zach's penthouse, only to be discovered there in the morning by Miles, who's come looking for Zach. Roger is summoned to Singapore, though Frankie stays in California. L.B. comes up missing.

## "The Outcast," March 13, 1986

Jason finds L.B. in the attic. Jeff and Jason reunite. Jeff and Fallon plan for their wedding to be in California. Dominique wants Monica to hire back Neil. Garrett tells Jason that his divorce could get expensive. Fallon and Sable tangle over the wedding plans. A private investigator hired by Connie tapes the conversation with Zach and Sable, who still haven't slept together. Miles and Zach strike up a "gentlemen's agreement" – Miles keeps mum about seeing Mum at Zach's place, and Zach says he'll help Miles with the Mahoney case. Miles shows up drunk at the engagement party. Monica hires back Neil.

## "The Wedding," March 20, 1986

Miles has a heart-to-heart discussion with Fallon. Jason gives Jeff the watch that belonged to Jason's grandfather, as Miles walks in. Blake arrives in California a day early for the wedding – to sign a deal with Zach Powers to cover any oil shipment that Colby Enterprises cannot. Spiros holds his mother's mysterious death over Zach's head. Fallon has joyful visits with Blake, then Steven. After a lovely wedding ceremony for Jeff and Fallon, Lt. Braden shows up and arrests Miles for Mahoney's murder.

**"The Honeymoon," March 27, 1986**
Miles is booked into the L.A. County Jail. Fallon and Jeff enjoy wedded bliss in Jamaica, while Bliss and Sean escape with plans to elope. Jason comforts Sable during Miles' ordeal. Jason confronts Zach, telling him he'll truck Blake's oil rather than letting Powers Shipping pick up the slack. Roger returns to Frankie, saying he turned down his Singapore assignment, but they share heated words over Jason. Monica senses something else is wrong with Miles. Connie invites Frankie to stay at the Colby poolhouse, then Frankie confronts Sable about Roger's Singapore transfer. Fallon and Jeff get an ominous reading from a fortuneteller. Miles pleads not guilty to murder.

**"Double Jeopardy," April 10, 1986**
Frankie tells Jason that she and Roger are divorcing. Moretti questions Jeff in Captain Livadas' death in Greece. Bliss backs out of her quickie engagement to Sean. While Wayne is away having the surgery that will hopefully give him back his sight, Monica hops back in the sack with Neil. Sean takes the Florida job he was previously offered. Sable continues to resist Zach, harboring hopes of a reunion with Jason. Moretti shows up at the opening of the new wing of the Colby Collection to arrest Jeff for the murder of Livadas.

**"A Family Affair," April 17, 1986**
This time, Jeff is booked into the county jail. Connie and Sable tangle again. As she's finishing up her divorce trip to Acapulco, Frankie rethinks her apprehension about Jason. Jason sees an upsetting newspaper story about the murder cases and storms into Moretti's office. Jeff has his arraignment then returns home. Sable manages to sleep by Jason's side, then makes it out to be more than it is with Frankie the next morning. Bliss goes to Zach's office looking for Sean and meets Spiros instead. Jason offers Zach the shipment of Blake's oil – if he'll drop the cases against Jason's two sons. Zach then tries to do a little murder investigating on his own. Miles confesses to Monica that he blacked out on the night of Mahoney's murder. Frankie tells Jason she'll marry him.

**"The Recording," May 1, 1986**
Connie strategizes over Jason and Sable's divorce, inviting Zach to her office to taunt him that he'll never get a piece of Colby Enterprises. Sable tags along as Jason and Frankie fly to Greece to help Jeff. Connie gives Jason the tape of Sable and Zach in their clandestine chatter. Jason discredits the witness against Jeff, freeing him. Miles disappears – he's gone to Dr. Paris to try to retrieve through hypnosis his memory of the night of Mahoney's murder. Wayne returns to town – with his sight.

### "Anniversary Waltz," May 15, 1986
Sable plans to lie for Miles on the witness stand. Neil gives Monica a key to his home. Jeff and Miles work together to track down the tools from his totaled car, and shed light on Moretti's "murder weapon." Spiros hits on Bliss at her surfing competition. Fallon thinks she's pregnant. Wayne walks in on Neil and Monica kissing. Sable surprises Jason with an anniversary party, then Jason surprises Sable with the tape of her and Zach. Bliss hops into bed with Spiros. Sable runs to Zach at his yacht. Jason comes there, also, for a confrontation with Zach. As the two men wrestle with Zach's gun on deck, it goes off and Sable is shot.

### "Checkmate," May 22, 1986
As Sable recuperates in the hospital, Zach tells Jason that he loves Sable. But later Sable says goodbye to Zach. With no longer any case against Miles, Moretti turns his attention to Sable's "accident." Jason gives Sable the tape of her and Zach, and she flaunts it in Connie's face. Zach accuses Spiros of framing him in the double Colby murder charges. Monica walks in on Neil – and his wife. Jason tells Sable he's divorcing her, then packs and takes off for the Dominican Republic with Frankie. Sable turns to Moretti. Fallon confirms her pregnancy – but she's further along than she thought. Monica's plane crashes. As Jason and Frankie are about to depart, Jason is arrested – for "beating" Sable, who really fell down the Colby staircase after he left.

### *Season 2 – 1986-1987*

### "The Gathering Storm," September 24, 1986
Monica is rescued by a forest ranger. Jason is let out on bail. Miles encounters a mysterious woman in an elevator. Fallon wants to know who the father of her baby is. Sable's whole family wants her to stand down from her lies about Jason. Even Arthur Cates cautions her. Sable then offers herself up to Zach, at last, hoping to secure false testimony from him against Jason regarding the accidental shooting on his yacht. Channing Carter shows up at the Colby mansion under the guise of doing a story on it for her uncle's home design magazine.

### "No Exit," September 25, 1986
Miles has dinner with Channing – and dreams of Randall. Jason and Frankie spend the night together, as Sable, who just stormed out on Zach, looks on. Dominique tells Monica she's selling Titania Records and her hotel to help Blake out of a bind. Now that Zach won't back her lie, Sable recants her story against Jason to Moretti. Fallon tells Jeff about the rape and the possibility that Miles is the baby's father. Garrett appeals to

Dominique to see Jackie, then after her rejection once again, nabs a new assignment from Jason as the head of the New York office. Sable tries to make good with Jason, Jason kicks her out, but then she passes out just as she's about to leave the mansion for good.

## "Jason's Choice," October 2, 1986
Sable's collapse buys her more time at the Colby estate. Zach buys Dominique's hotel and Titania Records. Dominique then appeals to Jason for Blake and the pipeline deal. Monica hands Zach her resignation from Titania. Channing moves into the Colby mansion to do a magazine story on Sable's surrounds, then she promptly moves in on Miles. The Colby kids plead Sable's case to Jason. Learning that Sable got a "stay" of execution from Jason, Frankie demands that he choose between them.

## "The Matchmaker," October 16, 1986
Jason gives Sable divorce papers, and they work out a deal whereas she keeps living in the Colby mansion. Jeff gets upset and starts a fight with Miles after seeing him talking to Fallon; Jeff comes just short of spilling the secret over the baby's questioned parentage. Bliss meets a Russian ballet dancer and is very intrigued. Jason asks Monica to take Garrett's old job as his general counsel. Zach, the proud new owner of the Excelsior Hotel, tells Sable he can teach her how to wield the business power she'll gain from her divorce with Jason. Miles proposes to Channing, and they fly off to Las Vegas, soon followed by the agitated Lucas Carter – and Sable, whom he has managed to agitate, too.

## "Something Old, Something New," October 23, 1986
Monica tells Jason about the plane crash and her involvement with Neil. Jason's "old friend" Cash Cassidy calls from Washington. Monica does some digging into Zach's file by visiting Mahoney's widow. Cash brings Jason the news that Washington will back his IMOS satellite project, and Jason holds a press conference with the news. Jason then meets with Channing, his new daughter-in-law, with some secrets from her past, but then decides to forget about it for Miles' sake. Cash comes to the party Sable throws for Channing and Miles, and Monica is uneasy, since she was involved with Cash years earlier.

## "The Gala," October 30, 1986
Sable prepares for the gala debut of her new dance company. Channing tries girl-talk with Fallon. Monica dwells on her past with Cash, even after reading Connie's reassuring letter. Jason works with Cash on the satellite project. Channing feels the pressure from Sable and Miles to have a baby and finally explodes to Miles that she's barren. At the gala, a drunken

Miles still pines for Fallon, and he and Jeff fight in the pool. A flustered Monica runs to Arthur Cates to make sure he's never told anyone that she had Cash's child eight years ago.

### "Bloodlines," November 6, 1986
Frankie wants to feel useful around Jason, and he finally gives her a job with his satellite project. Channing tells Miles a tale of teenage rape and abortion and infection, then secretly takes her next birth-control pill. Sacha's strict control is suffocating Kolya. Sable asks Jason to put both her and Miles on his board of directors. Jason wants to take Cash off the satellite project, but Zach wants to assure he stays on. Cash's wife reminds Monica of their "agreement" years ago. Sable discovers that the paternity of Fallon's baby is questioned.

### "Deceptions," November 13, 1986
Sable acts on her newfound knowledge of Fallon's baby, consulting with Arthur Cates. Jason asks Jeff to keep an eye on Cash in the satellite project. Sable tells Miles that Fallon's baby is his, then Miles confronts Fallon. Bliss tells Kolya she can't see him anymore. Sable tells Jason about Fallon's baby, and Jason sends Jeff out of town and talks to Miles. Then Miles confronts both Jeff and Fallon, and fighting ensues. Miles falls over the edge of the Colby Towers heliport.

### "And Baby Makes Four," November 27, 1986
Security guards arrive just in time to help Jeff lift Miles up from the ledge of the building. Kolya sneaks away from Sacha's prying eyes to see Bliss, and he sets off the Colby estate alarm. Monica sees the Cassidy family arrive at the airport and meets little Scott. Miles overhears Channing criticizing Fallon and puts Channing in her place. Adrienne gets increasingly nervous about Monica's contact with Scott, telling Cash that it was Connie Colby who talked her into adopting the little boy – Monica's child – eight years ago.

### "Bid for Freedom," December 4, 1986
Fallon and Jeff go skiing, and Miles and Channing end up at the Colby Lodge with them. Bliss and Kolya sneak off to spend some time together. Zach asks Sable to marry him. Cash and Monica take Scott to a rocket launch. Adrienne appeals to Jason about Cash's involvement in the satellite project. Zach and Sable help Bliss secret Kolya away to freedom, but when Sacha and his men corner Kolya, he jumps off the hotel ledge.

### "Sanctuary," December 11, 1986
Kolya survives the fall, and when Sacha catches up to him, he requests

political asylum in the U.S. But Anna has been taken away. Fallon is having pains, and Channing purposely doesn't call a doctor for her. Francesca arrives and discovers Channing's deception. After a strange conversation with Adrienne, Monica demands to Arthur Cates to tell her who adopted her son. Fallon's pains are a false alarm. Monica calls Connie and gets the truth about her son – that he is Scott Cassidy. Jason takes in Kolya. Monica confronts Cash about Scott.

## "Reaching Out," December 18, 1986

Jason learned that Connie wired herself $2 million in India. Monica tries to resign from the satellite project, but Jason won't accept it. Cash puts Zach in his place for trying to blackmail him. Zach tells Sable that Scott Cassidy is Monica's child, then Sable goes to Monica and finds out the story from her. Kolya speaks to Anna, who's under duress with Sacha in Russia. Jason can't reach Connie, and he sends Jeff and Miles overseas to look for her and Hutch.

## "Power Plays," January 1, 1987

Sable sets out to snatch her first grandchild out of the Cassidys' hands. Jason is named Man of the Year. Sable corners Adrienne over lunch, then Adrienne later yells at Monica for it. Lucas' lawyer is skulking around the Colby mansion, blackmailing Channing into spying for him. Sable brings in a ballerina from New York to replace Anna as Kolya's partner – and it's a woman Kolya once knew. A tabloid story from one of Lucas' papers vexes Jason and his relations with the Soviets over the satellite project. Sable attends her first board meeting, promptly voting against Jason on the first issue. Cash tries to convince Monica to make a family with him and Scott. Jason gets the news from Miles and Jeff – Connie is dead.

## "The Legacy," January 7, 1987

The Colbys try to untangle the mysterious deaths of Connie and Hutch and their meeting with a man called Hoyt Parker. Zach pays his respects along with the other mourners at Connie's funeral. Cash tells Adrienne he wants to call it quits. Connie leaves her voting shares and seat on the board to Miles. Georgina taunts Bliss with her past relationship with Kolya, then sets Bliss up to see her kissing Kolya. Adrienne poisons Scott's mind against Monica. Now in California, Hoyt Parker follows Jason and Frankie to the Colby ranch in Eureka – and aims a gun at them.

## "The Home Wrecker," January 15, 1987

*Michael Parks as Hoyt Parker is added to the opening music.*
Hoyt shoots at Jason and Frankie and misses. Buoyed by his Aunt Connie's faith in him, Miles sets out to give Jeff a run for his money. Scott

runs away after Cash announces that he's divorcing Adrienne. Cash proposes to Monica, and Adrienne gets drunk and tells Jason that Scott is Monica's child. Georgina continues her taunting of Bliss, pretending to have a relationship with Kolya. Zach gives Sable an engagement ring.

### "Manhunt," January 22, 1987
Monica and Cash find Scott in the outer-space observatory. Jason feels dejected that Monica never told him about her son. Knowing how upset Bliss is, Kolya asks Sable to replace Georgina as his partner. Frankie receives a threatening anonymous phone call from Hoyt Parker. Jeff investigates the life of Vietnam vet Hoyt Parker by visiting his mother. Jason is shot at during a press conference for his satellite project, but Cash pushes him out of the way and takes the bullet.

### "All Fall Down," January 29, 1987
A jealous Channing picks a fight with Fallon. Surgeons have a tough time removing the bullet from Cash. Zach presses Sable for an answer to his proposal, but she sees the news about the attempt on Jason's life and runs off. Jason gives Frankie an engagement ring. Hoyt secretly buys up massive shares of Colby stock, and Jeff accuses Zach of the takeover attempt. Channing pleads with Jeff to help her with the Miles and Fallon situation. When Cash wakes up, Monica admits her love to him. Jeff and Fallon fight, and as he walks out, Fallon falls down the stairs. Miles finds her, and sees Channing standing up the stairs, and thinks Channing pushed her.

### "Guilty Party," February 5, 1987
Fallon is rushed to the hospital, while Jeff chases Hoyt Parker after intercepting a call meant for Hoyt – from Zach Powers – at the hotel bar. Fallon is forced to have a C-section, and a baby girl is delivered. Miles confirms that it was Hoyt Parker who bought up all the Colby stock, then Jason confronts Zach over Zach's involvement with Hoyt. L.B. tells Miles that he was the one who left the marbles on the stairs when Fallon fell. The doctor tells Miles and Jeff that the baby's life is in danger.

### "Fallon's Baby," February 12, 1987
Adrienne tells Cash she's leaving, and Sable tells Cash she wants to use Adrienne's past treatment for substance abuse to fight for custody of Scott. Jeff tells Channing to stay away from Fallon and the baby, which spurs Miles to yell back at Jeff. Hoyt digs through newspaper accounts of the Colby trials and tribulations. The baby's condition improves. Jeff bribes the hotel clerk where Hoyt stayed. Bliss suggests to Kolya that they marry. The test results come in – Jeff is the baby's father.

### "Answered Prayers," February 26, 1987
Sable drags her feet signing the divorce papers. Fallon and Channing try to work out a truce. Channing tosses out her birth-control pills. Sable signs the divorce – but pleads with Jason not to marry Frankie. Miles tells Channing he appreciates the way she has stood by him. Zach and Sable vacation in Morocco as Zach keeps pressing for Sable to marry him. Just as Frankie and Jason are about to say "I do," Frankie sees Phillip among the guests and faints.

### "Return Engagement," March 5, 1987
Fallon warns Jeff about Phillip and how Connie used to speak of him. Jason and Phillip argue, but then Jason gives him a job. Anna calls Kolya and pretends to tell him their mother is dying, but her coded words tell Kolya that it's a trick by the Russian government. Against Jason's wishes, Jeff decides to give Phillip his shares of Colby Enterprises. As Jeff tracks Hoyt Parker, Jason finds something very familiar about the handwriting sample. Miles discovers Channing's birth-control pill pack. Phillip surprises Frankie at the poolhouse, and soon they are kissing – as Sable looks on.

### "Devil's Advocate," March 12, 1987
Frankie tells Jason she wants Phillip out of the house for the sake of their relationship. Jeff buys his own family a house, but Fallon doesn't want to move. Phillip gets an ominous call from the lawyer of a syndicate that "wants its money." A handwriting expert confirms for Jason that Phillip is Hoyt Parker. Jason asks for help from Roger Langdon at the British Consulate, and on a tip from him, visits Hoyt Parker's mistress in Singapore. Channing talks herself back into Miles' good graces. Phillip lures Frankie into another kiss. Fallon has second thoughts about moving – and signs on her own house. Scott overhears Adrienne saying that Monica is his natural mother. Jason hosts a black-tie family production – with special guest star Maya Kumara – and exposes Phillip as Hoyt Parker.

### "Betrayals," March 19, 1987
Phillip explains to everyone how he assumed the identity of his deceased friend Hoyt Parker. Frankie tells Jason she "needs some time." Jeff decides not to give Phillip his Colby shares, but he will lend Phillip $300,000 to cover his debt. Monica tells Sable that Zach was the one who schemed with Adrienne, and Sable gives Zach the big kiss-off. Adrienne tells Sable that she's taking Scott away and will fight Sable with everything she has if Sable tries to stop her. Kolya asks Sable to be let out of his contract so he can join a dance company in New York, then Kolya tells Bliss he wants to get married. Phillip sells his $2 million in Colby shares to Zach. Jason finds Frankie and Phillip kissing in bed.

### "Dead End," March 25, 1987

Jason dukes it out with Phillip on the lawn. The bickering of Miles and Jeff ruins the fun of a going-away party for Bliss and Kolya. Fallon gets strange feelings and strange phone calls. Lucas Carter antagonizes Jason about his "bastard grandson," then he turns his animosity toward Channing, who deflects it, happily, by telling him she's pregnant with Miles' child. Sable tells Zach that the two of them were just not meant to be. Phillip asks Sable to lunch then lifts her Colby Enterprises access card so he can sneak in and photograph Jason's IMOS files for Zach. Zach then tries to steal the file copies from Phillip's room, but he finds instead the gun Phillip used to try to kill Jason at Eureka. Frankie retreats to the seaside to think, and as Jeff comes to find her, she's jumped off the pier.

### *Finale:* "Crossroads," March 26, 1987

Jeff rescues Frankie from drowning. Fallon sees a strange light in the sky. Zach leaks out the word that Phillip is the one who tried to kill Jason at Eureka, and Jason tells Phillip to leave town. Phillip does, but he kidnaps Frankie, too. Thrilled that Channing is pregnant, Miles decides to throw a party, but Channing calls him to say she's skipping town and getting an abortion. Scott says goodbye to Monica, telling her he's glad she's his mother. Sable kidnaps Scott from school. After their car crashes, Phillip disappears and Frankie, badly injured, tells Jason to take care of Sable. And, in perhaps the most disappointing plot twist for any fan who wants to believe that the show's producers find fans intelligent, Fallon is abducted by a UFO when she heads to Mexico to help Frankie. *Yikes.*

---

### Behind the scenes

> "Planning what Alexis would wear to scheme and seduce was enormous fun. I spent hours with Nolan (Miller) in the wardrobe department designing outfits with an eye on what Alexis was up to. The duller the scene, the more outrageous her clothes, and vice-versa."
> — Joan Collins, in her autobiography, *"Second Act"*

# "Dynasty Reunion: Catfights & Caviar"
### Airing on CBS, May 2, 2006

*The intro to this reminiscing occasion is done in the same style as the regular intro of the two shows. A photo is shown of the actor or actress during the show's run, then it is joined by a modern photo.*

The setting was casual, though the dress was certainly nice (Joan Collins and Linda Evans in Nolan Miller, of course). Cast members gathered at the Filoli mansion, filming site for the Carrington mansion scenes in the show, and chatted over champagne, their conversation interspersed with clips from the series. Collins arrived through the Filoli's front door and was greeted by Evans, who'd just come down the grand staircase. After the first commercial break, they were joined by Pamela Sue Martin and Al Corley, also descending the staircase. Gordon Thomson later entered boldly through the double doors. After subsequent commercial breaks, Catherine Oxenberg came down the stairs to join the group, then Collins and Evans chatted about their catfights (and a montage of the show's catfights was shown with Pat Benatar's "Hit Me With Your Best Shot" playing over it). John Forsythe finally made his appearance at the end of the reminiscing. Interview clips of other cast members, such as Pamela Bellwood and Emma Samms, were also shown. Some notable quotables:

**Joan Collins**
"My most exciting time in 'Dynasty' was when we became the No. 1 show. We loved the enthusiasm that everybody had for the show. We loved the fact that we were on the magazine covers and everybody was talking about the show. We felt we were invincible."
*To Evans:* "I think not just you and me, but John, were such pivotal parts of it, because he was so totally devoted to Krystle. You had this great relationship all the way through the show. He was very protective of you."
*On Alexis:* "I'm constantly defending her, because I liked her, and so did the audience."
*On the Moldavian Massacre:* "We had no idea who was going to live or die." *(Evans then mentions the sprinkling of blood on the actors in the massacre scene.)* "The more blood we had, the less chance we had of coming back."
*To Evans:* "Those catfights, I'm still in agony over all of them. ... Let's drink to the catfights! And you always started them. I always said, Alexis doesn't fight with her fists, she fights with her tongue. ... The first one was the pillow fight. The feathers flying all over the place. And at the end, what was it that you said?" *(The clip is shown: "If you want a rematch, just whistle, if you can.")* ... "The fight scene that everyone seems to remember the most is the lily pond."

## Linda Evans

"I think that everybody's under the illusion that if you're rich you have no problems, and we showed them that it's a complex life."

"The response to the clothes was over the top. Every time I walked down the street, some woman would come up to me and say, 'I loved your outfit,' 'Where did you get this?' 'Where did you get that?'"

"What an amazing, amazing life experience. I wouldn't have changed it for anything in the world. How wonderful to experience it. How wonderful to have lived it. How wonderful to have had it."

*To Collins:* "People always thought of us as archetypes. ... I think, actually, though, that we represent both sides of every woman. ... I must say I don't think 'Dynasty' could have been the success we were without you. I'm so glad they brought your character into it."

"You have to admit that after five years, they had no idea what to do with our characters. I had to play my double, have a Southern accent and red hair."

*To Collins, on the catfight with Krystle's "twin," Rita:* "That was probably one of the most difficult things I'd done in my life. ... It was exhausting. I must say, it's much more fun beating you up! ... You were threatening to my life, to my husband, to someone that I love. And I would allow you and allow you, until one day you crossed over that threshhold."

## John Forsythe

*On Blake:* "He was such a strong character, so varied, so multifaceted. If he had problems, it was within the family."

"Joan Collins was a tremendous plus to the show. I expected that she was going to be good, but not to the extent that she was. She was a powerhouse."

"At the airport, I was bustling along, and this woman stopped me and she hit me with her purse. I asked her what's wrong, and she said, 'I don't like the way you're treating Krystle!'"

### Gordon Thomson
"One of the nastiest things Adam ever did, and one of the toughest things I found to do, inside, was rape. ... I really was a son-of-a-b--ch."
"I must say, bad and evil as I appeared to be, I couldn't hold a candle to you, Joan."
*On the Moldavian Massacre:* "I was given a joke T-shirt: 'I survived Amanda's wedding.' "

### Pamela Sue Martin
*On leaving the show:* "I just felt like I'd been inside a studio for a long time and it was time to get outdoors."
*On Forsythe:* "He treated me like a daughter because *(smile)* ... I was always misbehaving."

### Catherine Oxenberg
*On the show:* "It really was a prototype for dysfunctional, wealthy people, and that larger-than-life behavior is always fascinating."
*To Collins:* "You're the first person to turn the word 'b--ch' into a compliment. ... She used to call me Little B--ch, and I called her Big B--ch."

### Al Corley
*On leaving the show:* "There are a lot of pressures in doing TV shows and a lot of pressures from sponsors. They didn't want it to be too gay, they had to be less gay ... I just felt like at that point it was hard to go any further with the character."
"I had no idea how important this character was to a lot of people."
*To Collins:* "My favorite over-the-top, when I was on the show, was when you killed Lloyd Bochner." *(Laughs, then the clip is shown of Cecil's love-nest heart attack)* "You said you liked being on top!"

### Jack Coleman
"At first I tiptoed around a little bit like, oh, I'm the new Steven. Ultimately, after a week or two, it was just sorta, here I am."
"The show had a star quality."

### Emma Samms
"'Dynasty' was about a very rich family, and the joy of it was, that all their money didn't make them happy."
"To have been offered the job on 'Dynasty' was a dream come true, and I always at all times felt incredibly grateful to be there."

## Credits

### "Dynasty"
*Airing January 12, 1981 to May 11, 1989, on ABC*

| | |
|---:|:---|
| Creators | **Esther and Richard Shapiro** |
| Creative consultants | **Eileen and Robert Mason Pollock** |
| Executive producers | **Douglas S. Cramer, Esther and Richard Shapiro, Aaron Spelling** |
| Executive supervising producers | **E. Duke Vincent, David Paulsen** |
| Supervising producers | **Eileen and Robert Mason Pollock, Elaine Rich, E. Duke Vincent** |
| Producers | **Aaron Spelling, E. Duke Vincent, Esther and Richard Shapiro, Douglas C. Cramer, Edward DeBlasio, Diana Gould, Dennis Hammer, Edward Ledding, Camille Marchetta, John B. Moranville, Philip L. Parslow, David Paulsen, Elaine Rich** |
| Associate producers | **Ed Ledding, John B. Moranville, Carol Rubin** |
| Co-producer | **Ursula Alexander** |
| Directors | **Dwight Adair, Gwen Arner, Gabrielle Beaumont, Bruce Bilson, Jeff Bleckner, Burt Brinckerhoff, Georg Stanford Brown, Jerome Courtland, Edward DeBlasio, Harry Falk, Lorraine Senna Ferrara, Kim Friedman, Curtis Harrington, Laurence Heath, Michel Hugo, Shelley Hull, Jerry Jameson, Timothy King, Richard Kinon, Alf Kjellin, Michael Lange, Philip Leacock, Nancy Malone, Don Medford, Irving J. Moore, Eileen and Robert Mason Pollock, Robert Satlof, Robert Scheerer,** |

| | |
|---|---|
| | Ralph Senensky, Bob Sweeney, Robert C. Thompson, Kate Swofford Tilley, Glynn R. Turman |
| Writers | Richard and Esther Shapiro, Susan Baskin, Daniel King Benton, Stephen Black, Donald R. Boyle, James Harmon Brown, Katherine Coker, Mart Crowley, Edward DeBlasio, Loraine Despres, Joanna Emerson, Priscilla English, Barbara Esensten, Diana Gould, Scott M. Hamner, Laurence Heath, Don Heckman, Stephan Kandal, Stephen and Elinor Karpf, Norman Katkov, James W. Kearns, Chester Krumholz, Rita Lakin, Jeffrey Lane, Roberto Loiederman, Will Lorin, Camille Marchetta, Leah Markus, Susan Miller, Dick Nelson, David Paulsen, Samuel J. Pelovitz, John Pleshette, Ron Renauld, Mann Rubin, A.J. Russell, Michael Russnow, Jeff Ryder, Frank Salisbury, Paul Savage, Robert Seidenberg, Joel Steiger, Henry Stern, Harold Stone, Noreen Stone, Dennis Turner, Elizabeth and Richard Wilson, Shimon Wincelberg |
| Executive story consultants | Edward De Blasio, Chester Krumholz, Eileen and Robert Mason Pollock |
| Executive script consultant | Edward De Blasio |
| Editors | Tita Bell, Joanna Bush, Kenneth Miller, Ron Renauld, Robert Wolfe, John Woodcock |
| Film editors | Dick Darling, Jim Faris, Kenneth Miller, Michael S. Murphy, John M. Woodcock A.C.E. |

| | |
|---|---|
| Supervising film editor | **Michael S. McLean A.C.E.** |
| Music by | **Bill Conti, John David, Gerald Fried, Ken Harrison, Artie Kane, Marvin Laird, Ben Lanzarone, Dennis McCarthy, Angela Morley, Peter Myers, Lance Rubin, Mark Snow, Fred Steiner, Duane Tatro, Richard Lewis Warren, Fred Werner** |
| Directors of photography | **Michel Hugo A.S.C., Richard L. Rawlings A.S.C.** |
| Art directors | **John E. Chilberg II, Frank Swig, Paul Sylos, Tom Trimble** |
| Executive production manager | **Norman Henry** |
| Costume designer | **Nolan Miller** |

### "Dynasty: The Reunion"
*Airing October 20 and 21, 1991, on ABC*

| | |
|---|---|
| Producer | **Elaine Rich** |
| Executive producers | **Aaron Spelling, Douglas S. Cramer, Richard and Esther Shapiro** |
| Executive supervising producer | **E. Duke Vincent** |
| Director | **Irving J. Moore** |
| Writers | **Richard and Esther Shapiro, Edward DeBlasio, Robert and Eileen Pollock** |
| Production designer | **Elayne Ceder** |
| Film editor | **Barry L. Gold** |
| Costume designer | **Nolan Miller** |

### "Dynasty Reunion: Catfights & Caviar"
*Airing May 2, 2006, on CBS*

| | |
|---|---|
| Producer | **Gary Tellalian** |
| Executive producers | **Michael Levitt, Henry Winkler** |
| Supervising producer | **Greg Sills** |
| Director | **Michael Dempsey** |
| Writers | **Xaque Gruber, Stephen Pouliot** |
| Costume designer | **Nolan Miller** |

## "Dynasty II: The Colbys"
*Airing November 20, 1985 to March 26, 1987, on ABC*

| | |
|---:|:---|
| Creators | **Richard and Esther Shapiro, Eileen and Robert Pollock** |
| Developers | **William Bast, Paul Huson** |
| Executive producers | **Aaron Spelling, Douglas S. Cramer, Richard and Eileen Shapiro** |
| Executive supervising producer | **E. Duke Vincent** |
| Supervising producers | **Eileen and Robert Pollock** |
| Producers | **William Bast, Dennis Hammer, Paul Huson, Christopher Morgan** |
| Associate producers | **Ursula Alexander, Shelley Hull, Marko Joelson, Stephen K. Rose** |
| Directors | **Gwen Arner, Gabrielle Beaumont, Roy Campanella, Jerome Courtland, Harry Falk, Kim Friedman, Curtis Harrington, Richard Kinon, Don Medford, Robert Scheerer** |
| Writers | **William Bast, Paul Huson** |
| Teleplay writers | **Bruce Bilson, Oliver Clark, Mart Crowley, Rick Edelstein, Frank V. Furino, Maryanne Kasica, Elliott Lewis, Charles Pratt Jr., Donald Paul Roos, Carol Saraceno, Michael Scheff, E. Doris Silverton, Jeffrey Smith, Dennis Turner** |
| Executive script consultants | **Rick Edelstein, Donald Paul Roos** |
| "The Colbys" theme music by | **Bill Conti** |
| Other music by | **John E. Davis, Ken Harrison, Dennis McCarthy, Angela Morley, Peter Myers** |
| Directors of photography | **Richard L. Rawlings A.S.C., Tony Askins** |
| Art director | **Jack Chilberg** |
| Film editor | **Larry Strong A.C.E.** |
| Costume designer | **Nolan Miller** |

## Up for Debate

One of the funnest aspects of juicy television shows like "Dynasty" and "The Colbys" is the next day's water-cooler talk (or perhaps, first-hour Government class talk, as it was in BRB's case!). As we delight in the escapades of our favorite characters, we can't help but analyze and nitpick and study. That's the reasoning behind this feature for BRBTV, "Up for Debate." Submitted, for your consideration, are the following points of debate. It's obvious there are many of you "Dynasty" experts out there; you've emailed BRBTV! Send any thoughts you have to dynasty@brbtv.com, and they might be included in the next electronic edition of "Dynasty High"! (That's one of the reasons it's called an "interactive" PDF!)

- **Who is the real Steven?**

Steven's character wasn't the only one that saw a change of talent. But this character was crucial to the show's success, and in setting it apart from other television shows at the time. Steven is the "token" gay character – a major source of conflict in the Blake Carrington storylines – but he has many facets that go way beyond his gayness. He is the sensitive one of the Carrington clan. He is well-read, a scholar, at least in Al Corley's interpretation. And he is the one with the moral conscience in the family. He is the first one to welcome Krystle, because of his kindness of heart. Dare we say that Jack Coleman played him more confused? Softer? More flustered? And that Corley portrayed him as more jaded, pointed and angry? With a firmer sense of his convictions? (And sorry, but Corley was *so* much hotter! *Meow!*) What was your concept of the character of Steven, and which actor captured him more accurately? Discuss!

- **Who is the real Fallon?**

OK, you just knew we had to follow up the Steven question with the Fallon question. I mean, just look at these two Fallons. How much more dramatically *different* could they be? One is a pencil-thin, smart-mouthed, spoiled-brat, slutty tiger; the other, a buxom, sweet, English-accented, victim of a girl. We all probably can guess which Fallon you'd rather have lunch with (or maybe not!), but which Fallon is the better component of the "Dynasty" series? Which Fallon was needed most in this show?

- **What's the difference between Alexis and Sable?**

Both are dastardly. Both are beautifully preserved, "slightly older" females, and fabulously dressed! *(Puh-leeze! They dress circles and figure-8s around Krystle and Frankie!)* Both are fiercely protective mothers. Both have an English accent! Both appreciate art – Alexis paints it, and Sable buys it for her Colby Collection. Both are accomplished businesswomen, though dare we say ... that Alexis craves more corporate power than Sable does? Sable never really pursues power in the workplace; Zach has to encourage her to do that when she divorces Jason. Alexis, on the other hand, is busily scratching and clawing her way into any business interests she can get during the entire run of "Dynasty," motivated, of course, by her hatred of Blake. In fact, both females can often be motivated by hatred and spite, directed at whomever they perceive as their enemies at the time, but Alexis is slightly more savvy. Alexis is more stealth – she can very easily hit you without your ever knowing it. She is cooler, sneakier in her schemes. And Alexis is less ruled by her emotions than Sable is. Don't you agree? Or do you?

- **Is Frankie a tramp?**

Quite frankly, we were confused when we first kept hearing Sable call Frankie a tramp. *Sweet* Frankie? *Innocent* Frankie, often the victim of Sable's schemes? But when Phillip came back from his assumed death and also called Frankie a tramp, we had to wonder ... OK, why does everyone think Frankie's a whore? She can't say no when Phillip pours on the charm and nostalgia. She certainly can't say no when she and Jason starts to "reunite." She's been married to several different men, not including Jason. But a tramp? Is she really so malicious? "Tramp" is just such a malicious word! Isn't a tramp someone who comes on to anyone she sees, not caring whom she hurts? We don't think that's Frankie. Perhaps Frankie is just a little confused when it comes to men. Right?

- **Which "Dynasty" character showed the most personal growth during the run of the show?**

We're going to pose this answer for you: Sammy Jo, *by far*. As long as you don't count the reunion movie! Discuss!

- **Is Alexis still secretly in love with Blake?**

Some may say this is an easy question – a resounding yes! Alexis is accused of this particular crime by Dex, several times, and denies it. She sets out to destroy Blake personally and professionally many times. But after Blake and Daniel Reece are in a plane crash, she is devastated with worry. Then there's that whole amnesia incident overseas! And the two of them did still get along for quite a while after that. The very last episode, even, begins with the two of them making peace again. We know that it's not a "love" thing for Blake – his heart belongs to Krystle. But Alexis?

- **Was color an issue in the controversy over Dominique's family connection to Blake?**

Now, I must preface this by saying that I viewed these episodes from two sets of eyes: one set of eyes was a teenager in the 1980s, so naive to the world, and another set of eyes belonged to the mid-30s independent chick of the new millennium, having lived in the big city and experienced so much of the world! ... *So* ... Consider that Blake doesn't want to acknowledge Dominique at first. He sees her as a possible scammer. Now, of course, you can see *anyone* as a possible scammer, regardless of color or religion or breed of favorite pet. And Dominique, faced with Blake's denial of her, actually never directly references her color as a possible reason. When I saw the storyline in the '80s, I read it completely as a color snobbery on Blake's part. Now ... not so sure. Maybe color was not really an issue. Any issue of color is handled rather gingerly where Dominique is concerned. She dates both men of color and Caucasian men, and nothing is thought of it. She is simply a rockin' accomplished female who can score anyone. It has been said in the media (around the time that "Melrose Place" aired, in the 1990s) that Aaron Spelling was always reluctant to add color to his casts. *Hmm* ... We're not so sure of that, either ... What do you think?

- **Who's your favorite recurring character?**

Morgan Hess in his tacky suits? Dr. Edwards with his fatherly demeanor toward Adam? Gordon Wales with his consistent, pinpointed aggression? Dean Caldwell with his whatever?

- **OK, c'mon ... out with it ... What's your favorite Alexis outfit?**

You can just run with this one.

- **Can you be a moral person and still enjoy "Dynasty" and "The Colbys"?**

You know the feeling ... you're sitting there, engrossed, in front of the boob tube, feeling not only a few brain cells dying, but feeling yourself becoming somehow ... tainted ... corrupted ... dirtier? Do you *really* want to know how Alexis pulled off that business deal? Do you feel that it will somehow *change* you? Hmmm ... **BRBTV** asserts that yes, you still can be a moral person who enjoys these shows. In fact, we're of the firm belief that you can actually *turn it around*, make it work for you. Case in point: Krystle Carrington. Just watch how she handles each situation, particularly the ones involving Alexis. Keep that focus on Krystle; it will help.

# Fun & Useless Information

Sort of a combination of "where are they now?" and "where did we go then, anyway?" — with some other cool stuff thrown in, here's the chapter of what BRBTV fondly terms "fun and useless information" ...

## John Forsythe

Certainly you recognize John Forsythe's voice from ABC's '70s hit "Charlie's Angels," before he showed his face as our patriarch, Blake Carrington. The role of Blake was originally played by George Peppard in the "Dynasty" pilot, but we're glad for the choice the producers eventually made.

The son of a Wall Street businessman, Forsythe was born John Lincoln Freund in Penn's Grove, New Jersey. According to the Internet Movie Database (IMDb), he graduated from Abraham Lincoln High School in Brooklyn, New York in 1934. He attended the University of North Carolina. He had a contract with Warner Bros. in his early acting days, which paused when he entered the Army Air Corps in World War II. After the war, he helped found the Actors Studio.

He got his acting start in the 1940s and '50s and even had his own "John Forsythe Show" in 1965. His very first role was in 1943's "Northern Pursuit," a part that was uncredited, but he went on to the Kraft Television Theatre, the Cosmopolitan Theatre, the Starlight Theatre, the Ford Theatre Hour and much more. In fact the "theatre" and "playhouse" circuit was very much his thing throughout these earlier years.

For his work on "Dynasty," Forsythe received Golden Globe Awards in 1983 and 1984. In 1985, he endorsed one of the "Dynasty" fragrances, a men's cologne line called "Carrington." He's reprised his "Charlie's Angels" role for the motion pictures, to the tune of $5 million each. That's a nice raise, considering he reportedly got $40,000 an episode during the original series. In October 2006, Forsythe announced he had colon cancer.

BILLIE RAE BATES

# Linda Evans

Of course you remember Linda Evans as Audra Barkley on ABC's "Big Valley," long before she became Krystle Carrington. (Barbara Stanwyck, incidentally, who was matriarch Victoria Barkley of that show, became the matriarch of "The Colbys.") Born Linda Evanstad in Hartford, Connecticut, she attended Hollywood High School with "Hart to Hart" star Stefanie Powers. Long before "Dynasty," as a teenager, Evans shared the screen with John Forsythe, guest-starring on ABC's sitcom "Bachelor Father" as a girl who develops a crush on Forsythe's character, Bentley Gregg, in an episode appropriately titled "A Crush on Bentley" in 1960. It was her first official role.

She went on to roles on 1965's Frankie Avalon / Annette Funicello vehicle "Beach Blanket Bingo" and episodes of ABC's "The Adventures of Ozzie & Harriet" and "The Untouchables" and CBS' "My Favorite Martian," before venturing on to the "Big Valley."

Just 38 years old when she was cast as Krystle, the lovely Evans quickly came to personify beauty beyond youth. Through the "Dynasty" years her star rose in a mind-blowing way, but after the show went off the air she kept a relatively low profile. Her romances were always publicized, however, from her late-'60s / early-'70s marriage to actor and director John Derek to her dating musician Yanni in the '90s.

More recently, she marketed a line of skin-care products, Rejuvenique, a mask for toning facial muscles. According to the IMDb, she attended the nuptials of Prince Charles and Camilla Parker-Bowles.

In 2006, she took to the stage with her "Dynasty" costar Joan Collins for "Legends," a much-publicized reunion for the two that plays on their catfighting days in Denver. They do portray rival actresses in the stage production's revival, after all!

# Joan Collins

Joan Collins, who brought serious power to the series as Alexis in the second season, had the great fortune to star in what many "Star Trek" fans consider the finest episode of the classic TV series, "City on the Edge of Forever." The character, Edith Keeler, even has an action figure. Collins played the sexy villain Siren in the 1960s "Batman" TV show. (Can you believe that the producers of "Dynasty" originally only planned to have her in six episodes?)

Born Joan Henrietta Collins in England, she was the eldest of three children. Her father, Joe Collins, was a theatrical agent, and her mother, Elsa Bessant, a dancer. In her autobiography, Collins writes of a privileged middle-class upbringing with traditional values. She enrolled in the theatrical school Cone-Ripman at age 12, and studied acting at London's Royal Academy of Dramatic Arts.

Her filmography is extensive, dating all the way back to the early '50s and no doubt boosted by her uncanny similarities to superstar Elizabeth Taylor. She started out playing a beauty queen contestant in 1951's "Lady Godiva Rides Again," and went on to 1953's "Turn the Key Softly," 1955's "Land of the Pharaohs" and much more. She continued both TV and movie work through the ensuing decades. Her sister, well-known author Jackie Collins, brought her into the movie adaptations of a couple of her novels, 1978's "The Stud" and 1979's "The Bitch" (a moniker Collins probably couldn't shake if she tried – and wouldn't necessarily want to!). Joan has written many books of her own, both fiction and nonfiction.

Reportedly romantically linked to Hollywood heavies like Warren Beatty, Dennis Hopper and Ryan O'Neal, Collins posed for Playboy magazine at age 50. She has by no means taken on a post-"Dynasty" idleness. She did a guest stint on CBS' "Guiding Light" in 2002 and has had a recurring role on the UK's drama "Footballers' Wive$."

## Pamela Sue Martin

And then there's Pamela Sue Martin, ABC's supersleuth Nancy Drew in 1977-78, right before "Dynasty" launched and she created the role of Fallon Carrington.

Born in Westport, Connecticut, Pamela Sue Martin graduated from Staples High School in February 1971. At age 17, she began a modeling career in New York, according to her official website, before being lured into acting. Her ground-breaking role was in the film "The Poseidon Adventure" in 1972, at only age 19. After she made it even bigger as Nancy Drew, she did an episode of ABC's "Love Boat" and "Fantasy Island" before landing in Denver for "Dynasty."

She's pretty much been flying below the acting radar since leaving "Dynasty," only making a couple brief TV appearances, including one on Fox's "That '70s Show." She toured the United States and Canada in a stage production of "Beau Geste." She also wrote, produced and starred in the 1985 film "Torchlight."

Martin has just written an autobiography, her manager tells **BRBTV**, called "The Spirit of the Matter." "It's about what it felt like for me to walk into fame so early and why I walked out," she told TV Guide for a February 2005 issue. "It's kinda Marianne Williamson meets Erma Bombeck."

She also did some commentary for the 2005 DVD release of the first season of "Dynasty." She provided commentary for the special features on the DVD release of "The Poseidon Adventure." She is involved in organizations such as PETA, Save the Whales and Greenpeace, her website says. She also spent a decade playing polo with the Piaget Celebrity Polo Team.

In 2006, she played a character named Linda Kennard on Showtime's "The L Word."

# John James

John James has had a perhaps quieter career than his castmates. He made the run of "Fantasy Island" and "The Love Boat" episodes on ABC before "Dynasty," but has lay pretty low since.

Born Herb Oscar Anderson in Minneapolis, James' dad was a legendary radio personality of the same name, according to his IMDb bio. James studied at Manhattan's American Academy of Dramatic Arts. His first role was in the soaps realm: CBS' "Search for Tomorrow," where he played the third Junior Bergman in the late '70s. He also played Rick Decker on CBS' "As the World Turns" in 2003-'04.

He has been married since 1989 to Miss Australia 1978 Denise Coward, and they have two children, according to Wikipedia. He has lived with his wife and children on a 230-acre farm in Cambridge, N.Y., where he worked with a local theatre group. His children, Laura and Phillip, are getting a little taste of Hollywood themselves: they worked with their dad as production assistants on the set of the 2006 film "Illegal Aliens," in which James plays a character named Big Tony.

James returned to the soap world in summer 2006, as Dr. Jeff Martin on ABC's "All My Children," playing the ex-lover of Erica Kane and adoptive brother of Tad Martin.

## Behind the scenes

> Our most difficult casting task actually centered on the role of Jeff Colby. We had looked and looked at dozens of actors and didn't really feel right with any of them.
> — *Aaron Spelling, in The Hollywood Reporter*

# Al Corley

He isn't doing a whole lot of acting these days, but he can still be found behind the scenes. Al Corley, the original *(and hottest!)* Steven Carrington, served as executive producer of "Behind the Mask: The Rise of Leslie Vernon," a horror film directed by Scott Glosserman.

The Wichita, Kansas-born Corley once served as a doorman at New York's Studio 54, according to his IMDb bio. He even tried his hand at music, with the electro-pop song "Square Rooms" in 1985.

Corley showed up in castmate Pamela Sue Martin's film "Torchlight." He also starred in the 1991 "Dynasty: The Reunion" (to our great relief) and the 2006 reminiscing special. He married actress and painter Jessika Cardinahl in 1989, and they have three children.

# Jack Coleman

Jack Coleman, our second Steven Carrington, starred in the TV movie "Cow Belles" on the Disney Channel in 2006.

Born in Easton, Pennsylvania, Coleman spent his pre-"Dynasty" days on daytime soap "Days of Our Lives" as the second Jake Kositchek. He kept up fairly solid work after "Dynasty" left the airwaves, with appearances on CBS' "Touched By An Angel," "Diagnosis Murder" and "Burke's Law." More recently, he's done guest shots on CBS' "CSI: Miami" and f/X's "Nip / Tuck." In 2006, he was working on the film "Beautiful Loser," plus he got a rather-sinister role in NBC's unique new drama "Heroes."

In 1996, Coleman married Beth Toussaint, who played Tracey Lawton on "Dallas" (see "Destination: Dallas," **BRBTV**'s sister book to "Dynasty High").

## Emma Samms

The woman who played Fallon Carrington later, Emma Samms, made her way first romancing Luke Spencer and Robert Scorpio as Holly Sutton in the early 1980s on the ABC soap "General Hospital." She even reprised her role on the soap in 2006.

A Londoner like her "Dynasty" mummy, Samms was born Emma Samuelson and had one sister and two brothers. (She cofounded the Starlight Children's Foundation as a tribute to her brother, Jamie, who died of aplastic anemia at age 8, according to her IMDb bio.) Samms once worked as a certified emergency medical technician in Los Angeles.

Samms has twice turned down the offer to be a centerfold in Playboy. Married three times, she has two children, Cameron and Beatrice. "The Emma Samms persona is a suit I put on for work," she has said. "Who I really am is the wife and mother and daughter and sister and friend."

## Pamela Bellwood

Pamela Bellwood, who played Claudia Blaisdel, did a number of guest appearances on TV shows in the '70s and '80s, including CBS' "Mannix," NBC/ABC's "Police Story" and ABC's "Baretta" and "The Love Boat." She starred in quite a few TV movies in the '80s. Born Pamela King in New York City, Bellwood studied acting at New York City's Neighborhood Playhouse. Reportedly, her "Dynasty" character's death occurred when she became pregnant in 1986. She did offer some thoughts on "Dynasty" for the 2006 reunion, "Catfights & Caviar."

Billie Rae Bates

# Gordon Thomson

Gordon Thomson, who came along a little later in the series as long-lost son Adam Carrington, was one of three different Mason Capwells on the NBC soap "Santa Barbara."

Born in Ottawa, Ontario, Canada, Thomson graduated from Montreal's McGill University with honors, according to his IMDb bio. At first, he wanted to work in architecture or law *(a lawyer like Adam? hmm ...)*, but decided later to pursue acting.

He starred in the also-defunct NBC soap "Sunset Beach," and he even once did a spin as archaeologist Aristotle Benedict White on ABC's equally defunct "Ryan's Hope" in 1981-'82. He's appeared on Fox's "Beverly Hills, 90210," CBS' "The Nanny" and "Murder, She Wrote," and even a 1983 episode of ABC's "Fantasy Island." Thomson reportedly could not get time away from the "Santa Barbara" set to appear in the 1991 "Dynasty: The Reunion." More recently, he did a tiny speaking role in 2006's "Poseidon," which was, of course, the remake of the film where his "Dynasty" sibling Pamela Sue Martin appeared. This actor, who's done some pretty conniving roles, has been quoted as saying, "I think we all have a dark side to us. I find that I can't trust sunny-natured people, people who are constantly sunny. I think that's major denial."

In May 2006, USA Today asked Thomson what he thinks might have happened to his character Adam over the years. He joked, "He has three grown children he is estranged from, and one baby daughter whom he has called Fallon Alexis."

# Heather Locklear

We simply can't go any further without mentioning the '90s queen of the nighttime soap, Heather Locklear, who OWNED Aaron Spelling's "Melrose Place" -- apartment building *and* TV show. She cut her conniving teeth as Sammy Jo on "Dynasty," and when she came sliding down the bannister, right into Alexis' face, at the tender age of 19 in real life, we knew good old Mr. Spelling was onto something big.

Born in Westwood, California, the youngest of four children, Locklear is a cousin of Donald Trump's second wife, Marla Maples. A rejection from her high school cheerleading squad pointed her toward the drama club and the world of acting. She graduated from Newbury Park High School in Newbury Park, California. She attended UCLA for a short time, according to her IMDb bio, then continued her acting dream instead of a bachelor's degree in psychology. Her father, William Locklear, has served in various UCLA high-level administrative positions.

Locklear has the distinction of maintaining roles on two different series at once: her "Dynasty" days were doubled with her starring role as Stacy Sheridan on ABC/CBS' "T.J. Hooker," with William Shatner. She joined back up with Shatner on "Boston Legal" in 2005. This star of ABC's "Spin City" has seen her personal life in the tabloids often enough, after marriages to rock stars Tommy Lee of Motley Crue and Richie Sambora of Bon Jovi. She has one daughter, Ava Elizabeth.

Locklear has more recently been involved in the ABC pilot "Women of a Certain Age," along with the 2007 film "Oranges." Certainly not many actresses can nail so many winning roles in a long-term, consistently fabulous career.

# Diahann Carroll

Diahann Carroll, a shining light as Dominique Deveraux, has been very active on stage and screen. She had her own musical variety miniseries on CBS in 1976. She played the title role in "Julia" on NBC in the late '60s, breaking ground as the first black female to star in her own comedy series.

*Diahann Carroll, photographed by Carl Van Vechten, March 1955.*

Born Carol Diahann Johnson in the Bronx, New York, Carroll attended the New York City High School of the Performing Arts, along with Billy Dee Williams, according to Wikipedia.

Her film work includes "Claudine," for which she received a 1974 Best Actress Academy Award nomination, 1954's "Carmen Jones," 1961's "Paris Blues," 1959's "Porgy and Bess," 1967's "Hurry Sundown," the 1979 TV movie "I Know Why The Caged Bird Sings" based on Maya Angelou's hit book, and 1997's "Eve's Bayou."

She appeared on "On Stage America," a syndicated variety show from 1984. She had a recurring role as Marion Gilbert on the NBC sitcom "A Different World," and in 2002 appeared in the series "The Court." She also, incidentally, has designed purses, carried at stores such as JCPenney.

In October 1995 she starred on stage as Norma Desmond in the Toronto premiere of Andrew Lloyd Webber's hit musical "Sunset Boulevard," according to her official website. Carroll made her Broadway stage debut starring in Harold Arlen and Truman Capote's "House of Flowers," and after seeing her in this production, Richard Rodgers created the Broadway production "No Strings" as a starring vehicle for her, her website bio says, for which she won a Tony Award. She also starred on Broadway in the award-winning play "Agnes of God."

The lovely songstress opened a new U.S. tour in April 2006 at Michael Feinstein's well-known New York nightclub. Carroll, who was married over the years to casting director Monte Kay, restaurateur Freddie Glusman, editor Robert DeLeon, and most famously, singer Vic Damone, told Parade magazine in 2006, "I was always married to my career, so I wasn't very good at being married."

# Catherine Oxenberg

OK, now get this. Catherine Oxenberg, who played the show's equivalent to royalty, Amanda, who married a prince, and who *also* as an actress has played Princess Diana in a TV movie, actually has connections to royalty. Oxenberg's mother is second cousin to Prince Charles *and* Oxenberg was actually proposed to at one time by the dashing Prince Andrew.

Born in New York City and raised in London, Oxenberg was named after ancestor Catherine the Great (Empress Catherine II, Tsarina of Russia), according to her IMDb bio. She attended St. Paul's School, where she graduated summa cum laude, and was admitted to Harvard University, according to her official website. She transferred to Columbia University after deciding to pay her own way through college and start modeling. She was photographed for the covers of Vogue, Glamour, Cosmopolitan, Harper's Bazaar, Redbook, Good Housekeeping and many others. Like her on-screen mummy, Oxenberg has a sister, Christina Oxenberg, who is a novelist.

Named on the Harper's Bazaar list of America's 10 Most Beautiful Women in 1985, just as she was beginning her "Dynasty" time, Oxenberg also starred in the 1987 TV movie "Roman Holiday" and reprised her role as Princess Diana in the 1992 TV movie "Charles and Diana: Unhappily Ever After." It was rather fun to see her star with "Dynasty" castmate Emma Samms in the 1994 TV movie, "Treacherous Beauties."

Oxenberg married actor Casper Van Dien in 1999 and starred with him in the Christian apocalyptic thriller, "The Omega Code." Her children are India Oxenberg, Maya Van Dien and Celeste Van Dien, with stepchildren Cappy Van Dien and Grace Van Dien. They all appeared together, as themselves, in Lifetime's "I Married a Princess" in 2005. In 2006, she was working on the TV series "Watch Over Me" with Van Dien.

## Behind the scenes

> I've done so much healing on myself, been through personal hell, through hell in my relationships; my children have been through so much, and we've gotten to a place of healing.
> — *Catherine Oxenberg, discussing turbulent times that included childhood abuse and a teen eating disorder, for a Scripps Howard News Service story, April 2005*

## Michael Nader

Can you believe Michael Nader appeared with "Dynasty" castmate Linda Evans years earlier in the 1965 film "Beach Blanket Bingo"? Yep, he played (what else?) a beach boy! The Los Angeles-born Nader attended Santa Monica College in Los Angeles and studied at the Actors Studio and Herbert Berghof Studio while in New York appearing in off-Broadway plays, according to his IMDb bio. He had a bit of a typecast going for a while there, playing a beach boy in 1963's "Beach Party," then the year after that playing a surfer boy in "Muscle Beach Party," a beach boy in "Bikini Beach" and a pajama boy in "Pajama Party"! He was *quite* the boy! Nader is well-known for his role as Dimitri Marick on ABC's "All My Children."

## Lloyd Bochner

Our own Cecil Colby, Lloyd Bochner, has pages and pages of solid TV and film credits, spanning from the 1940s to 2003, shortly before his October 2005 death. Born Lloyd Wolfe Bochner in Toronto, Ontario, Canada, he began his career on the radio in Canada when he was 11 years old. In his 20s, he launched into acting, and over the years he starred in episodes of CBS' "The Twilight Zone," "The Wild Wild West" and "Perry Mason," NBC's "Dr. Kildare," "Bonanza" and "The Man From U.N.C.L.E." and many more.

Bochner was originally cast to play C.C. Capwell on NBC's daytime soap "Santa Barbara" when it debuted in 1984, but he suffered a heart attack. The role went to his "Dynasty" castmate, Peter Mark Richman (and another "Dynasty" castmate, Paul Burke, who was Neal McVane, took over the C.C. Capwell role from Richman!). He and his son, Hart Bochner, both voiced roles for "Batman: The Animated Series" and its video movies. The elder was the voice of Mayor Hamilton Hill, and the younger was the voice of Arthur Reeves in "Batman: Mask of the Phantasm."

- You might recall **Richard Anderson**, who played Buck Fallmont, as Oscar Goldman on ABC/NBC's 1970s "Bionic Woman." Anderson started out with many, many film roles in the '40s and '50s and even more TV appearances since the '50s, including shows such as "Matt Houston," "Remington Steele" and CBS' "Simon and Simon."

- **Troy Beyer,** who played the young Jackie Deveraux, has come into her own, directing and starring in the 1998 movie, "Let's Talk About Sex." She had a recurring character, Whitney, on CBS' "Knots Landing," as well as film roles in "B.A.P.S." and "Weekend at Bernie's II," among others.

- **Tracy Scoggins,** who played Monica Colby on "The Colbys," has done a lot of other TV. She had a small part in a "Dukes of Hazzard" episode on CBS, and roles on CBS' sudsy "Dallas" and its two reunion movies. After "The Colbys," she played the saucy gossip columnist Cat on ABC's "Lois & Clark: The New Adventures of Superman." Meow! More recently, she's been involved in the horror flick "Mr. Hell" and the latest adaptation of the well-known Robert Louis Stevenson classic, "The Strange Case of Dr. Jekyll and Mr. Hyde."

- **Peter Mark Richman,** who played Andrew Laird here, crossed over to the "Dallas" realm as Maynard Anderson. He also was one of the men to play C.C. Capwell in NBC's daytime soap, "Santa Barbara." His TV appearances are extensive, especially in the '70s and '80s, from ABC's "The FBI" to CBS' "Barnaby Jones" and "Mission: Impossible" and beyond. He's just one of those faces you see in a whole lot of places. Richman, who assumed his first name, Peter, spiritually in 1971, has a long theater resume and is also a prolific novelist (see the titles at left), film writer and painter.

- The amazing, the incomparable, the wonderfully handsome *(and terribly revered by* **BRBTV** *— can you tell?)* **Ricardo Montalban,** who played Zach Powers on "The Colbys," needs no introduction. We all know him best as the kind host of ABC's original "Fantasy Island," another Aaron Spelling production. But before he donned that white suit, he bared his beautiful barrel chest in the landmark episode of the original "Star Trek" series, "Space Seed." He reprised the role in the second "Trek" movie, "The Wrath of Khan." Montalban, who was born in Mexico City, has an esteemed film and TV career dating back to the 1940s. He has starred most recently in the "Spy Kids" movies.

• **Billy Dee Williams**, who was the dashing Brady Lloyd here, was also the dashing Lando Calrissian in the classic "Star Wars" trilogy. Plus, he was the dashing, original *(and best!)* Harvey Dent in 1989's "Batman." Heck, he has also played the dashing Billy Dee Williams on TV shows such as CBS' 1970s "The Jeffersons" and Fox's 1990s "Martin" and "In Living Color." Williams is an accomplished painter of many years. **BRBTV**'s founder had the pleasure to meet and interview Williams when he appeared at the Motor City Comic Con in Novi, Michigan, in May 1999, and snapped this photo of him. More recently, Williams was starring with rap star Snoop Doggy Dogg in the movie "Hood of Horror," classified as "a hip-hop horror anthology."

• You must remember **Ted McGinley** (Clay Fallmont) as ABC's "Love Boat" photog? He also played Roger Phillips in ABC's "Happy Days" in the 1970s, as well as neighbor Jefferson D'Arcy on Fox's "Married With Children" in the 1990s.

• **Geoffrey Scott** (Mark Jennings) got his acting career kicked off with a guest shot on an episode of ABC's 1960s "Dark Shadows." He has had quite a good measure of gigs, before and after his time on "Dynasty." More recently, he played the president in the big-screen "Hulk" in 2003.

• **Grant Goodeve** (Chris Deegan) starred in ABC's "Eight is Enough" as David Bradford. He also had a recurring role on CBS' "Northern Exposure" and the WB's "7th Heaven."

• **Bo Hopkins** was a recognizable face before signing on at the very beginning of "Dynasty" as *The* Ex-Boyfriend, Matthew Blaisdel. He's done a whole heckin' lot of television, from his early days on NBC's "The Virginian" and CBS' "Gunsmoke" in the 1960s to 2003's flick "The Road Home." Many of his credits are Western-flavored *(could be that rockin' drawl!)* For more on Hopkins, see the Q&A segment in this chapter.

• Remember **Ken Howard**, who played a perennially frustrated Garrett Boydston here, as "The White Shadow" on CBS, 1979-81? He also played the leading character in the romantic comedy "Adam's Rib" in 1973 on ABC, and in the detective series "The Manhunter" on CBS in 1974-75. He took another crack at comedy with the leading role in "It's Not Easy" in 1983 on ABC. Plus, he hosted the "Dream Girl, U.S.A." contest for syndication in 1986. More recently, he played the (very) patient father of the Andrews sisters, Jane and Sydney, on Fox's "Melrose Place."

• **Bibi Besch** played a doctor in both "Dynasty" and "Dallas"; she also was Capt. James T. Kirk's long-lost love Carol Marcus in the second "Star Trek" motion picture, "The Wrath of Khan." Besch, who starred in CBS/ABC's soap "The Edge of Night" in 1969, died of breast cancer in 1996.

• Dashing evertan man **George Hamilton** (the evil Joel Abrigore) has done a lot of screenwork, notably as the vampire everyone adored in the film "Love at First Bite." Did you know he took a spin with adventure shows, in "Paris 7000" way back in 1970 on ABC? He did a role on the epic miniseries "Roots" on ABC in 1977. Later he was the lead character, Ian Stone, in "Spies" on CBS in 1987, a good role for the suavemeister. He's also done kooky commercials for Old Navy clothiers.

• For **Ali MacGraw** -- the photographer Lady Ashley Mitchell who chased Blake around -- art imitated life: She began her early career working in 1960 as a photographic assistant at Harper's Bazaar, as an assistant to the legendary fashion maven, Diana Vreeland, at Vogue, as a fashion model, and as a photographer's stylist, according to Wikipedia. Born Alice MacGrew, she was once married to Steve McQueen and had a groundbreaking role with Ryan O'Neal in 1970's "Love Story." She made her Broadway debut in 2006's London play "Festen."

• You might consider **Rock Hudson**'s "Dynasty" role as Daniel Reece his mainstream pop-culture bow, before he succumbed to AIDS in the late '80s. This hunk-with-a-secret had a vast film career dating back to the late '40s, epitomizing big-screen male stardom. This photo shows him in his earlier years.

BILLIE RAE BATES

- **Maxwell Caulfield**, our own Miles Colby, plays Mayor Schmitz in the docudrama "Living the Quake," a 2006 TV movie marking the 100th anniversary of the great San Francisco Earthquake.

- **James Farentino,** who was our Nick Toscanni, has done a lot of acting since the 1960s, even showing up on Aaron Spelling's "Melrose Place," though he's perhaps, unfortunately, better remembered for that whole Tina Sinatra thing. He was one of the last contract stars in the late '60s, with Universal, according to his IMDb bio. In 2003, he received rave reviews on the L.A. stage playing a Russ Meyer-like porn producer in "Boy Gets Girl."

- **Leann Hunley** scored (for a time) with Adam Carrington as Dana Waring. She's been taking roles since the 1970s, playing a chick warrior on ABC's "Battlestar Galactica" and a secretary on CBS' "Hawaii Five-O." After her "Dynasty" work, she kept on with the TV appearances. In 1998, she had a key role as Tamara Jacobs, the teacher who tempted Pacey on the WB's "Dawson's Creek."

- **Wendie Malick** (Carol Marshall) played Mitch Buchanon's ex-wife (and Hobie's mom) on the syndicated "Baywatch" and went on to NBC's sitcom "Just Shoot Me," among a whole lot of other TV stuff.

- "Star Trek" fave Kira Nerys, **Nana Visitor,** got to display her talents as a ballerina in the last season of "The Colbys" as the new partner of Kolya Rostov. She's the daughter of a choreographer and a ballet teacher.

- Cash Cassidy of "The Colbys," **James Houghton**, had some other sudsy experiences: notably on CBS' "Knots Landing."

- **Bert Remsen**, who played Jack Crager, the trainer for Peter DeVilbus' prized horse, Allegre, also played Dandy Dandridge on rival soap "Dallas."

- Debuting in France in fall 2006 before moving on to the U.K. and the U.S. after that, the film "Love and Other Disasters" stars none other than our own Sable Colby, aka **Stephanie Beacham**, who stomped her spiked heels all over both "Dynasty" and "The Colbys." Beacham shared the scenes with heartthrob Orlando Bloom and his big sister, Samantha Bloom, in the romantic comedy.

- **Lou Beatty Jr**. is known to us "Dynasty" fans as Rudy Richards in the 1988-89 episodes. That was one of his first roles, and he's kept up pretty solid work since then, including the recent movies "Driftwood" and "Welcome to Paradise."

- The enigmatic **John Saxon**, who starred as Rashid Ahmed in 1982 and 1984, has one of those "I've seen him in something! I just know it!" faces. Could be those hundreds of TV and film roles listed on his IMDb page! "Bonanza," "Night Gallery," "Gunsmoke," "The Rockford Files," "Wonder Woman," all the classics and more, spanning five decades. **BRBTV** got a chance to chat with Saxon at the Motor City Comic Con in Novi, Michigan, in May 2006 (the photo above), and asked him about his "Dynasty" days. Saxon reminisced about the AIDS scare of the 1980s, which haunted the "Dynasty" set with the shocking revelation about Rock Hudson. In the midst of the AIDS hysteria in Hollywood, Saxon said, Joan Collins was skittish about their romantic scenes. "She didn't want to kiss anyone," he said. Saxon, who also starred on CBS' primetime soap "Falcon Crest" as the father of Lorenzo Lamas' character (now *there* was some informed casting! Meow!), told **BRBTV** that of all the wealth of acting he's done, the role that stands out for him is his spin as Chuy Medina in 1966's "The Appaloosa," alongside Marlon Brando.

- **Katharine Ross** (Francesca Colby) is well-known for her roles in 1967's "The Graduate" and 1969's "Butch Cassidy and the Sundance Kid." She's had scattered acting gigs since "The Colbys," including "Donnie Darko" in 2001 and "Eye of the Dolphin" in 2006. Ross married actor Sam Elliott in 1984 and starred with him in the wonderfully creepy 1978 film "The Legacy" *(love the entrapment in the pool!).*

- And what can we say, really, about the legendary **Charlton Heston**, whose defining moment was certainly not his role as Jason Colby on our beloved sister soaps. Besides the wonderful first "Planet of the Apes" movie in 1968, he is well-regarded for his roles in the 1959 film "Ben-Hur," 1971's "The Omega Man" and "Airport 1975" (which, truth be told, was a 1974 film!). The 6-foot-3 dashing actor, born John Charles Carter, started this whole acting thing way back in the early 1940s, and became known in more recent years for his very public political stance on firearms and his post at the National Rifle Association.

- **Kevin Bernhardt**, known to us as Father Tanner McBride in the later years of "Dynasty," wrote the fourth "Rambo" flick, scheduled for 2007.

*No stranger to political causes: Charlton Heston at the Civil Rights March on Washington, D.C., in August 1963.*

- **Robert Symonds**, who tried so hard to counsel that wayward Adam Carrington as Dr. Jonas Edwards, is the stepfather of actress Amy Irving. He married actress Priscilla Pointer (Rebecca Barnes Wentworth of "Dallas") in 1980. Notably, he played Dr. Taney in "The Exorcist" in 1973. He also played a character named Martin Porter in a couple episodes of "Dallas" in the early 1980s, before his "Dynasty" gig. From "Dynasty," he went on to guest stints on shows such as CBS' "ER" and ABC's "Alias."

- **Mark Withers** has the fine distinction *(well, OK, he doesn't care, but we do!)* of being the first-known **BRBTV** quadruple shot. Not only was he the ill-fated Ted Dinard, lover of Steven Carrington, on "Dynasty," but he also appeared on all three of the other **BRBTV** shows: he played a private investigator on "Dallas," he played a character named Denis on the "Bad Day in Hazzard" episode of "The Dukes of Hazzard," and he was Dr. Evan Montclair on "Santa Barbara." *Yowza.* He's just an all-around 1980s guy.

- After his role as ever-dignified butler Joseph Aynders burned out on

"Dynasty," **Lee Bergere** went on to another primetime soap, CBS' "Falcon Crest," as Justin Nash. He'd already, by that point, done a lot of years of great TV roles, dating back to CBS' anthology "Studio One" in 1954.

• Miami-born brunette **Terri Garber** (not to be confused with blond actress Terri Garr -- we just *know* a lotta ya do that like we do!) seemed to be destined for great things with her spicy and saucy 1980s roles as Leslie Carrington on "Dynasty" and Ashton Main on ABC's beloved miniseries "North and South." TV Guide even named her "the hottest new vixen of the year" in 1985, after all. But Garber's been relatively low-key since then, doing an occasional guest stint and more recently the role of Iris Dumbrowski on NBC's "As the World Turns."

• **James Healey** went on from his role as Sean Rowan to play the sinister vigilante Derek Griffin on NBC's daytime soap "Santa Barbara." The Australian-born actor did a few roles after that, up until about 1996.

• We just knew **Christine Belford** looked familiar when she played Susan Farragut, the nanny with issues, on "Dynasty." Besides bearing a heckuva uncanny resemblance to Jaclyn Smith, Belford starred in a "Wonder Woman" episode that **BRBTV** just loved: She played Baroness Paula Von Gunther, sinister cape and all, in the 1976 episode "Wonder Woman Meets Baroness Paula Von Gunther." Belford just has one of those looks that's familiar, and for good reason: She's done a ton of TV work. She's been on "Diagnosis Murder," "Family Ties," "The Golden Girls," "My Two Dads," "Night Court," "Fantasy Island," just about anything you can name. She's married to actor **Nicholas Pryor**, who's had roles as a doctor on both "Dynasty" and "The Colbys" (remember when Jason got that chilling news that he was terminal?) and who played Nathan Billings on "Dallas."

• **Richard Hatch,** who proved a little too tempting to Claudia Carrington as Dean Caldwell, is best known as Apollo in ABC's "Battlestar Galactica." He's been in several "Galactica" projects over the years and has even written novels based on the series. Not to be confused with the inaugural "Survivor" winner of the same name, Hatch says in his IMDb bio, "I never thought of being an actor. I was far too shy, too insecure."

• Producer **Aaron Spelling**, the man behind "Dynasty," was a prolific powerhouse in the world of television, bringing us great stuff such as ABC's "The Love Boat," "Fantasy Island," "Charlie's Angels" and "Hart to Hart," Fox's "Melrose Place," NBC's "Sunset Beach," the WB's "Charmed" and much more. The Dallas-born visionary with the nickname Jerry Lane also took some memorable turns on the other side of the camera on shows such as "Gunsmoke" on CBS and his own "Beverly Hills, 90210" on

Fox. Spelling died on Friday, June 23, 2006, after suffering a stroke. He was 83.

• Just an amusing note: One of the delightful ongoing jokes on "Dynasty" is certainly the way **Alexis always confuses the names of her assistants** (and most or all of them are male, incidentally!). It is a fabulous touch, from a slightly feminazi perspective!

• Another ongoing joke: **Sammy Jo sliding down that silly bannister** in the Carrington mansion. She does it four times: 1. the unforgettable first time, she is brand-new to the mansion and gets the joy of bumping into Alexis; 2. the second time, it's Adam she bumps into, and a few sparks fly before he jogs off in his workout shorts; 3. then, she gets to meet Clay Fallmont for the first time at the bottom of the bannister, and of course, plenty of sparks fly that time, too; 4. finally, in the 1991 reunion movie, she slides down the bannister one last time, to the cheers of her son and other Carringtons.

• There was lots of **mystery parentage** during the run of both "Dynasty" and "The Colbys." Among the mystery parents, some discovered and / or changed during the show and some still a mystery: Dominique's father, Jackie's father, Amanda's father and mother, Sammy Jo's father, Adam's mother and father, Clay's father, Miles' and Monica's father, Jeff's father.

• Finally, some fun info about the **Carrington mansion**. Three homes were actually used to produce the opulent Carrington pad: one in northern California, one in Denver and one in Pasadena (which offered the shots of the pool and gardens). The main mansion of these associated with the Carrington clan, however, was the Filoli estate just south of San Francisco. The address of Carrington mansion, as shown in a letter from Ted Dinard to Steven Carrington in an early episode, is 173 Wessex Drive, Denver, CO 80364. (And did you know that the Mountain Gate Country Club in Los Angeles was used as a LaMirage location?)

Dynasty High

# Corporate ship-jumping

**Jeff, Adam and Steven could never seem to figure out just which company they'd like to work for! Talk about revolving doors! Here's our best record of the executive exiting and entering:**

### Adam Carrington
Starts out working for his mom, Alexis Colby, at Colbyco in November 1982, shortly after arriving to Denver. Jumps to Denver Carrington to work for his dad, Blake Carrington, in October 1983. Resigns from Denver Carrington and rejoins Colbyco in October 1986. Stays on while Alexis acquires Denver Carrington, then moves with her back to the Colbyco offices in December 1986. Comes back to Denver Carrington with Steven Carrington and Fallon Colby while Blake is campaigning for governor in 1987, then leaves again in March 1989. Is recruited by an evil consortium to spy at Denver Carrington in May 1988, which results in Blake losing the company.

### Jeff Colby
Starts out working for his uncle, Cecil Colby, at Colbyco in the early 1980s. Leaves the company in December 1981 when Alexis takes control and goes to work for Blake Carrington at Denver Carrington. Goes back to Colbyco to keep an eye on Alexis and Adam, November 1982. Jumps back to Denver Carrington in November 1983 to work for Blake. Goes to Colby Enterprises in California to work with Jason Colby in October 1985. Leaves California to return to Denver in 1987. Works as Blake's campaign manager in his run for governor, 1987.

### Steven Carrington
Works with Matthew Blaisdel on a Denver Carrington oil rig in 1981. Starts working for his mother, Alexis Colby, at Colbyco when he returns from the dead in March 1983. Serves on the board of directors of Denver Carrington in spring 1986. Leaves Colbyco in October 1986. Is chosen (over Fallon and Adam) by his father to run Denver Carrington in November 1987. Leaves Denver altogether in 1988. Works as an environmental activist in Washington, D.C., in 1991.

# A chat with Bo Hopkins

In the early days of "Dynasty," he was the handsome, blond, rough-cut Matthew Blaisdel, ex-boyfriend to Krystle Carrington. Nowadays, he's taken a role behind the scenes, producing movies. **BRBTV** caught up with Bo Hopkins in 2006 and posed a few questions to him ...

**By the time "Dynasty" came along, you had done a lot of television (especially a lot of Western stuff, like "Bonanza," "Gunsmoke" and "The Virginian"). How did you first hear about the role of Matthew Blaisdel on "Dynasty"?**

"Aaron Spelling's office sent a script to me on the set of 'Rodeo Girl.'" *(Hopkins played Will Garrett — to Katharine Ross' Sammy Garrett — in this 1980 film.)*

**Did you read for any of the other characters at the same time?**

"No."

**You always seemed to have such strong chemistry with Linda Evans in your role as Matthew. The two of you were emitting sparks in every scene in that first season of the show, and you were such a terrific tough-guy foil to the elder, seasoned, corporate magnate of Blake Carrington. What was your favorite part of playing Matthew? Was there anything you saw as a drawback to playing Matthew?**

"My favorite part: His honesty and integrity.
My least favorite part: He was always trying to get rich."

**Are there any similarities between Matthew Blaisdel and Bo Hopkins?**

"Pride."

**Who was the funnest person to work with on the "Dynasty" set?**

"Director Don Medford." *(Medford also served as director for "The Colbys," "Jake and the Fatman," "Airwolf," "Mrs. Columbo" and many others, from as early as the 1950s through the 1980s.)*

**What is your most vivid memory from the "Dynasty" set?**

"Filming the pilot at the Hearst Castle."

**How did you feel about Matthew's dramatic (and surprising) return to the show in 1987?**

"It was challenging."

**You had some other roles on Aaron Spelling's TV shows, such as "Charlie's Angels," "Fantasy Island" and "Hotel." Do you have any particular fond (or otherwise) memories of the late Spelling?**

"He was very energetic and he would make you want to do the part."

**What projects do you have going on these days?**

"I have opened a production company, and we have several movies in development."

**What's been your most fulfilling or personally important role, over the years?**

"'Judgement: The Court Martial of William Calley' with director Stanley Kramer." *(This 1975 TV movie, based on a real court case against an Army lieutenant in the Vietnam War, cast Hopkins as a prosecuting attorney; Harrison Ford and Ben Piazza also starred.)*

# Birthdays

| | |
|---|---|
| Pamela Sue Martin | January 5, 1954 |
| John Forsythe | January 29, 1918 |
| Katharine Ross | January 29, 1942 |
| Bo Hopkins | February 2, 1942 |
| Michael Nader | February 19, 1945 |
| Kathleen Beller | February 19, 1956 |
| Jack Coleman | February 21, 1958 |
| Geoffrey Scott | February 22, 1942 |
| James Farentino | February 24, 1938 |
| Susan Scannell | February 24, 1958 |
| Leann Hunley | February 25, 1955 |
| Stephanie Beacham | February 28, 1947 |
| Cassie Yates | March 2, 1951 |
| Gordon Thomson | March 3, 1945 |
| Ken Howard | March 28, 1944 |
| Ed Marinaro | March 31, 1950 |
| Ali MacGraw | April 1, 1938 |
| Michael Praed | April 1, 1960 |
| Kevin Bernhardt | April 2, 1961 |
| Billy Dee Williams | April 6, 1937 |
| Lee Bergere | April 10, 1924 |
| Peter Mark Richman | April 16, 1927 |
| John James | April 18, 1956 |
| Karen Cellini | May 13, 1958 |
| Richard Hatch | May 21, 1945 |
| Al Corley | May 22, 1956 |
| Joan Collins | May 23, 1933 |
| Deborah Adair | May 23, 1952 |
| Adrian Paul | May 29, 1959 |
| Ted McGinley | May 30, 1958 |
| Pamela Bellwood | June 26, 1951 |
| Grant Goodeve | July 6, 1952 |
| Barbara Stanwyck | July 16, 1907 |
| *(died January 20, 1990)* | |
| Diahann Carroll | July 17, 1935 |
| Lloyd Bochner | July 29, 1924 |
| *(died October 29, 2005)* | |

DYNASTY HIGH

## Behind the scenes

"You can sometimes buy them for half price. Aaron Spelling for a long time had this warehouse of clothes from 'The Love Boat' and 'Dynasty,' so a lot of production companies would come and rent the clothes, and we would wear 'Charlie's Angels' dresses if we could fit into them because they were very tiny — but I think they finally sold that off. But sometimes you buy it for half or you don't get them at all."

— *Heather Locklear, on whether or not she got to keep clothing from 'Dynasty,' on "Larry King Live" in September 1999*

| | |
|---|---|
| John Saxon | August 5, 1935 |
| Richard Anderson | August 8, 1926 |
| Kate O'Mara | August 10, 1939 |
| George Hamilton | August 12, 1939 |
| Emma Samms | August 28, 1960 |
| Catherine Oxenberg | September 22, 1961 |
| Heather Locklear | September 25, 1961 |
| Charlton Heston | October 4, 1923 |
| J. Eddie Peck | October 10, 1958 |
| James Houghton | November 7, 1948 |
| Troy Beyer | November 7, 1964 |
| Tracy Scoggins | November 13, 1959 |
| Rock Hudson | November 17, 1925 |
| *(died October 2, 1985)* | |
| Linda Evans | November 18, 1942 |
| Joseph Campanella | November 21, 1933 |
| Maxwell Caulfield | November 23, 1959 |
| Ricardo Montalban | November 25, 1920 |
| Wendie Malick | December 13, 1950 |
| Christopher Cazenove | December 17, 1945 |
| Terri Garber | December 28, 1960 |

# Websites

Have a fascination with Fallon?  A delight with Dex?  An amour for Amanda?  Here are some of the sites of the shows' stars.

### Joan Collins  est. 2001
JoanCollins.net
**Webmaster:** Darren M. Elly
**Email:** pkeylock@aol.com or ellyd04056@aol.com
**Fan-mail address:** 16 Bulbecks Walk, South Woodham Ferrers, Chelmsford, Essex, CM3 5ZN England
Billed as Joan Collins' official website, with biography, filmography, merchandising info and an extensive list of PR contacts.

### Pamela Sue Martin  est. 2005
PamelaSueMartin.com
**Email:** robert@pamelasuemartin.com
Martin's official site includes a brief biography and career rundown, with some photos of her more recent activities. You can buy autographed photos at the site.

### Michael Nader  est. 2001
MichaelNader.com
**Email:** webmaster@michaelnader.com
What is evidently a fan page features a filmography, interviews and articles (with nice color magazine covers) and tidbits on what he's doing nowadays.  (Was up, but then down at press time.)

### Catherine Oxenberg  est. 2003
CatherineOxenberg.com
**Webmaster:** webmaster@catherineoxenberg.com or ken@caspervandien.com
**Fan-mail address:** 9461 Charleville Blvd., Suite 380, Beverly Hills, CA 90212
**Secondary (official) fansite:**  www.geocities.com/caovdfc
This is very pretty, as far as official celebrity websites go, featuring a biography, resume and photo gallery, along with a separate "Dynasty" page.  One nice added element is a page of her favorite prayers (Oxenberg has been involved in Christian filmwork).  *You go, girl!*

### Peter Mark Richman
PeterMarkRichman.com
**Email:** actor.mgmt@petermarkrichman.com
**Fan-mail address:** Peter Mark Richman Productions, 19528 Ventura Boulevard, Suite 385, Tarzana, CA 91356; (818) 623-6476
This official site chronicles not only Richman's acting career, but also his work as an artist and a novelist. He sells autographed "Dynasty" photos at the site.

### Diahann Carroll   est. 2006
DiahannCarroll.net
**Email:** mail@diahanncarroll.net
**Fan-mail address:** Diahann Carroll, P.O. Box 57593, Sherman Oaks, CA 91403
Carroll's official site features nicely detailed biography and film credits, with illustrations. She's got a news page, as well as a TV page that tells where and when her TV roles are appearing now.

### Bo Hopkins   est. 2004
BoHopkins.com
**Email:** fanmail@bohopkins.com
Hopkins leads motivational seminars and acting workshops nowadays, and his official site includes info on that, as well as a biography and nice photos. His scrapbook page includes some stills from "Dynasty."

### Richard Hatch   est. 1995
RichardHatch.com
**Email:** webmaster@richardhatch.com
You really won't find a lick of "Dynasty" in this official site, but if you're a "Battlestar Galactica" fan, or just an all-around Richard Hatch fan, it's a good-looking site.

---

## Behind the scenes

> At a wrap party, they ran a film of Andrew Laird, my character, for kicks, walking and exiting through different doorways, and when I spoke I was dubbed in a different language — Japanese, Spanish, Italian, German, etc. Cuts from various countries. It was pretty funny.
> — *Peter Mark Richman, to BRBTV, 2004*

### Tracy Scoggins  est. 2001
TracyScoggins.com
**Webmaster:** Time Machine Collectibles / CR Management
**Email:** tmartin@bmi.net
**Fan-mail address:** 2109 S. Wilbur Avenue, Walla Walla, WA 99362; (509) 525-4387
Scoggins' official site is part of a network of official celebrity websites, featuring her filmography on the home page, as well as pages for photos, links and more.

### Michael Parks  est. 1998
MichaelParks.com
**Email:** webquery@michaelparks.com
This page is really simply a storefront for the music of this actor who portrayed Hoyt Parker on "The Colbys."

### J. Eddie Peck
JEddiePeck.com
**Email:** webmistress@jeddiepeck.com
**Fan-mail address:** J. Eddie Peck, c/o Peggy Goldsmith, 507 Oakley Avenue, Streator, IL 61364
This official site has had lots of hunky photos of the guy who played Alexis Carrington's lover Roger Grimes in flashbacks on the show, though it's been under construction for a time.

### Adrian Paul
AdrianPaul.net
Paul's nice-looking site includes a very detailed filmography and biography. He gives you the latest news on his projects, plus an online store.

### Ted McGinley
TedMcGinley.com
This website was classified as "Coming soon" at one point, but seems to have disappeared altogether, as of press time.

## Merchandise

Here's some of the merchandise relating to the TV shows "Dynasty" and "The Colbys" and their stars. There are a whole lot of books, as you can see below. If there's something you've seen that's not listed here, email dynasty@brbtv.com!

### Books related to "Dynasty" or its stars
- "Dynasty: The Authorized Biography of the Carringtons," hardcover and softcover, by Doubleday, 1984.
- "Dynasty," paperback novel by Eileen Lottman, 1983.
- "Alexis Returns," paperback novel by Eileen Lottman, 1984.
- "The Dynasty Years: Hollywood Television and Critical Media Studies," by Jostein Gripsrud, Routledge London & New York, 1995.
- "Glamour, Greed & Glory – Dynasty," paperback by Judith A. Moose and Paul D. Keylock, Signing Stars, August 2005.
- "Joan Collins Superstar: A Biography," by Levine, G K Hall & Co; large-print edition, June 1986.
- "Joan Collins," by John Kercher, Gallery Books, 1984.
- "Inside Joan Collins: A Biography," by Jay David, Carroll & Graf, May 1988.
- "Joan Collins: The Unauthorized Biography," by Jeff Rovin, Bantam Books, October 1984.
- "Hollywood Sisters: Jackie and Joan Collins," by Susan Crimp, Patricia Burstein, St. Martin's Press, March 1989.
- "A Touch of Collins: The Story of a Show-Business Dynasty," by Joe Collins, Columbus Books Ltd., October 1986.
- "Linda Evans," by Michael Freedland, Weidenfeld and Nicolson, 1986.

- "Diahann: An Autobiography," by Diahann Carroll, Ross Firestone, Little Brown & Company, April 1986.
- "Diahann!," by Diahann Carroll, Ross Firestone, Ivy Books, reprint edition, May 1987.
- "Beauty & Exercise Book," by Linda Evans with Sean Catherine Derek, Wallaby Books Inc., 1983.
- "Aaron Spelling: A Prime-Time Life," memoir by Aaron Spelling, St. Martin's Press, November 2002.

## Books by Joan Collins
- "Past Imperfect: An Autobiography," Simon & Schuster, 1984; hardcover by Random House Value Pub; April 1984; paperback by Berkley Pub Group; reprint edition, April 1985.
- "Future Terrific," Berkley Pub Group, April 1985.
- "Second Act," also autobiographical, G K Hall & Co; large-print edition, June 1998.
- "My Secrets," hardcover by Firefly Books Ltd. and Pan Macmillan, January 1994.
- "Infamous," hardcover by Penguin USA, March 1996; paperback by Onyx Books, March 1997; audiocassette by Brilliance Audio, abridged edition, April 1996.
- "The Joan Collins Beauty Book," Pan Macmillan, November 1, 1981.
- "Joan's Way: Looking Good, Feeling Great," Robson Books; hardcover by Chrysalis Books, October 3, 2002.
- "My Friends' Secrets: Conversations with My Friends about Beauty, Health and Happiness," Trafalgar Square.
- "Star Quality," Hyperion Press, November 2002.
- "Prime Time," hardcover by Linden Pr, September 1988; paperback by Arrow (A Division of Random House Group), December 22, 1988.
- "Too Damn Famous," hardcover by Chivers Press Ltd, September 30, 1996; paperback by Chivers Press Ltd., May 31, 1997; audiocassette and audio CD by Ulverscroft Large Print; January 2003.
- "Love & Desire & Hate," Simon & Schuster, February 1991; paperback by Pocket Books, reprint edition, December 1991.

- "Misfortune's Daughters," hardcover and paperback by Hyperion Press, March 2005.
- "Health, Youth and Happiness: My Secrets," an audio book by Dove Audio, 1994.
- "A Christmas Carol," by Joan Collins (designer), John Holder (illustrator), Charles Dickens; Penguin Putnam, May 1994.
- "The Railway Children" (Ladybird Picture Classics), by Joan Collins, E. Railway Children Nesbit, George Buchanan (illustrator), Jonathan Mercer (illustrator), Ladybird Books, March 1997; also available in audiocassette, audio CD and e-book. Collins has been involved in several other book projects for kids such as this.

## Other miscellaneous items spotted here and there
- "Forever Krystle" eau de toilette spray for women, fragrance, powder, bath and shower gel, etc., by the Design House of Carrington, 1984.
- "Carrington" spray cologne for men, which comes in a unique, dark, plastic decanter.
- "Scoundrel" cologne by Revlon, endorsed by Joan Collins, with accompanying promotional materials such as a button depicting Collins and reading "Dare to wear Scoundrel."
- Alexis doll, 24" by World Doll Inc., 1985.
- Krystle doll, 24" by World Doll Inc., 1985.
- Krystina Emma Carrington doll by Eugene, 21" tall, vinyl and cloth body with birth announcement and rhinestone necklace included, 1985.
- "Dynasty: The Happy Couple" jigsaw puzzle depicting Krystle and Blake, 551 pieces, 18" by 24", Maruca Industries, 1984.
- "Krystle" jigsaw puzzle depicting Krystle, 551 pieces, 18" by 24", Maruca Industries, 1984.
- Dynasty Collection tuxedo wear for After Six.
- "Dynasty" logo wall clock, 8.5" round, part of a series of pop-culture wall clocks for sale on eBay, 2006.
- John James' pop single "Painted Dreams / Sleeping In Your Arms Again" (white vinyl), 1985.

Try a search on eBay for "Dynasty TV" or "The Colbys TV" — it might be the only place you find items like these, short of your neighborhood garage sale. On eBay or similar online auctions, you'll also find autographed photos of the stars, press kits and script copies, plus an occasional videotape of the reunion movie or episodes, even a rather-bizarre and slightly dangerous-sounding CD of thousands of photos from the TV show ("from one collector to another"). Hmmm ....

Happy hunting!

*This glass brandy snifter, used on the "Dynasty" set, showed up on eBay in 2006.*

*This nine-inch collector's plate by the Royal Orleans Co. features Krystle, Blake and Alexis in full color and was manufactured in limited-edition, numbered quantities in 1985.*

*You can often snag yourself neat stuff like this on eBay: A Spring 1985 "T.V. Soap World Special" featuring Joan Collins on the cover and promising exclusive photos and articles on the show — at least on the show back in '85.*

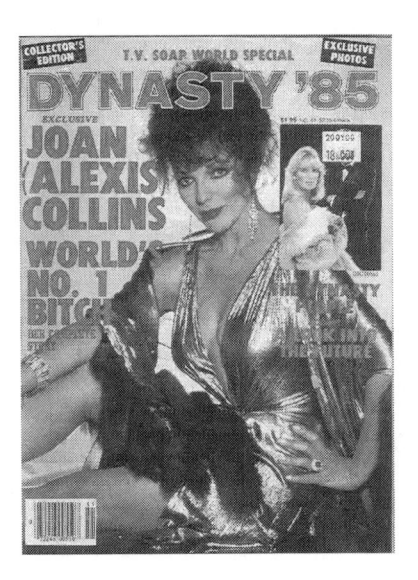

Another eBay item: A cream three-piece wedding suit with faux pearls and rhinestones around the waist — designed by Nolan Miller for a "Dynasty Collection." Meow!

Nolan Miller also put his name on "Dynasty"-themed dress patterns such as this one.

Not quite official, but fun: This wall clock takes the "Dynasty" text treatment of the DVD set and gives it a "monied" background.

With a cover featuring The Big Three (one of them under wraps, don't we know!), the first-season DVD of "Dynasty" was released on April 19, 2005 by 20th Century Fox. Its features include commentary by series co-creator Esther Shapiro on "Oil" parts 1-3 and Al Corley on "The Separation" and "The Testimony," plus an overview on creating the show and profiles of the Fallon and Steven characters. "Dynasty" fans went wild with the release, but when a second-season DVD was not forthcoming, many were miffed.

BILLIE RAE BATES

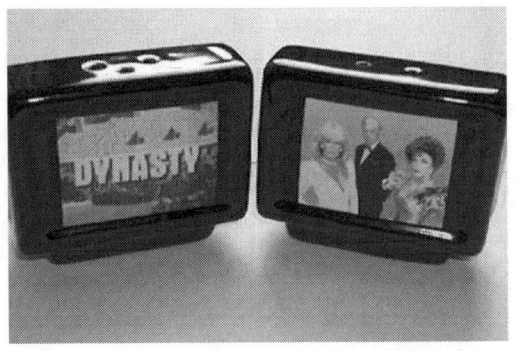

*These rare and rather interesting (!) ceramic salt and pepper shakers turned up on eBay, as did the signed script and photo below.*

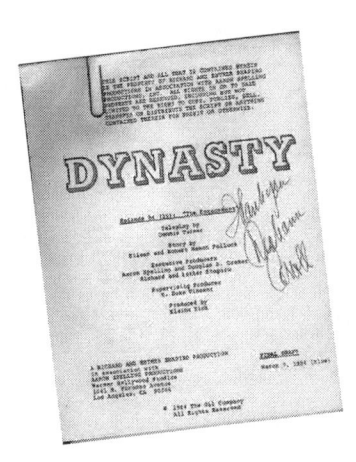

## Behind the scenes

" I remember we were having lunch, and I wasn't really good friends with her at the time. We sat at lunch and talked, and she was just getting started in her career. She was very concerned about getting jobs and asking me all these questions about jobs. "
— John Saxon, reminiscing with BRBTV about Joan Collins, Motor City Comic Con, May 2006

# Acknowledgments

The release of this book represents a big milestone in a trio of projects I began in 1998, with the advent of the **BRBTV** websites.  Believe me, I'm very grateful to have finished it!  This book comes from many years of love and hard work, and it comes at a time in my life where I'm very thankful for the blessings I've been given.  My Heavenly Father takes good care of me, so of course, I thank Him, first and foremost.

- Many thanks to the following for their help with this book:
    - ABC Television
    - Bo Hopkins and Evelyn Ehlers
    - Diahann Carroll and Jeffrey Lane
    - Dr. John C. Nardo
    - Eden Clark of Catherine Oxenberg.com
    - Joan Collins and her assistant, Paul Keylock
    - John Saxon
    - Michael Parks and Molly Lairamore of Listen Recordings
    - Pamela Sue Martin and her management
    - Peter Mark Richman and his assistant, Julie Harmon
- Thanks, also, to my very own Pastor Keith, for his love and support during this project!
- Much appreciation to Spence Beamon, Detroit musician and systems expert, for both technical and moral support.
- And I'm very grateful to the "Dynasty" fans out there who have emailed me at the **BRBTV** sites in the past five years ... you've inspired me, you've given me good feedback, you've asked me some great questions!  Most of all, though, you've shared a love for the trials and tribulations of the Carringtons and the many things we learn from them ...

*BRB*

# Bibliography of supplemental sources

Like the other books in the **BRBTV** book series, "Dynasty High" was compiled and written, first and foremost, from BRB's own viewing and love of the TV series (the episode synopses, for instance, are her own original content). **BRBTV** would like to acknowledge, however, the following supplemental sources, besides those various sources attributed within the text, for extra fun facts and tidbits on the show:

- The Internet Movie Database (IMDb.com)
- TV Tome / TV.com
- Tim's TV Showcase (timvp.com/tv.html)
- Wikipedia.com
- About.com
- "The Complete Directory to Prime Time Network and Cable TV Shows" by Tim Brooks and Earle Marsh, Ballantine Books, 2003
- "The Soap Opera Encyclopedia" by Christopher Schemering, Ballantine Books, 1985, 1987
- "Soap Opera History," contributing author Mary Ann Copeland, Publications International Ltd., 1991
- "People Weekly Entertainment Almanac," People Books, Time Inc.

Made in the USA